Praise for And Now I See...

"The reading of this book is like a guided visit to some vast treasure house where we are invited to explore the rich heritage of Christian thought. With the eyes of artists and the insights of poets, we walk with saints, philosophers, and theologians, challenged to move from blindness and fear to freedom and vision through Christ. At the end of the visit, we realize that we have actually begun, with renewed energy and enthusiasm, a journey — a pilgrimage — along the path of faith and conversion, trust, and love. This is a book 'for all seasons'!"

— AGNES CUNNINGHAM, SSCM, theologian
and author of *Prayer: Personal and Liturgical*

"Robert Barron, an inspired writer, illuminates the teachings of 'the great tradition,' showing how they coalesce with the best literary witnesses to liberate us to our true selves. His reflections range from the philosophical to the poetic, themselves inspired by the riches of the tradition they unearth."

— DAVID B. BURRELL, CSC, Hesburgh Professor of
Philosophy and Theology, University of Notre Dame

All I know is
I was blind,
and now I see.

JOHN 9:25

AND NOW I SEE...

A Theology of Transformation

ROBERT BARRON

A *Crossroad* Book
The Crossroad Publishing Company
New York

The woodcut on p. ii and the part openings is "He Smeared the Man's Eyes with Mud, Jn 9:6" from Helen Siegl, *Blockprints for Sundays, Cycles A-B-C,* new revised edition, copyright © 1984, 1990 Pueblo Publishing Company, Inc. Reprinted with permission of Liturgical Press, Collegeville, Minn.

All biblical citations are from the Jerusalem Bible.

The Crossroad Publishing Company
370 Lexington Avenue, New York, NY 10017

Printed in the United States of America

Library of Congress Cataloging-in-Publication Data
Barron, Robert E., 1959-
    And now I see – : a theology of transformation / Robert Barron.
        p.   cm.
    Includes bibliographical references.
    ISBN 0-8245-1753-9 (pbk.)
    1. Theology, Doctrinal – Popular works. 2. Spiritual life –
Catholic Church. 3. Catholic Church – Doctrines.   I. Title.
BX1754.B345 1998
230 – dc21   98-13578

4   5   6   7   8   9   10   02

To
Msgr. William J. Quinn,
Mentor, Friend, Great Soul

CONTENTS

Part 3
THE HEALING

Prelude

CHANGE YOUR WAY OF SEEING

Christianity is, above all, a way of *seeing*. Everything else in Christian life flows from and circles around the transformation of vision. Christians *see* differently, and that is why their prayer, their worship, their action, their whole way of being in the world have a distinctive accent and flavor. What unites figures as diverse as James Joyce, Caravaggio, John Milton, the architect of Chartres, Dorothy Day, Dietrich Bonhoeffer, and the later Bob Dylan is a peculiar and distinctive *take* on things, a style, a way, which flow finally from Jesus of Nazareth. Origen of Alexandria once remarked that holiness is seeing with the eyes of Christ, Teilhard de Chardin said, with great passion, that his mission as a Christian thinker was to help people *see*, and Thomas Aquinas said that the ultimate goal of the Christian life is a "beatific vision," an act of *seeing*.

In the strange and strikingly beautiful account of the healing of the man born blind in John's Gospel, we find an iconic representation of this coming to see. Jesus spits on the ground and makes a mud paste which he then rubs onto the man's eyes. When the man washes his eyes in the pool of Siloam as Jesus had instructed him, his sight is restored. The crowds are amazed, but the Pharisees — consternated and skeptical — accuse him of being naive and the one who healed him of being a sinner. With disarming simplicity the visionary responds: "All I know is I was blind, and now I see." This is precisely what all Christians say when they have encountered the light of Christ. It was St. Augustine who saw in the making of the mud paste a metaphor for the Incarnation: the divine power mixing with the earth, resulting in the formation of a healing balm. When this salve of God made flesh is rubbed onto our eyes blinded by sin we come again to see.

This book is about coming to vision through Christ. It is about the

transformative power of the rich, complex, and variegated tradition
that flows from Jesus of Nazareth, the enfleshment of God.

But what is it precisely that Christians see, and how do they come to
see it? What is the "mystical" sense which stands stubbornly at the
heart of all Christian experience? To answer these questions, I rec-
ommend that we turn to the first chapter of the earliest Gospel, that
of Mark. After his baptism and temptation in the desert, Jesus goes
into Galilee and begins to preach. The first words out of his mouth,
as Mark reports them, serve as a sort of summary statement of his life
and work: "The time has come, and the Kingdom of God is close at
hand. Repent and believe the Good News" (Mark 1:15).

The moment has arrived, the privileged time, the *kairos;* something
that human beings have been longing for and striving after and hoping to see has appeared, and the time is now for a decision, for action.
Jesus' very first words are a wake-up call, a warning bell in the night, a
summons to attention. This is not the time to be asleep, not the time
to be languishing in complacency and self-satisfaction, not the time
for delaying tactics, for procrastination and second guessing. In the
Byzantine liturgy, we find the oft-repeated call to "be attentive," and
in the Buddhist tradition, there is a great emphasis placed on wake-
fulness. In the fiction of James Joyce, we often find that moments of
spiritual insight are preceded by a great thunderclap, the cosmic alarm
shocking the characters (and the reader) into wide-awakenness. The
initial words of Jesus' first sermon are a similar invitation to psychological and spiritual awareness: there is something to be seen, so open
your eyes!

But what is it that he wants us to notice? What is this astonish-
ing state of affairs that must not be missed? "The Kingdom of God is
close at hand." Now there have been libraries of books written on the
subject of the "Kingdom," some suggesting that it refers to a political
realignment of Jewish society, others that it signals a purely spiritual
condition beyond the world, still others that it points to a change of
heart in the individual. To my mind, the metaphor of the Kingdom, in

its poetic richness, is legitimately open to all of those interpretations, but it has a primary referent *in the person of Jesus himself.* Jesus wants us to open our eyes and see *him,* more to the point, to see what God is doing in and through him. He himself *is* the Kingdom of God coming into the world with transformative power.

In Jesus of Nazareth, the divine and the human have come together in a salvific way, and this reconciliation *is* the long awaited Kingdom of God. Though there are many themes that run through the Hebrew Scriptures, there is one motif that is consistent and persistent: the passionate and aching desire for deliverance, the cry of the heart toward the God from whom the people feel alienated. If only the power of rebellion and sin were ended and the friendship of God and human beings reestablished, peace, *shalom,* all-pervasive well-being would reign. What Jesus announces in his first sermon in the hills of Galilee, and what he demonstrates throughout his life and ministry, is that this wild desire of his ancestors, this hope against hope, this intimate union of God and humanity, is an accomplished fact, something which can be seen and heard and touched.

Now the Gospel writers agree that the Kingdom of God, the enfleshment of the divine life in human form, the Incarnation, *is not something to be admired from the outside, but rather an energy in which to participate.* This is, tragically, one of the most overlooked dimensions of Christian thought and experience. If we open our eyes and see the light, we too often stop at the point of admiration and worship, lost in wonder at the strange work that God has accomplished uniquely in Jesus of Nazareth. But Jesus nowhere in the Gospels urges his followers to worship him, though he insistently calls them to *follow* him. One of the surest ways to avoid the challenge of the Incarnation, one of the most effective means of closing our eyes, is to engage in just this sort of pseudo-pious distantiation. But the Gospels want us, not outside the energy of Christ, but in it, not wondering at it, but swimming in it. In John's Gospel, Jesus speaks of himself as the vine *onto which we are grafted like branches,* and he compares himself to food *which we are to take into ourselves.* These beautifully organic images are meant to highlight our *participation* in the event of the Incarnation, our concrete citizenship in the Kingdom of God. It was the great medieval mystic Meister Eckhart who commented that the Incarnation of the Word in Jesus of Nazareth long ago is of no interest and importance unless that same word becomes incarnate in us today.[1]

We have been summoned to attentiveness, and we have heard the word announcing the coming together of the divine and human. But what is it that enables us truly to hear and respond? How can we see the light that has been so unexpectedly and suddenly turned on? Again we consult Jesus' opening speech in Mark's Gospel: "repent and believe the Good News." The word so often and so misleadingly translated as "repent" is *metanoiete*. This Greek term is based upon two words, *meta* (beyond) and *nous* (mind or spirit), and thus, in its most basic form, it means something like "go beyond the mind that you have." The English word "repent" has a moralizing overtone, suggesting a change in behavior or action, whereas Jesus' term seems to be hinting at a change at a far more fundamental level of one's being. Jesus urges his listeners to change their way of knowing, their way of perceiving and grasping reality, their perspective, their mode of *seeing*. What Jesus implies is this: the new state of affairs has arrived, the divine and human have met, but the way you customarily see is going to blind you to this novelty. In the gnostic Gospel of Thomas, Jesus expresses the same concern: "The Kingdom of God is spread out on the earth, *but people do not see it*." Minds, eyes, ears, senses, perceptions — all have to be opened up, turned around, revitalized. *Metanoia*, soul transformation, is Jesus' first recommendation.

But what exactly is the problem with the way we think and see? To give an adequate answer to that question we would have to work our way through the whole of the Bible and the Christian tradition, for the attempt to name and heal spiritual blindness is one of the basic motifs of our religion. But perhaps a simple answer can be given in these terms: we see and know and perceive with a mind of fear rather than with a mind of trust. When we fear, we cling to who we are and what we have; when we are afraid, we see ourselves as the threatened center of a hostile universe, and thus we violently defend ourselves and lash out at potential adversaries. And fear — according to so many of the biblical authors and so many of the mystics and theologians of our tradition — is a function of living our lives at the surface level, a result of forgetting our deepest identity. At the root and ground of our being, at the "center" of who we are, there is what Christianity calls "the image and likeness of God." This means that at the foundation of our existence, we are one with the divine power which continually creates and sustains the universe; we are held and cherished by the infinite love of God. When we rest in this center and realize its power, we know that, in an ultimate sense, we are safe, or, in more classical religious language, "saved." And therefore we can let go of fear and begin to live in radical trust. But when we lose sight of this rootedness in God, we live exclusively on the tiny island of the ego, and lives become dominated by fear. Fear is the "original sin" of which the church fathers speak; fear is the poison that was injected into human consciousness and human society from the beginning; fear is the debilitating and life-denying element which upsets the "chemical balance" of both psyche and society.

To overcome fear is to move from the *pusilla anima* (the small soul) to the *magna anima* (the great soul). When we are dominated by our egos, we live in a very narrow space, in the *angustiae* (the straits) between this fear and that, between this attachment and that. But when we surrender in trust to the bearing power of God, our souls become great, roomy, expansive. We realize that we are connected to all things and to the creative energy of the whole cosmos. Interestingly, the term *magna anima* shares a Sanskrit root with the word *mahatma*, and both mean "great soul." What Jesus calls for in *metanoia* is the transformation from the terrified and self-regarding small soul to the confident and soaring great soul. The seeing of the Kingdom, in short, is not for the pusillanimous but for the magnanimous.

In that wonderful story of the calming of the storm at sea, we witness some of the spiritual dynamics of fear and trust. Making their way across the lake in their tiny boat, the disciples stand symbolically for all of us journeying through life within the confines of the fearful *pusilla anima*. When they confront the storm and the mighty waves, they are immediately filled with terror, convinced that they are going to drown. Similarly, when the trials and anxieties of life confront the ego, the first reaction is fear, since the ego is fundamentally persuaded that there is nothing "under" it or "behind" it, no power beyond itself upon which it can rely. In the midst of this terrible *Sturm und Drang,* this inner and outer tension, Jesus, Mark tells us, is "asleep on a cushion," that is, utterly at peace, centered, at rest. Jesus stands here for the divine power which is "asleep" within all of us, indeed within the very confines of the ego. He symbolizes that divine energy which remains unaffected by the fear-storms generated by the grasping ego. Continuing to read the story at a spiritual level, we see that it is none other than this divine power which successfully stills the storm and calms the waves: "he rebuked the wind and said to the sea, 'quiet now; be calm'" (Mark 4:39). This beautiful narrative seems to suggest that if we but awaken to the presence of Christ within us, if we learn to live and to see at a deeper level, if we live in basic trust rather than fear, then we can withstand even the most frightening storms. When, at the close of the story, Jesus asks the bewildered and exhausted disciples, "Why are you so frightened? How is it that you have no faith?" (Mark 4:41) he is wondering why they have not yet let go of the ego mind, the mind of fear, why they have not yet experienced the *metanoia* necessary for living in the Kingdom of God.

Thus our examination of Jesus' programmatic opening homily in Mark's Gospel reveals the following: open your eyes; see the coming together of the divine and the human; learn to live in the power of that incarnation (the Kingdom) through *metanoia*, through the changing of your attitude, your orientation, your way of seeing. But Jesus' great speech does not end with the call to *metanoia;* rather, it explicitly names the state of being in the Kingdom of God, the goal and end point of the change of heart: "believe the Good News." Now like the word *metanoiete,* the term *pisteuete* (believe) has been terribly misunderstood over the centuries, coming, unfortunately, to mean the dry assent to religious propositions for which there is little or no evidence. Since the Enlightenment and its altogether legitimate insistence on rational responsibility, faith, in the sense just described, has come into disrepute. It seems to be the last refuge of uncritical people, those desperate to find some assurance with regard to the ultimate things and thus willing to swallow even the most far-fetched theories and beliefs. Happily, "belief" in the biblical and traditional sense of the term has nothing to do with this truncated and irresponsible rationality. "To believe," as Jesus uses the term, signals, not so much a way of knowing as a way of *being known*. To have faith is to allow oneself to be overwhelmed by the power of God, to permit the divine energy to reign at all levels of one's being. As such, it is not primarily a matter of understanding and assenting to propositions as it is surrendering to the God who wants to become incarnate in us. In Paul Tillich's language, "faith" is being grasped by Ultimate Concern, permitting oneself to be shaken and turned by the in-breaking God.

Hence when Jesus urges his listeners to believe, he is inviting them, not so much to adhere to a new set of propositions, but rather to let go of the dominating and fearful ego and learn once more to live in the confidence of the *magna anima*. He is calling them to find the new center of their lives *where he finds his own,* in the unconditional love of God. One of the tragic ironies of the tradition is that Jesus' "faith," interpreted along rationalist lines, serves only to boost up the ego, confirming it in its grasping and its fear: I *have* the faith, and you don't; do I *really* understand the statements I claim to believe? The state of mind designed to quell the ego has been, more often than not, transformed into one more ego game. "Believing" the "Good News" has nothing to do with these games of the mind. It has everything to do with radical change of life and vision, with the simple (and dreadfully complex) process of allowing oneself to swim in the divine sea, to find the true self by letting go of the old center.

One of the most remarkable accounts of this conversion is the story of the healing of the blind man, Bartimaeus, in the Gospel of Mark. Physical blindness is, for Mark as well as for John, an evocative symbol of the terrible blindness of the soul which all of us sinners experience. When the *pusilla anima* reigns, when the *imago Dei* is covered over, we see within the narrow spectrum of our fearful desires. Blind Bartimaeus, sitting helplessly by the road outside of Jericho begging for alms and attention, expresses this hopeless and darkened-over state of soul. When he hears that Jesus of Nazareth is in the vicinity, he begins to cry out, "Son of David, have pity on me" (Mark 10:48). The original Greek here is *eleeson me,* beautifully reflective of the liturgical cry of the church, *Kyrie eleison,* Lord have mercy. Bartimaeus gives voice to the prayerful groaning of the whole people of God for release from the imprisonment of the small soul. Though he is reprimanded by the crowd, Bartimaeus continues to shout, until finally Jesus calls out to him. This is the summons that echoes from the very depths of one's own being, the call of the *magna anima,* the invitation to rebirth and reconfiguration.

Inspired by this voice, convinced that he has discovered the pearl of great price, the *unum necessarium,* Bartimaeus jumps up, throws off his cloak and comes to Jesus. In the early centuries of the church, those about to be baptized were invited to strip themselves of their clothes, symbolizing thereby their renunciation of their old way of life. In Mark's story, the blind man prepares for inner transformation by throwing off the cloak of his old consciousness, his old pattern of de-sire, the lifestyle which has rendered him spiritually blind. Then, at the feet of Jesus, Bartimaeus hears the question that all of us hear in the stillness of the heart, the question which comes from the divine power within and which subtly but firmly invites us to transformation: "What do you want me to do for you?" God beckons us, but God never compels us. Then, in one of the simplest and most poignant lines in the Scripture, Bartimaeus says, "Master, I want to see again." Desperately in the dark, hounded by the demons of desire, caught in the narrow passage of ego-consciousness, Bartimaeus wants to see with a deeper, broader, and clearer vision. In his pain, and also in his con-fidence, Bartimaeus stands for all of us spiritual seekers, all who hope against hope that there might be a way to live outside the tyranny of the ego. He wants precisely what we have been exploring here: a new attitude, a new perspective, the *magna anima.* And Jesus' answer to Bartimaeus, "Go, your faith has saved you," is perfectly in line with the "inaugural address" which we have been analyzing. What saves the blind man is the *metanoia* which culminates in faith, the shift in consciousness from ego-dominance to surrender. What restores the vision of the spiritual seeker is the throwing off of the old mind and the adoption, through God's grace, of a divine mind. Of course, the story ends with Bartimaeus, "following Jesus up the road." It ends, in a word, with discipleship. Once the soul has been transfigured, the only path that seems appealing is the one walked by Christ, that is to say, the path of radical self-offering, self-surrender. Fired by the God-consciousness, in touch with the divine source within us, drinking from the well of eternal life, we are inspired simply to pour ourselves out in love.

❖

Jesus of Nazareth embodied the Kingdom of God and made possible a new way of seeing which enabled others to enter into the energy of that Kingdom. The first Christians were those who were intoxicated by this vision and felt their lives transformed by it. The epistles of Paul and the Gospels are the first written accounts of the experience of being grasped by the power of Jesus Christ. It is terribly important to remember that they are by no means objective, disinterested narratives, biographies, or histories; rather, they are presentations of the process of *metanoia,* "showings" of how Jesus Christ changes lives and minds. What Matthew, Mark, Luke, John, and Paul do consistently is to hold up icons of the New Being, pictures of the Christ, in the hopes of affecting *metanoia* in their readers. In the spiritual traditions of the Christian East, there is great emphasis placed on the role of icons or sacred pictures. When we meditate on an icon of the Virgin or of Christ, we allow ourselves to be drawn into the "field of force" of that picture, letting the icon to work on us through a type of spiritual osmosis. There is something similar at play in the epistles and the Gospels: like the Master himself, the first Christian writers are interested, above all, in changing attitudes, in awakening faith.

In his magnificent letter to the Christians in Rome, St. Paul says: "I am not ashamed of the Good News. It is the power of God saving all who have faith" (Rom. 1:16). This is a beautiful summary of the spiritual dynamics I have been describing throughout this introduction. Paul boldly and unabashedly holds up the image of the Good News (the Kingdom of God, the coming together of the divine and human) because he realizes its enormous transformative power for those who have the vision (the faith) to see it. There is another wonderful and pithy summation of the energy of *metanoia* in Paul's letter to the Galatians: "It is no longer I who live but Christ who lives in me." The Apostle is announcing to his audience that he has experienced the *metanoia,* the shift in consciousness, brought about by contact with Jesus Christ: it is no longer the petty and fearful ego which dominates, but rather the power of Christ, the *magna anima.* When Paul speaks of justification or salvation throughout his epistles, he is referring, above all, to this reordering of the person through the power of the Incarnation.

Paul and the evangelists were the first Christian "theologians," that is, those seeking to say a *logos,* a word, about what God has done in Jesus of Nazareth. Their "words" are always in imitation of *the Word,* who is Christ himself, the embodiment of the Kingdom of God. Thus, their "theologies" are, as we have hinted, not primarily rational, philosophical investigations of the nature of God, but instead efforts in the direction of life transformation, re-presentations of the energy of the original Word. In this sense, Christian theology, in the beginning, had an unmistakably "evangelical," missionary, practical flavor.

This "metanoetic" function is perfectly evident in the theology which grew out of the New Testament tradition and flourished in the first centuries of the church. In the patristic period, the most prominent theologians were pastors, bishops, catechists, and monks — and not what we would call "academicians." No theologian of the early church was writing for an academic audience or to receive tenure or to be published in technical journals of theology. On the contrary, they were writing (to be sure, at a very sophisticated level) for the spiritual benefit of the people they were concretely serving. Theology was, like preaching and pastoral care, for the sake of salvation.

In this context, it is helpful to consider the example of Origen, the third-century catechist of the Christian church at Alexandria. This ingenious pastor and teacher speaks of theology as *theoria.* Obviously, we have derived our word "theory" from this Greek term, but we must beware of identifying the two. For the ancient Greeks, and for Origen, *theoria* designated, not abstract knowing, but rather mystical vision and contemplation, the type of seeing that awakens and sustains wonder. For these ancient thinkers, one did not engage in *theoria* in order to satisfy the curiosity of the mind, but to assuage the deepest longings of the spirit. In his homilies, his scriptural studies, and his voluminous theological works, Origen of Alexandria offers his readers a "theoretical" vision of Jesus Christ; he holds up an icon of the Lord and hopes thereby to change the souls of his audience.

St. Athanasius, the embattled and feisty fourth-century bishop of Alexandria, was the impassioned defender of the Christological formulas of the Council of Nicea. Against the powerful, numerically superior, and well-organized opposition of the Arians, Athanasius proclaimed the legitimacy of the *homoousios* teaching, the conviction that Jesus is "one in being" with the Father, fully divine. To safeguard this doctrine, Athanasius not only engaged in fierce theological polemics, but he also withstood public humiliation, exile, and the constant threat of violence. When we read the account of Athanasius's travails today, we are tempted to smile, perhaps a bit condescendingly. Why, after all, would a man go through so much simply to defend an idea, a dogma? Our confusion is the result of our profoundly truncated understanding of the nature of ideas. Athanasius did not put his life on the line for the Nicean formula simply because he thought it was a relatively adequate rational expression of Christian belief. He stood *contra mundum,* defending Nicea ferociously *because he believed that the salvation of the Christian community depended on that doctrine.* To fudge the teaching, as the Arians had, was not only to misplay a theological language game, but to compromise radically the dynamics of inner transformation in the minds and hearts of believers. Like his contemporaries and like the New Testament authors, Athanasius was convinced that "theoretical" icons have a saving power only when they are painted correctly.

St. Augustine, arguably the greatest mind in the history of the church, was the bishop of the town of Hippo in North Africa. By our standards, Hippo was a large parish, and Augustine its busy pastor, concerned with preaching, catechetics, and all the details of administration. His theological works fill several library shelves and are carefully examined today, for the most part, by students and professors of theology. But, once again, Augustine himself was not writing for such a rarefied audience. He endeavored to write "words about God" in order to move his flock closer to an *experience* of the God who is, in Augustine's own magnificent phrase, *interior intimo meo* (closer than we are to ourselves). Thus in his best known work, the *Confessions,*

Augustine moves from metaphysics to poetry to psychological autobiography in an effortless rhythm. We might be puzzled by this mixing
of genres, but given Augustine's wholistic sense of the purpose of theology, it is perfectly natural. He would undoubtedly be puzzled by our
inability to see the links between ideas and life, between *theoria* and
the stirring of the spirit. Even his most technical theological work, the
tortuously argued and densely complex *De trinitate,* was composed in
order to lure the Christian into the energies which constitute the divine power. The principal aim of the work was not the clarification
of the mind, but the transformation of the spirit into a Trinitarian
pattern.

Even St. Thomas Aquinas, supposedly the most "rationalist" of the
medieval thinkers, remains entirely patristic in the basically spiritual
orientation of his theology. If we attend carefully to the opening question of Thomas's masterpiece, the *Summa theologiae,* we find that the
purpose of *sacra doctrina,* theology, is the elevation of human beings toward their final end, the contemplation of God. Aquinas also
speaks of theology as a mystical participation in the intimate knowledge which God has of Godself. And how is this knowledge arrived at?
It is mediated through God's perfect revelation in Jesus Christ, God's
surprising, overwhelming, and unpredictable disclosure of the depth of
divine love in the Incarnation. In short, theology, for Thomas, is a
raising up of the human spirit to a new intensity of vision and insight
through the power of Jesus Christ; it is a type of *metanoia.*

If one had asked Origen, Athanasius, Augustine, or Aquinas to
distinguish between his technical theology and his "spirituality," he
would have been at a loss. He would probably not even have understood the question. For the great thinkers of Christianity, from the
New Testament period up through the Middle Ages, the "metanoetic"
quality of theology was taken for granted. But a split between what
we call today "spirituality" and "theology" began to open up sometime around the beginning of the fourteenth century, that is to say, in
the period just after the death of Thomas Aquinas. Theology, words
about God, became increasingly a formal academic discipline, taught
alongside of law and medicine in the great universities, whereas spirituality, reflection on the experience of God in one's life, became a

more or less underground concern of monks and mystics. In their effort to find intellectual respectability, theologians endeavored to conform to the more and more objective and disinterested style of the academy, thus consciously putting aside feeling, personal commitment, the focus on conversion. It is interesting to me that, according to the general consensus, Catholic theology went into decline just after this tragic rupture occurred, deteriorating into a cold and arid scholasticism, ready-made answers for technical questions unrelated to anyone's lived experience of the faith.

It wasn't until the twentieth century that the terrible division between theology and spirituality was addressed by Catholic theologians. The thinkers associated with the controversial *nouvelle théologie* (the new theology) — Henri de Lubac, Jean Daniélou, Karl Rahner, Hans Urs von Balthasar, and others — sought to return to the biblical and patristic sources that had given form to Catholic thought. And what they saw in the Bible and in the fathers was precisely the dynamic that we have been exploring: theology, not as a lifeless game of question and answer, but as seeing, as transforming, as a catalyst for soul conversion.

❖

One of Andrew Greeley's "laws" is that whatever Catholics drop, someone else eventually picks up. Around the time of the Second Vatican Council, Catholics began dropping the language of "soul," convinced that it had unfortunate dualistic overtones, and, in accordance with Greeley's prediction, it has been picked up all over the popular culture. *Care of the Soul,* Thomas Moore's book dealing with the cultivation of one's depths, sat atop the *New York Times* best-seller list for months; Joseph Campbell, the comparative mythologist who has been enjoying a posthumous vogue in recent years, was an unabashed celebrator of soul. And C. G. Jung, whose thought has penetrated the culture in so many ways, wrote a book entitled *Modern Man in Search of a Soul.* "Soul" has proven to be such a stubbornly useful term precisely because it names something which can be named in no other way. It refers, not to the mind alone or to the "spirit" alone or to the emotions and passions alone, but rather to the center and deepest point *of the whole person*. Soul is that point of contact with the divine, that power which is opened up through metanoia and faith. It is the "interior castle" of Teresa of Avila, the even more evocative "inner wine cellar" of Meister Eckhart and the *point vierge,* the virginal point, of which Thomas Merton speaks.

What I want to show in this book is precisely *how* theological teachings, doctrines, dogmas, and stories function "metanoetically," how they transform souls. One of the earliest and most passionate designations of Jesus in the Gospels is *Soter,* a word rendered in Latin as *salvator.* The *salvator* is the bearer of the *salus,* or health. The use of this title shows that Jesus was appreciated by his first followers as a healer, one who "salves" sin-sick people, who doctors souls. The first great theologians saw their work as an extension of this soul-healing power of Jesus of Nazareth: holding up the icon of his life, teaching, death, and resurrection has a soothing, transforming, healing effect on a disordered mind. I want to look at the teachings of theology as medicines for the deepest dimension of the human being. I want to read the great motifs of the theological tradition as expressions of what St. Bonaventure called the *Itinerarium mentis in Deum* (the journey of the spirit into God). I want to take the books of theology off of the dusty shelves of libraries and put them to use in service of the people of God. For it is my conviction that doctrines are powerful agents of transformation and that they have, for too long, been bottled up. It is as though we were in possession of vaccines to cure the most dreaded diseases of humankind *and refused to allow them to be used.*

Accordingly, I will look at some key theological themes of our tradition under three general headings: anthropology, doctrine of God, and Christology. Theological *anthropology* teaches us who we are in the presence of the divine, that is to say, at the level of *soul.* It analyzes the soul and learns its movements, its longings, its hopes, its typical problems, its anxieties. Just as the medical doctor studies biology in order to learn how the body functions, so the theologian or pastor studies anthropology in order to learn what makes souls sick or healthy. In the terms of our discussion, the theological anthropologist examines the dynamics of *metanoia* and awakening to faith.

The doctrine of God seeks to articulate the nature of the divine power which alone can bring healing and peace to our souls. It tries to speak of that reality which stands as the goal of our deepest longing and as the terminus of our most impassioned quest. The one who thinks about God endeavors to find the cure, the elixir, the Holy Grail, the object of "faith."

And Christology is the science which studies the coming together of the longing and its fulfillment, the reconciliation of the divine and the human, the achievement of the Kingdom of God. As such, it stands at the very center of our project. To analyze Jesus Christ is to understand the Good News in all of its concreteness and freshness, and to see with greatest clarity the height and depth, the length and breadth of the *magna anima*. To see Jesus is to know, in repentance, what is wrong with us, to glimpse, in hope, what is beautiful in us and to taste, in ecstasy, the God who summons us to union.

In the course of this study, we will range widely through the Christian tradition, drawing on authors as diverse as Dante, G. K. Chesterton, Flannery O'Connor, Thomas Aquinas, Origen, Hans Urs von Balthasar, James Joyce, William Faulkner, and Paul Tillich. We will use different styles and highlight widely divergent approaches, moving, as Augustine did, from literature to autobiography to abstract metaphysics to spirituality and back again. Some will probably find certain sections of the book more appealing than others, certain authors and approaches more congenial to their taste. With this I have no quarrel. The Christian tradition stubbornly and patiently walks around the icon of Christ, seeing it, describing it, speaking of it in various ways and with various audiences in mind, convinced that no one word, no one take, is sufficient to exhaust the "infinite richness of Christ." This book stands in that tradition and confidently adopts that pluralist style. It was John Henry Newman who said that the mind is brought to assent, not so much through any one clinching argument, but through a series of probable arguments converging and tending in the same direction. It is in accord with this "illative" approach that we proceed.

We will attempt to read the teachings of great literary, spiritual and theological figures "metanoetically," that is to say, as extensions of the healing energy contained in Jesus Christ. We shall present the Christian tradition, in its myriad manifestations, as an icon of Christ and hence as an agent for the transformation of soul and the opening up of vision.

"I was blind but now I see."

Part I

The Riven Self

Chapter One

The Mind of Fear

Beginning with Dante

We are staggering to the end of the bloodiest and most brutal century in history. Having witnessed the horror of the Holocaust and the brutal political murders of tens of millions in Soviet Russia, Communist China, and the Cambodia of the Khmer Rouge, having seen the near-successful attempts at genocide in Tibet, the Ukraine, and Rwanda, the ferocious and unending internecine religious wars in Ireland and the Holy Land, having noted the indiscriminate slaughter that followed upon the atomic bombings of Hiroshima and Nagasaki and the casual killing that takes place every day in the streets of major cities around the world — having witnessed all of that, it is exceedingly difficult for a twentieth-century observer to take seriously any program of human perfectibility, whether proposed by classical philosophers, religious enthusiasts, or the confident theorists of the Enlightenment. There seems to be something profoundly and dangerously *wrong* with us, a flaw that cannot be wished or thought away, an ineradicable darkness of the heart, a sickness of soul.

And the depth psychologists of our century have uncovered for us the frightening and uncontrollable abysses within us, those reaches of the soul that remain stubbornly strange, untamable, often contemptuous of the pretensions of the sovereign mind. We have been forced to surrender the conviction that we are serenely presiding over our lives, disposing of ourselves rationally, ordering the powers within purposefully and consciously. We have been compelled to admit that we are largely strangers to ourselves. When we look within (if we dare), we now see, not a well-ordered kingdom, but a chaotic blur of energies, a zoo from which most of the animals have escaped. When we

19

turn to the artists of our time to understand the human condition we find the shifting planes and split identities of Picasso's portraits, the multivalent and disquietingly off-centered inner monologues of Joyce's characters, the hopeless wait for Godot at the heart of Beckett's play, the confusion of Bob Dylan's helplessly rational Mr. Jones, the hauntingly silent scream of Edvard Munch's painting. Yes it seems as though our confidence is gone, lost as we are in Auden's Age of Anxiety.

And which of our modern poets is it who so pointedly gives voice to the feeling of our time: "so I find it to be a law that when I want to do right, evil lies close at hand. For I delight in the law of God, in my inmost self, but I see in my members another law at war with the law of my mind and making me captive to the law of sin which dwells in my members. Wretched man that I am! Who will deliver me from this body of death?" It is, of course, no modern figure at all, but rather the Apostle Paul speaking passionately to the tiny Christian church gathered in Rome in the middle of the first century. Paul knew all about the darkness that grips us from within, the uncontrollable forces that mock and shame us, the conflicts and rifts that madden us. With a perceptiveness that uncannily anticipates the depth psychologists, Paul saw through the rationalist optimism of the Greek philosophers. Plato felt that knowledge is the key to virtue, that if one only *understood* with clarity, one would be morally upright; and Aristotle thought that wisdom in combination with habituation would produce right action. Neither saw what Paul saw: the inner beast that undermines the finally pathetic attempts of reason to master the moral situation. Neither saw with requisite insight the terrible warfare that rages within the human person, rendering us riven, alienated, an enemy to ourselves.

Paul perceived exactly what so many artists, poets, playwrights — and ordinary sufferers — of our time have so clearly seen: the power of original sin. It is ironic that the very doctrine which the Enlightenment *philosophes* ferociously attacked as a holdover from a superstitious time effectively named the dark power that ultimately undid the Enlightenment project itself. What so many Christian theologians of the twentieth century indicated was just this arrogant bracketing of original sin and the concomitant overconfidence in the human capacity to create the earthly paradise. The overwhelming calamities of the century, they felt, served as a sort of judgment on this hubris and ignorance. It is my conviction that an indispensable spiritual exercise is to look, with honesty, calmness, and critical intelligence at the daunting darkness indicated by the doctrine of original sin. To ignore this admittedly puzzling teaching is to see only half the truth about ourselves and hence to undercut our spiritual progress. If we are called to "change our minds," we have to admit that there is something the matter with them; if we are to be saved, we must *feel* in the richest sense possible what it means to be lost. In short, an indispensable spiritual exercise for Christians is to sense the agony of the *pusilla anima*.

But original sin does not tell the whole story. If there is something irreducibly *wrong* with us, there is also, the gloominess of one-sided pessimists notwithstanding, something inescapably and stubbornly *right* about us. And our terrible century itself witnesses to this unquenchable light. The demonic fury of the Holocaust was followed by the emergence of a Jewish nation and the development of a post-Holocaust theology of hope against hope; the shocking destructiveness of the Second World War was followed by an even more shocking economic and political rebuilding; the dawn of the nuclear age prompted a profound reevaluation of our attitude toward just war and a critical examination of the roots of armed conflict; the institutionalized violence against the colonized peoples of India led to the liberating protest of Gandhi, and the systematic oppression of blacks in the United States stirred to eloquence the prophetic voices of W. E. B. Du Bois, Malcolm X, and Martin Luther King; Freud and Jung showed us the darkness and confusion within and then assured us that the journey through that frightening inscape would bring us to a peace of soul never before experienced; the Picasso who gave us the harsh cry of *Guérnica* also gave us the gentle sweetness in the portraits of his children; the Joyce who spoke so agonizingly of the breakdown of our overly rationalized confidence also places in the mouth of Molly Bloom the emphatic and ecstatic "Yes" to existence that closes out

Ulysses; the Bob Dylan who sang of the splintering and disintegrating of consciousness also sings of the "master's hand / in every leaf that trembles and in every grain of sand." It was Chesterton who remarked that the only problem more puzzling than the question of evil is the question of the good. What accounts, in the end, for our confidence in the face of the overwhelming warrant for despair? Why do we keep breathing in and out; why do we go on even when everything around us says, "Stop?"

The Christian answer to these questions is contained in the doctrine of the *imago Dei.* There is indeed something terribly the matter with us, and there is, at the same time, something foundationally good, something "divine" at the heart of us, a power or principle that keeps us hoping and living and striving. As the weed pushes its way through the harsh cement of the city sidewalk, so the human soul grows stubbornly and almost inexplicably toward the light.

When Jesus uttered his call for *metanoia,* he was assuming the presence of what our tradition has called original sin, and he was also presupposing the *imago,* some elemental goodness, some capacity for change and transformation. And people came to Christ, drank in his words, revelled in the provocativeness of his gestures, precisely because they felt the same tension of sin and *imago Dei* in themselves: they were sick, but they recognized what would make them well. Thus, the proper starting point for any healthy Christian theological anthropology is a clear sense of the togetherness of original sin and likeness unto God, for without the first, *metanoia* is unnecessary, and without the second, it is impossible. Thus, just as we must *look at* the dark face of our own sin, so we must *look at* the beauty that is God's enduring presence within us. Both of these facts must be seen, accounted for, experienced if effective *metanoia* is to take place. We must know and, more to the point, feel in our bones, what is wrong in us; we must look it in the face and acknowledge it with uncompromising honesty. Without this "searching moral inventory," without this journey into our own inner Hell, we will not feel the compunction to shift our way of being and seeing. And, at the same time, we must awaken to what is god-like in us, what is rich and fecund and unbroken, what is in continuity with the saving designs of God. Without this clear sense, we will fall into complacency or hopelessness and see *metanoia* as, at best, a cruel illusion. Yes, the *pusilla anima* must be acknowledged, but the *magna anima* must be hoped for with confidence.

Now the tools proposed for this essential and two-pronged spiritual exercise are the doctrines of original sin and *imago Dei*. It is the wager of the spiritual and theological tradition that the contemplation of these icons will effect a metamorphosis, a shift in the way we see ourselves and the God who has come to save us. Without a sufficient immersion in the transformative power of the doctrine of original sin, a person will come to see himself as divine, as the unconditioned center of his universe; and without a sufficient exposure to the doctrine of the *imago*, a person will appreciate herself as hopelessly perverse and hence the object of the relentless pursuit of the judging God. When the delicate equilibrium between these two doctrines is lost we confront, therefore, the idols of the ego as god and God as crushing competitor.

First we shall engage in the spiritual work of looking at our sin. We shall do so with the help of three icons from the Christian tradition: a medieval poem, a biblical myth, and a doctrinal statement. Using very different rhetorical forms and with different audiences in mind, these three "showings" of sin perform the same soul-doctoring function. They all bring us face to face with the inner darkness; they all convince us of our helplessness; and they all consequently open us to grace. Having explored the nooks and crannies of the *pusilla anima*, we shall look, with hope, at the *magna anima*. Let us begin the work.

Many have commented that Dante's *Divine Comedy* is basically a celebration of seeing. The pilgrim is led from the deepest obscurity at the beginning of the poem to a blinding light at the end, and along the path from darkness to illumination, he is compelled to look at truths about himself and the world with ever deeper vision and comprehension. The *Commedia* is a mystagogic itinerary, an account of the spiritual journey from confusion and dissolution to clarity and centeredness. It would not be far from the truth to claim that the *telos* of the *Divine Comedy* is what we have been calling *metanoia*, change of vision and consciousness. It is therefore appropriate that we begin our analysis of the transformative power of doctrine with Dante's great epic.[2]

The *Divine Comedy* opens in the darkness of a deep wood in the year 1300. The narrator, "midway along the journey of our life,"[3] suddenly finds himself alone and lost, far from the "straight path" on which he had been traveling. The fearsomeness of that moment — "a bitter place; death could scarce be bitterer" — is such that he can barely bring himself to speak of it.[4] In 1300, Dante was thirty-five, indeed "midway" between birth and death, at that terrible crossroad spoken of by so many psychologists and spiritual writers, a time of crisis and decision, of depression and fear. At midlife, many people awaken to the fact that they are lost, that the goals and styles and attitudes of the first half of life no longer satisfy, no longer "work." In the language of the Jungians, they know that the ego, the center of the rational consciousness, is not master in its own house and cannot simply command achievement and positive affect as it once could. The midlife period is a desert trek, an undersea journey or, in Dante's image, a wandering in the deep woods.

As is so often the case in spiritual literature, it is precisely at this painful moment, at this time of confusion unto death, that the journey properly begins. It is almost a commonplace among the masters of the soul that to start from any other position — from success, adulation, confidence, pleasure — is to skew the journey in the direction of the self-elevation of the ego. As is so often emphasized in the Twelve-Step programs, it is only the experience of "hitting bottom" that can prompt the salvific upward movement. Having reached the lowest point, Dante makes the simple move that will eventually lead to his salvation:

> I raised my head, and saw the hilltop shawled
> in morning rays sent from the planet
> that leads men straight ahead on every road."[5]

In the depths of the woods of depression and fear, Dante looks up and sees; he refuses to stay mired in his pain and rather spies the goal of his desire, the mountain of God, washed in the light of glory. He tells us that this vision alone caused his "terror to subside." Again, this sort of flash of insight is commonly described by the spirit masters. At the very beginning of the journey, the spiritual seeker spies, with great clarity, the goal of his quest, and this vision fires him with tremendous enthusiasm and even impatience. In the *angustiae* of the small soul, one sees the possibility of the *magna anima* and is eager to realize it. The mistake, of course, is to think that arriving at and climbing the mountain are relatively simple tasks.

And this is Dante's errant strategy. With eagerness, firmness of purpose, and even a touch of arrogance, he leaves behind the terrible darkness of the woods, "taking one last look," and begins his confident climb up the shining mountain. But immediately he confronts three beasts — a leopard, a lion, and a wolf — and they utterly block his ascent, indeed forcing him fearfully back down the slope. The animals are evocative of the love of pleasure, fierce pride, and ravenous greed that inhabit the soul of the pilgrim and prevent him from any sort of rapid rise to the level of consciousness of God. Having appreciated his lost state and having glimpsed the goal of his quest, Dante now sees the *sins* that block him, the evils he must confront if he is to come to self-transformation. The wild beasts convince him, much to his chagrin, that his beginner's enthusiasm must be tempered and that a hard work lies ahead of him. Frustrated, frightened again, Dante knows that he cannot make it up the mountain on his own power, and this ego surrender is indispensable, the condition for the possibility of the itinerary that will follow. To lift oneself out of spiritual malaise is self-contradictory, for the cause of the malaise itself is the dominance and overconfidence of the ego. The thrashing about of the *pusilla anima* is no way to produce the *magna anima*.

In accord with the natural rhythms of the spiritual life, it is precisely when Dante finds himself once again in direst need, once again at his wits' end, that help arrives:

> While I was rushing down to that low place,
> my eyes made out a figure coming toward me
> of one grown faint, perhaps from too much silence.[6]

In line with the common Eastern adage "when the student is ready, the teacher comes," Dante's psychopomp, mystic guide, shaman appears just when the pilgrim is ready to receive him. The wise man's faintness is a wonderful touch. Dante has been so preoccupied with the concerns of the first half of life that he has rarely allowed his inner mystic guide to speak. The "wise old man" of his own unconscious is, accordingly, weary from too much silence. The Roman poet Virgil introduces himself and calmly informs Dante that he will never succeed in climbing the mountain of light directly: "but you must journey down another road . . . if you ever hope to leave this wilderness." The road that he proposes is the terrible route that leads through Hell, that place of "second death," the realm of the lost souls. The confrontation with sin that began on the mountain now must be dramatically intensified. Dante must *see* in its fullness the range and power of human sin; he must look at *himself*, careful to gauge and measure the destructiveness that dwells within. What Dante presents as a geographical journey downward toward the center of the earth is a symbolic evocation of the inner itinerary down to the depths of the soul, to the heart of darkness. The mind of fear must be plumbed before the mind of trust can emerge.

Prompted by grace and guided by poetic wisdom, Dante enters into the Hell of his own disordered soul and carefully picks his way through the spiritual wasteland, seeing, mourning, and learning. It is eminently clear that this process is a painful and arduous one, a sort of dark night of the soul. As they approach the gate of Hell, Virgil encourages Dante with these words:

> Here you must leave all distrust behind;
> let all of your cowardice die on this spot.[7]

Confronting one's own shadow, the spirit masters concur, is always a dangerous business, and the road to healing is always blocked; hence courage is called for. In accord with the beautifully imagined geography of the *Divine Comedy*, he will descend through numerous "circles" or levels, each one providing the context for ever more errant expressions of the spirit. Mimicking the "feel" of sin, the constriction of the heart, each successive circle becomes tighter, more suffocating.

As he descends through Hell, Dante sees three basic divisions in the types of evil punished: sins of incontinence, sins of violence, and sins of fraudulence. In visiting each circle and witnessing the increasingly intense suffering of the damned, Dante sees the variegated complexity of his own sinfulness. Like the passions of the incontinent, his passions are disordered and frequently uncentered; like the violent, he aggressively holds off those who would threaten his own primacy; like the fraudulent, he undermines his own soul for the sake of selfish gain. As he moves through the levels of Hell, Dante sees ever more nefarious and focused expressions of his own corruption of soul. There is something relentless, nearly cruel, about this journey, and frequently Dante asks Virgil to spare him a particular sight or smell. Sometimes the pilgrim is so overwhelmed by what he sees that he swoons, only to awaken to more horror. Onward they go until all of the symphony of sin is heard, until all of the terrible icon of dissolution is revealed.

The pilgrim arrives at last at the very pit of Hell, a place where ice rather than fire dominates. The frozen landscape speaks of the lifelessness, constriction, and coldness of sin, the paralysis of the heart that is the chief consequence of egotism. At the center and deepest ground of Hell, buried to his waist in ice, presides Satan, the great beast, the one-time angel of light whose pride had destroyed him. His angel's wings have been transformed into the wings of a bat which beat the air unceasingly, producing the atmospheric conditions of this underground, upside-down world. Satan has three heads, and in the mouth of each writhes a sinner: Brutus, Cassius, and Judas, the archetypal traitors. Evidently for Dante, the betrayal of a friend for the sake of personal gain remains the chief perversion of the soul, far graver than any sin of incontinence or violence.

But it is the figure of Satan himself—the embodiment of the spiritual attitude of sin—that is worthy of special attention. At the center of Hell, Satan is a perverse mockery of the one who is the center of the universe. Thus the devil's three heads are an echo of the three persons of the Trinity, and his immobility in the ice is a lampoon of God's perfect unchangeability. A theme that is strongly rooted in Scripture and tradition is that of sin as perverted deification, turning oneself into God. Sinners make themselves the unconditioned absolute and hence live in a realm of illusion and shadow (like so much of the Inferno). And more to the point, they become a caricature of the divine, pathetically aping and parroting the true God but getting the impression comically wrong. Thus Satan "reigns" impotently and motionlessly at the heart of his dark kingdom.

Following Aquinas and others, Dante held that the goal of the human spirit is to soar upward and outward in the direction of the fullness of reality. As we have seen, the geography of Hell moves in the opposite direction, toward greater and greater narrowness, culminating in the single point where Satan himself is frozen in place. His angelic wings, originally evocative of the sailing upward of the healthy soul, now beat in vain, symbolizing the pointless efforts of the soul locked in sin:

> not feathered wings but rather like the ones
> a bat would have. He flapped them constantly,
> keeping three winds continuously in motion.[8]

Instead of contributing to flight, these wings serve only to make the atmosphere around Lucifer colder, just as the spiritual efforts of the egotist radiate coldly outward. This is a vivid evocation, of course, of the smallness of the *pusilla anima*. When we live in fear, we close in on ourselves, inhabiting, in the end, a kingdom precisely as large as the narrow confines of our egos.

And Satan chews on the three great traitors, punishing them to be sure, but also intensifying his own suffering:

> In each of his three mouths he crunched a sinner
> with teeth like those that rake the hemp and flax,
> keeping three sinners constantly in pain.[9]

It is so characteristic of the sinner to "chew" on old resentments, bitterness, past hurts, refusing either to swallow them or spit them out, never resolving them but only allowing them to deepen and fester. "Tormenting" those who have caused him pain, he only increases his own agony. And Dante saw another typical mark of sinners, namely, the tendency to punish precisely those who most resemble the sinners themselves, to project their own negativity outward. Thus Lucifer punishes most sharply those who, in their treachery and pride, are the mirror of Lucifer.

In Dante's vision, all the devil does is cry, from each of his six eyes:

> He wept from his six eyes, and down three chins
> were dripping tears all mixed with bloody slaver.[10]

This Lucifer has nothing to do with the Satan of Milton's *Paradise Lost* or with the Mephistopheles of Goethe's *Doctor Faustus* or even with the devil of C. S. Lewis's *Screwtape Letters*. All those figures are marked by a certain elegance and charm, a personal presence of some persuasiveness and authority. They are effective seducers and mighty rulers, forces to be reckoned with. Dante's devil is, on the contrary, a pathetic figure, someone who is just basically sad. Like a person in chronic depression, Dante's Lucifer stays helplessly in one place, mulls unproductively over past resentments, and weeps unceasingly. Neither charming nor seductive, the heart of darkness is, after all, rather pitiful and dull. This Dantean symbolic evocation of the psychodynamics of sin strikes me as far more effective than Goethe's, Milton's, or Lewis's. In its relatively superficial expressions, sin can have a certain seductive, glamorous power, but Sin itself, the source of moral evil, is essentially empty, banal, impotent, since it is nothing but an illusion, a false perception. Sins can be intriguing and captivating; Sin is just sad. It is interesting to note in this context that so many of the lesser devils and evil spirits whom Dante encounters on his journey through Hell are far more titillating, mobile, and powerful than Satan himself.

Of course what Dante has uncovered here is the dark and empty heart of his own sinful spirit. He has now seen the source, the deepest ground, of all of the errant expressions of the small soul that have bedeviled him: gluttony, pride, anger, sensuousness, pusillanimity, etc. He has discovered the dynamo that has energized all of his sinfulness, the beast within, and all it can do is weep. The heart of darkness is not an overpowering force; rather it is a pathetic sadness, a tortured creature weeping and wailing in self-reproach. Aquinas and so many other masters of the spirit hold that sin is a perversion, a bending, a corruption of a will that is fundamentally good. As such, it is best described as a negation, essentially an illusion. And there is, it is safe to say, cause for rejoicing here. Like a child who discovers that the monster under his bed is only a figment of his imagination, Dante sees that the pit of his own Hell is far more pitiful than frightening, a power that can be mastered through vision and compassion.

It is captivating how the *Inferno* ends. After arduous adventures and swoon-producing confrontations with horrors beyond description, Virgil and Dante calmly grasp the flanks of Satan and move down his body until they escape from the confines of Hell.

> He grabbed on to the shaggy sides of Satan;
> then downward, tuft by tuft, he made his way
> between the tangled hair and frozen crust.[11]

Sad Satan can do nothing to stop them; indeed he seems barely to notice them. Dante escapes from Hell because he has thoroughly *seen* it, even to the point of witnessing the helplessness of Lucifer himself. He conquers Hell by *embracing* it in the richest sense possible, hanging on to the sides of Satan. As is urged by so many of the spiritual masters, the evil within has to be seen and concretely confronted, faced, wrestled with. One must press one's nose up against the hairy sides of sin and embrace it if one is to conquer it. It is wonderful to note that as Virgil and Dante climb *down* the flanks of Satan, they reach a point where they suddenly and inexplicably begin to climb *up*. Having grasped on to evil and faced it, having climbed down as far as he could possibly go, Dante commences the upward surge. There is no way up but down; there is no pathway to the stars except that which leads through Hell; the route to *metanoia* is through the thorniness of sin.

What has Dante searched out in the course of his itinerary? He has seen the full range of disorder in his spirit, sins both actual and potential, and he has ultimately explored the very root of sinfulness itself, the comical/tragic anti-god which is the fearful and impotent *pusilla anima*. Like a patient undergoing psychoanalysis, he has descended (properly inspired and guided) into the darkness and narrowness of his inner life in order to unmask the demons that lurk there. He has tracked down the evil spirits to their deepest spring, uncovering in the end the "original," that is to say, originating Sin of sins. And in this process, he has come to a real liberation. Only after this necessarily horrible journey is he able to begin the task of purgation and renewal. Interestingly, throughout his sojourn, Dante frequently felt a sort of sympathy for the suffering souls whom he confronted, and Virgil, his mystic guide, consistently upbraided him for this sentiment, reminding him that these sinners were in such a state because of the divine justice. We might be tempted to side with Dante here, but our perspective shifts when we recall that the poem is speaking of the inner life. The aberrations of consciousness that we confront within must not be sympathized with or tolerated; they must be seen and unmasked. It is a profound temptation to coddle and toy with our tendencies toward hatred, violence, self-destruction, and fear, but like the demons in the Scripture whom Jesus ruthlessly and pitilessly expels, the devils within us must be confronted and commanded.

Just as Dante uses geography to evoke dimensions of the spiritual life, so he uses chronology. The dark night of the soul with which the *Commedia* begins takes place on Good Friday, the day of crucifixion. The sojourn in Hell happens on Holy Saturday, the day corresponding to Christ's time in the bowels of the earth, his own journey into Hell. And when Virgil and Dante emerge from the cave to see once more the light of the stars, it is Easter Sunday morning, the day of resurrection. The *Divine Comedy* is patterned according to the paschal mystery of Christ's passage from death to life, or better, *through* death to life. It is essential to the Gospel writers and to Dante that the *only* way to the glory of resurrection is through the suffering of the cross and the descent into the earth of sin.

Chapter Two

ORIGINATING SIN

The Tumble out of the Garden

Like Dante's great work of Christian poetry, Christian dogmatic the-ology is structured according to the rhythm of the paschal mystery. Doctrines — like Gospel stories and spiritual itineraries — have a mystagogic function: they are to move believers from errant, sinful con-sciousness to a renewal of soul; they are to draw them through death into life. Their purpose, in a word, is "metanoetic," soul-transforming. Just as Dante's transformation begins with the experience of being lost, Christian theology begins, logically, with the awakening to crisis, with the sense that there is something dramatically wrong with us. Chris-tianity is not a nature mysticism or system of contemplation; rather, it is a salvation religion which proposes a solution to a fundamental existential problem. Without a feel for the problem, Christianity's an-swer seems absurd. Thus, as we saw in the introductory chapter, it is essential, as a first step, to wake-up, to break out of self-complacency, to sense, with dramatic intensity, that all is not right.

The doctrine that is meant to effect this wake-up and to facilitate the process of coming to grips with negativity is that of original sin. By looking profoundly at this icon of the spiritual life, we see more precisely what it means to be lost, *and* we begin to discern the path that must be followed if we are to put ourselves aright. The teaching on original sin is meant, not to depress us or convict us of our worth-lessness, but, quite to the contrary, to give us reason to hope, to shed some light when we find ourselves "alone and lost in a dark wood." The icon of original sin is designed to force us into our own inner Hell, to look at and name what is aberrant and self-destructive in us, and its spiritual power is not exhausted until we have gone, like Dante, to the very depths and found the Lucifer, the beating of whose wings renders cold the entire inner atmosphere. Only when we have successfully named and conquered that power are we in a position to move up the mountain of purgatory, to awaken the image of God within us. Like Virgil, the doctrine of original sin is a mystagogue, relentlessly pushing us to honesty and spiritual nakedness, forcing us to see all that must be seen. As Dante tried so often to avoid certain sights in Hell, so we sinners try, by any means possible, to look away from the darkness within. We cast the blame on our neighbors, on society, on our psychological blocks, on the church, on God, assiduously avoiding the honest assessment of ourselves which alone will lead to liberation. The icon of original sin is a mirror to the dark soul, a glass in which we see uncompromisingly reflected the disorders of our consciousness.

Though the doctrine of original sin as such was developed, largely by Augustine, in the patristic period, its roots are profoundly biblical. In the first pages of Genesis, we read the story of the Fall, a mythic projection back to the beginning of time (*in illo tempore*) of the basic dynamic of sin. In the sin of Adam and Eve, the author of Genesis is seeking out the fundamental or "originating" energy of all sin, that Satan at the deepest ground of each person's inner Hell. It is worth our while to attend closely to the narrative moves of this almost too familiar account, trying as best we can to read it "naively," as if for the first time, without the full weight of the theological tradition conditioning our interpretation at every step.

We are told that God formed the first human being out of the dust of the earth and blew into his nostrils the breath of life. Next God planted a garden in the East, a place watered by four rivers, and placed the man in the garden giving him the command to till the soil and care for this paradise. In Eden there were two trees of special note, namely, the tree of Life and the tree of the knowledge of good and evil. Of the second, the man was told by God not to eat lest he die, although he was given free rein to eat of any other tree, including presumably the tree of Life. Realizing that it was not good for the man to be solitary, God created from the earth beasts and animals of all kinds, and though Adam named them, none proved to be a worthy companion. So from the rib of Adam, God fashioned the woman, Eve, and she became the man's partner. Both were naked, but utterly unashamed of their nakedness. At this point, the shrewdest and subtlest of God's creatures, the serpent, enters into the scene and begins to lure the woman in the direction of eating of the tree of knowledge. Assuring her that God has prohibited the fruit of this tree only out of jealousy, he convinces her to violate the divine command. She eats of the tree and then shares the fruit with her husband. Immediately their eyes were opened and, realizing their nakedness, they covered up their genitals, presumably out of shame: "they sewed fig leaves together to make themselves loincloths" (Gen. 3:7).

This classic story has been interpreted in myriad ways over the centuries, as an account of the tumble from dreaming innocence to dangerous experience, as a cautionary tale concerning the perils of sex, as a symbolic evocation of the transition from unitary to divided consciousness, as a condemnation of pride and a call to obedience. What I want to offer is a reading that, without necessarily excluding any of the above-mentioned insights, emphasizes the rise of sin precisely in the incapacity to trust, to live in relation to the alluring Mystery of God.

Adam is made from the dust of the earth and receives the breath of life from God. There is a kind of elemental dualism discernible here: the first human being is both material and spiritual, both drawn upward from the earth and endowed with the energy of the divine. Unlike the angels, Adam is ontologically split, a child, if you will, of both heaven and earth. However, and this is most important to notice, this split identity is not in itself evil or the source of evil; like all of the Lord's creatures, Adam is good — and his very complexity is essential to his goodness. The Genesis account never follows the all too easy path of identifying the battle between good spirit and evil matter as the source of human suffering and depravity. The best spirits in the Judeo-Christian tradition have always firmly resisted the temptation to move in this interpretive direction. Indeed, this spiritual animal is given the garden of paradise — with all of its sensual delights — as his proper field of operation. God delivers to the first human beings the positive command to enjoy and savor the goods of creation, including and especially the beauty and pleasure of each other. Thomas Aquinas speaks for at least one side of the tradition when he says that Adam and Eve experienced the fullness of sexual pleasure in the garden precisely because their bodies and spirits were in such natural harmony. No Manichaeism there. Furthermore, they are commanded to cultivate the garden, implying that they are to exercise their gifts of mind and will and imagination to bring their world to full flourishing. In their enspirited bodiliness, in loving communion, and in the realization of their natural powers and potentials, human beings are as God meant them to be.

In his splendid spiritual meditation *The Divine Milieu,* Pierre Teilhard de Chardin speaks of the "divinization of human activities."[12] He bemoans the pious tendency to denigrate our activities, accomplishments, and achievements in the interest of greater "spiritualization," as if a concentration on what human beings can do is tantamount to pride. On the contrary, he argues, we glorify God inasmuch as we cooperate with God's creation of the universe through our inventiveness, our curious intelligence, our bold dreams. In fact, the "cultivation of the garden" in which God has placed us constitutes an intense spiritualization of our humanity. Teilhard speaks here for the mainstream of the tradition stretching back to the Genesis account of creation: to be intelligently, bravely, imaginatively at work and play in the world, fully exerting our powers, is to give glory to the Creator God and to realize ourselves. Science, technology, poetry, architecture, literature, philosophy, engineering, diplomacy, sports, government, genteel conversation, wit — all of the flowers of civilization — are praiseworthy, humanizing, and sacred. There is nothing in Genesis to justify either a puritanical repression of the sexual or a pessimistic, moralizing denigration of human excellence.

But then there is the prohibition. Yes, they may eat of any of the trees of the garden, enjoying themselves and exercising their dominion fully, but of the tree of the knowledge of good and evil they are forbidden to eat. Some would argue that all prohibitions — all thou shalt nots — belong to a child's world, to a primitive form of consciousness prior to the dawning of real engagement and responsibility. From this perspective, the seemingly arbitrary command not to eat of a particular tree is a sort of fearful childish memory of the race, a dreadful taboo imposed on us in our minority, a primal terror of up-setting parental authority. In the interpretations of Kierkegaard and Paul Tillich, we find something of this: the command not to eat of the tree of knowledge is the expression of humanity's fear of leaving the garden of innocence and inexperience. And thus it is that Adam and Eve fall so quickly, so effortlessly, as if they were following a positive impulse, the forward evolution of the psyche. Without entirely repu-diating this interpretive strain (there is indeed a child's world quality to the Genesis account), I would prefer to move in another direction, emphasizing what Augustine saw: the temptation inherent in the very godlike exercise of our powers.

Legitimately at play in the garden of the Lord — tasting, master-ing, enjoying — the first humans, in this very divinization of their activities, begin to wonder whether they are not the complete masters of their lives, whether they are not in a position to see and control even the deepest things. Feeling what Paul Tillich memorably called *Schöpfungslust* (the exuberance of being a creature), they move in the direction of self-deification, becoming through their own achieve-ments the center and ground of their lives. It is here that we see why God has forbidden the eating of the tree of the knowledge of good and evil. This is by no means a prohibition against knowledge per se, born, as the Enlightenment would have it, of a typically religious obscuran-tism. As we have seen, the pursuit of knowledge, even to the limits of human capacity, is entailed in the permission to enjoy and culti-vate the garden. It is not science as such that is prohibited, but the *knowledge of good and evil,* that is to say, the final and unsurpassable understanding of the whole that God alone possesses. Where does the universe come from and what is its final destiny? What is the deepest meaning of my own life? Why is the cosmos, with all of its light and darkness, all of its shadings and ambiguities, all of its unresolved ten-sions and puzzles, organized the way it is? Where is the human race being led? What is the very essence of God?

To seek the answers to these questions, to desire to grasp with rational clarity those things that the infinite mind of God alone can see, is to eat from the tree of the knowledge of good and evil. In forbidding the first humans to eat of this tree, God is teaching them that, after the full flowering of their achievements and activities, they are invited, not to be active, not to accomplish, but to surrender in trust. The story implies that we human beings can — to a remarkable extent — *achieve* success and joy through our efforts but that the deepest and most enduring happiness is possible only through the nonachievement of faith in a power beyond ourselves. We can, to some degree, understand who we are, what the universe is, and even who God is, but the fullness of this knowledge is, necessarily, beyond the powers of a limited soul, and thus we have access to it only through a suspension of our grasping and a deep relaxation of the spirit in trust. Action, then passivity; striving, then letting go; doing all that one can and then being carried; breathing in and then breathing out — only in this rhythm is the spirit realized. Our lives, in the end, are not about us, but about a power beyond us. Is God, strictly speaking, denying us the knowledge of good and evil? No, God is rather insisting that such knowledge comes, not through grasping but through being grasped. In fact we Christians know that the goal of the Incarnation is precisely to lure us, through Christ, into such intimacy with God that we see and know God as God is. It is not the "what" but the "how" of this knowledge that is carefully regulated in the garden.

At the very beginning of the *Summa theologiae*, Thomas Aquinas makes an observation that is perfectly in line with this spirituality of Genesis. In the opening article of the opening question of the first part of his masterpiece, Aquinas wonders why there must be a revealed science beyond the rational sciences articulated by Aristotle. After all, since philosophy seems to explore with great clarity even the deepest things of God, it seems that we have no need of divine assistance in our knowing. Thomas's answer is simple. We require a revealed science precisely because we have been oriented by nature to an end that surpasses our natural powers to see and to understand. We seek some-

thing that we cannot in principle attain through our own powers.[13]
Here again is the rhythm: there is nothing wrong with science or with
intellectual mastery, but the deepest, richest, profoundest level cannot
be reached through those means. Grasp all you want, but at the end
of the day, you must be lured. As many have commented, the events
at the end of Thomas's own life witness to this truth. In December
of 1273, after a career of stunning intellectual achievement and literary effort, Thomas Aquinas simply stopped writing. When his friend
Reginald pressed him to continue, Thomas responded laconically, "I
cannot; everything I've written seems like straw compared to what has
been revealed to me." After decades of striving to know, something of
decisive importance was *given to him;* he spent a lifetime breathing in,
and at the end he learned how necessary it was to breathe out.

And we find something similar in Teilhard. After insisting on the
divinization of our activities, Teilhard reminds us that our lives take
on real spiritual power only in the progressive divinization of our pas-
sivities. Life, he thinks, is divided into two unequal sections, the first
given over to accomplishment and the second — far more important than the first — to acceptance by another. In the second period,
we allow ourselves to be "hollowed out," prepared for transformation
through the power of God.[14] In this "passivity" we participate most
profoundly in the *milieu divin.* In his remarkable speech to Peter by the
Sea of Galilee, the resurrected Jesus says to the leader of the disciples: "I tell you most solemnly, when you were young you put on your
own belt and walked where you liked; but when you grow old you will
stretch out your hands, and somebody else will put a belt around you
and take you where you would rather not go" (John 21:18). Is he not
telling Peter that his life will be transfigured only when, at the end of
his legitimate cultivation of the garden, he allows himself to be culti-
vated? And is all of this not implied in the tension between the joy of
the garden and the command not to eat of that one tree?

At the heart of the originating sin is the refusal to accept the
rhythm. What the serpent, the cleverest of God's creatures, awakens
in the mind of Eve is the temptation to radical autonomy, to complete
self-mastery. He makes the surrender to God appear, not as an invitation to deeper life, but as a denigrating and dehumanizing act. The

snake's opening gambit is intriguing: he asks the woman, "Did God say, 'You shall not eat of any tree of the garden?'" One can almost imagine the feigned look of shock on the serpent's face as he formulates this question. He seems to insinuate that God must be a strange and difficult lawgiver, desirous of keeping his rational creatures under strict control. Is his question not subtly planting in the mind of Eve the beginnings of resentment toward God, of rivalry with God, and, above all, of *fear* of God? How could God have imposed prohibitions on his children and what must his reasons be?

Though undoubtedly troubled by the question, Eve, childlike innocence still intact, answers directly: "We may eat of the fruit of the trees of the garden, but God said, 'You shall not eat of the fruit of the tree which is in the midst of the garden, neither shall you touch it, lest you die.'" Specifying the nature and limited range of the divine prohibition, she, for the moment, keeps at bay the general fear of God which the serpent had tried to awaken, but the snake is not so easily put off. He assures her that she will not die if she eats of the tree and that, in point of fact, it is God's fear and jealousy of *her* that prompted this arbitrary commandment: "for God knows that when you eat of it your eyes will be opened and you will be like God, knowing good and evil." At the root of the snake's temptation is the assumption that God and human beings are essentially rivals, involved in a desperate zero-sum game of competition and mutual antagonism. We ought to be fearful of God because he crushes us with his commands, and God ought to be afraid of us because we might supplant him with our knowledge; God doesn't want us to be like him because his majesty would then be compromised, and we don't want to remain in ignorance because our existence would then be threatened. To be at the expense of another, to be over and against, to be through clinging, these are all the marks of the sinful stance of soul. Fear of the other is the cause and the consequence of sin.

Eve is awakened to self-consciousness through the words of the serpent and through her action, but to a warped and illusory self-consciousness, to an awareness of herself as an isolated ego threatened by an imposing and overbearing divinity. She has become "like" God in order to protect herself from God; she has changed herself into the "supreme" being in order to hold her own against the other highest reality. So she eats of the fruit proffered to her by the serpent and, with remarkable ease, convinces her husband to do the same. In this moment, in this autonomous grasp at godliness, in this excessive exercise of their legitimate spiritual power, the first human beings sin. At the heart of it is mistrust of the Mystery and a concomitant disenchantment of the world. "And immediately their eyes were opened and they realized they were naked." Ingeniously, the author of Genesis identifies the first and most devastating result of the fearful clinging which is sin: shameful self-consciousness. Having turned to themselves out of fear of God, Adam and Eve "know" their nakedness and vulnerability. They have left the garden of dreaming innocence, and they have come to self-possession (which is all to the good), but they have come to know themselves, not as the beloved children of the Mystery, but as frightened supreme beings, exposed, susceptible to verbal assault and insinuation.

Shamed and frightened, they "make loincloths so as to cover themselves." Covering, defending, making armor, hiding — all are characteristics of the beleaguered ego now precariously at the center of the universe. From the standpoint of the ego-fortress produced by fear, the other can be seen only as an enemy or potential enemy, and one's own life can be appreciated only as something vulnerable to invasion and hence as something that must be covered up, concealed, defended. Once more, it is entirely appropriate that the author of Genesis keeps us in the symbolic field of sexuality here. Our first parents cover up their genitals immediately after they have eaten of the tree, that is to say, they hide what is most intimate and personal, what is, in fact, the mode of deepest union with the other. Once the ego reigns at the center, the very act which should be a celebration of self-forgetfulness becomes frightening and dangerous and shame-producing. From the perspective of fear, sexual intimacy — and all of its attendant emotional engagement — is the single most dangerous human act, the one most fraught with perils, since it puts the ego at greatest risk.

Now when the first sinners sense the presence of God making his way through the foliage of the garden, they instinctively hide themselves, thus playing out the fear that the snake had placed in the mind of Eve. To their now unconditioned and centralized egos, the divine must appear as a threat and a rival, one from whom escape is the proper strategy. It is incorrect to interpret their action as simply the childish avoidance of the arbitrary punishment that they know will follow the transgression of the divine command. There is something much more subtly "adult" at work here, namely, the conscious and willful desire to establish independence from God, to find a place where the press of God will not be felt. Having grasped at godliness unsuccessfully, they now try to hide from God, and in these two moves, we see the very essence of the originating sin.

The great insight of the author of Genesis, of course, is that there is no place to hide from God. The Creator effortlessly foils his creatures' pathetic attempt to conceal themselves and he confronts them: "Where are you?" Adam's answer is of enormous spiritual moment: "I heard the sound of you in the garden, and I was afraid because I was naked, so I hid." The first human being, the original sinner, witnesses to the basic dynamic of egotism: in clinging to myself, he implies, I realized how terribly vulnerable I am (nakedness) and how much of a threat you are to me (and so I hid). Covering up and hiding are the principal consequences of the fearful enthronement of the ego, and the spiritual/moral desert in which all of us human beings live is the result of those simple but devastating "original" moves. Our entire social, economic, political and military establishment can be seen as the frantic and finally self-defeating attempt to cover up our nakedness, to protect our egos.

We surround ourselves with objects, gadgets, toys, condominiums, VCRs, designer clothes, Pentium computers, insured bank accounts, political parties, and atomic weapons — all of them descendants of the loincloth sewn together by Adam and Eve. All of these are, to the sinful soul, defense mechanisms, armor plating, means of concealing the very capacity for love which is the one thing that will authentically save us from our fear. And the ranginess and creativity of our sinfulness — all the circles of Hell described by Dante, our violence, our betrayal, our blasphemy, our prejudice, our butchery, our quiet resentment, our refusal to forgive — all of those are the offspring of our first parents' concealment in the shrubbery and underbrush of Eden. All of our perversion of soul is the consequence of a desire to escape from God, to make ourselves isolated sovereigns in the garden.

One way to read the magnificent 139th Psalm is as a lament of the sinful ego:

> Where can I run from your love?
> If I climb the heavens you are there
> If I sink into the grave, you are there.
> If I take the wings of the dawn
> and dwell at the sea's furthest end,
> even there your right hand holds me up.

Could the psalmist be giving voice to the sinful *desire* to flee from the press of the divine, to find *someplace* where God is not, some ground where he can stand without the threat of God's intervention? Could this not be another version of Adam's desperate and finally futile attempt to conceal himself from the sight of God? On this reading, the psalm itself is an ironic, almost playful, acknowledgment that this hiding game of the self-elevating ego is hopeless, that there is, in the end, no place to run, and that, just perhaps, the proper attitude is one of laughing surrender to this hound of heaven who will not be put off the trail.

As the story of the Fall unfolds, the author of Genesis displays the consequences that follow from this fearful grasp of the ego and the concomitant dread of God. When God challenges Adam, "Have you eaten of the tree of which I commanded you not to eat?" the man blames his wife and, by implication, the God who brought her into being: "It was the woman you put with me; she gave me the fruit and I ate it." And when the woman is confronted, she conveniently passes the buck to the snake: "The serpent tempted me, and I ate it." The sovereign ego cannot accept blame or responsibility; it must defend itself at all costs, holing up in its protective fortress. In fact, it deflects attacks by objectifying the other and then projecting its own guilt onto the now dispensable scapegoat. Thus the man demonizes the woman and the woman demonizes nature, and both indirectly demonize the divine author of finitude. Each actor in the story has, by the end, been effectively boxed in, isolated from the others, set apart. Here is the *pusilla anima* in all its glory: having lost the link to Mystery, the ego loses the link to all things in the cosmos. It is now a very small place, *curvatus in se.*

The Zen scholar D. T. Suzuki commented on the Judeo-Christian system:

> God against man / man against God;
> man against woman / woman against man;
> humans against nature / nature against humans
> — funny religion!

His observation, of course, has its roots in the Genesis account we have just been studying, but it seems to me that he has missed its tragic irony. This universe of conflict and mutual antagonism is the *consequence of sin* and by no means the intention of the Creator. We do in fact live in a world characterized by these wearying battles between objectified humanity, nature, and divinity, but such a world is the construct of the fallen consciousness, an illusion created by the fearful egos of men and women. The metaphysical reality hiding behind the veil of illusion is the realm of unity, of God in the world and the world in God. Mutuality, interpenetration, love is the true ground of being that has been obscured by the objectifying tendency of the self-elevating ego. And the purpose of the Judeo-Christian religion is to shift consciousness so as to recover an authentic vision of the universe in accord with God's intentions. *Pace* Suzuki our religion is not content with or tolerant of this awful tension between God, humanity, and nature, but it does force us to see the fallen mind which has produced such a state of affairs — hence the iconic value of this strange story of the garden.

In staring at the tragedy of Adam and Eve, we confront the Satan buried in the ice of our own sinful hearts. We see the awful parody of God that reigns fearfully behind all of the particular expressions of our sin; we see at the very core of our being the pathetic ego-god who grasps and then hides, who does all in his power to avoid the saving lure of the true God.

Chapter Three

THE DOCTRINE OF ORIGINAL SIN
The Fathers of Trent

What we have seen so far has been a preparation for the consideration of the "icon" of the doctrine of original sin. Dante and the author of Genesis are trying to uncover Sin, that is, the grounding, originating, elemental disorder that lies behind all of the moral and spiritual disorders of the human condition. Each has implicitly argued that seeing this sin clearly for what it is and what it is not is essential to the process of rising above it. Each in a real sense has a sort of "sympathy" for sin, an acknowledgment that sin contains within it a moment of grace, an opening up of the spirit toward freedom and responsibility. But each just as clearly repudiates sin in its demonic negativity, in its egotistical self-destructiveness. In Dante, it is ice-encased Satan, the mighty angel now immobilized and able only to weep, who symbolizes this poignant ambiguity. In the Book of Genesis, it is the serpent — the cleverest of God's good creatures and the lure into egotism — who plays the same role.

As I have argued, too often the dogmas and doctrines of the church are presented in such an abstract and disembodied way that their transformative power is largely overlooked. What I have tried to do is prepare the ground by approaching the teaching on sin through narrative and imagery, through the vivid and provocative stories presented by Dante and the author of Genesis. In so doing, I have hoped to bring the metanoetic or soul-transforming elements of the doctrine into sharper focus. The doctrines and official teachings of the church are nothing but distillations of basic spiritual experience, highly concentrated and focused expressions of the dynamics of soul-doctoring as they have been felt and practiced in the life of the believing community. We *feel* and sense and tell stories about sin long before we formally theologize about it. I want to pour some of the water of story and experience on the seeds of dogma in order to make them flower.

We shall begin with the doctrinal formulas that came out of the Council of Trent concerning original sin and the justification of the human being. These statements, carefully fashioned as a response to the challenges of the reformers, have become classic expressions of Catholic anthropology. For too long, they have been the subject of purely academic or dogmatic debate, pitted against the Protestant counterpositions and either passionately attacked or passionately defended. When they are approached from the standpoint of soul-doctoring, they are lifted up beyond the level of partisan controversy and take on a heretofore unsuspected resonance and power.

In the first paragraph of Trent's decree on original sin, we find affirmed the view that the sin of the garden entailed a loss of "holiness and justice" and the incurring of the "wrath and displeasure of God."[15] Implied in the first couplet is the imbalance, the disorder that occurred because of sin. It was Origen who maintained that holiness is seeing with eyes of Christ, that is to say, knowing the world from the perspective of the divine. When the ego enthroned itself in the originating sin, when it placed itself at the center of the cosmos and thereby objectified all around it, it necessarily lost holiness, the divine perspective or take on the world. The vision of the sinner is skewed because she sees herself as an isolated individual, set apart from God and other creatures, and threatened with "invasion" from without. In the ego fortress, one appreciates oneself and one's world as "secular," untouched by the divine, unholy. In one of his most celebrated remarks, Paul Tillich observed that the surest sign of the perdurance of original sin is the fact that the house of worship exists alongside of the bank and the theater and the statehouse as a separate entity representing a separate realm of being. In a properly configured world, the entire "secular" realm would be "sacred," since all things would be seen as grounded in the holiness of God's reality. But in the perspective of the sinner, there is a sharp distinction between the holy and the profane, between super-nature and nature, since God has been sequestered as a dangerous rival. The awkward tumble out of dreaming innocence into egotism has indeed resulted in a loss of holiness or "wholeness" of vision. We now live in a universe marked by profanization and secularization, conditioned by a "divided" consciousness.

Trent also tells us that sin resulted in the loss of justice. This term is of tremendous importance in the tradition, finding particularly powerful expression in the debates surrounding the significance of the cross. Thus in St. Anselm's *Cur Deus Homo,* the theory is developed that Christ's death on the cross reestablished the original justice that had been lost through sin. What does "justice" mean in this context, and why is such a "legalistic" word employed to describe a religious dynamic? The fathers of Trent, like Anselm and the New Testament authors, turn to this term because it is a way of designating a quality of *relationship.* Justice occurs when there is right harmony or balance in a group. Thus there is "justice" in a society when the rapport between the members of that community is mutual, harmonious, and equal, and when the give-and-take between the group as a whole and its leadership is similarly balanced. There is "justice" in the soul when the various powers and inclinations of the psyche — mind, spirit, passion — find adequate and mutually satisfying expression. Thus, in Plato's classic definition, justice, both political and psychological, is "rendering to each his due."

Now how has justice been lost through sin? The self-elevation of the ego has destroyed the subtle and delicate balance between the divine and the human, a harmony and justice that will be reestablished only in Christ. What was lost through the clinging of the ego is the harmony and play between two self-emptying loves. As we shall see more clearly later in this book, God is most himself when he lets go of himself in love of another, and the human being is most herself when she abandons fear and rises above the demands of the ego. Fulfillment comes in forgetting; safety comes in courting risky love; sense of self comes through ignoring self. This high-wire act of mutual trust and abandonment, this shared throwing of caution to the wind, is the "justice" that ought to exist between the divine and the human; it is the balance, the "rendering to each" that is the condition for the possibility of joy. And, if Trent is right, it is this joyful acrobatic harmony that has been spoiled by the originating sin of fearful egotism.

Now the Tridentine document also tells us that this upsetting of the balance of justice incurs the "anger and displeasure of God." This symbol of divine anger is one that is only too easy to miscon-strue in an emotive direction, as if God had been in a good frame of mind prior to sin and had then passed into a grumpy mood in the wake of sin, or as if human failure had caused the touchy and fickle God to fall into a snit. There is something more than vaguely pagan in such a reading of the divine anger: the volatile God must be appeased and mollified by some sacrifice or offering if he is to be, once again, "pleased" with us. Christians describe God as "angry" in the wake of sin because sin has so dramatically separated them from the divine source. When two people are angry, they stay away from one another; they refuse to communicate, withdrawing into separate quarters. The self-elevation of the ego results in just this kind of seg-regation of the divine and the human. From the illusory perspective of the regnant ego, God does indeed appear as distant and threaten-ing, and thus the ego *feels* afraid of God and senses the "displeasure" of God.

This is none other than the feeling that prompted Adam and Eve to flee from the divine and to hide themselves. Obviously, this sense of God's anger has a salvific purpose, namely, to make the sinner so un-comfortable that he is lured back into union with God, but it remains one of the terrible and disconcerting consequences of the originating sin. As we have lost holiness, or saneness of vision, so we have lost peacefulness in our rapport with the divine; we have settled into a stance of suspicion and mistrust vis-à-vis God, and what this *feels* like is mutual anger. Just as St. Ignatius in his *Spiritual Exercises* urges the exercitant to feel the pain of his sin, so the doctrine of originating sin forces the believer to sit in the presence of the "angry" God and to sense the terrible injustice or imbalance that has settled into place. This exercise awakens the sinner, stirs her out of self-complacency and sets her on the path toward *metanoia*. Thus the anger of God is properly seen as the painful but necessary salve for the sick soul.

Now it is in the second paragraph of Trent's decree on original sin that we confront one of the most important yet controverted points in the theology of sin: the view that the fall of our first parents affects us, their descendants, "staining" us and marking us. As was hinted above, the *philosophes* of the Enlightenment found this aspect of the doctrine of original sin particularly distasteful, since it seemed so utterly without basis in fact, so superstitious and unreasonable. How could sin be passed on from generation to generation like a bacillus or a virus? How could we be held accountable for the fall of our mythic forebears? Trent is quite clear on this score: "If anyone declares that the sin of Adam damaged him alone and not his descendants...let him be anathema." And it furthermore asserts that the sin of Adam was passed on to us "by propagation and not by imitation," that is to say, not simply through the setting of a bad example that has been repeated down through the ages, but rather through a quasi-biological process of reproduction. The originating sin has infected each member of the human race, reaching into the minds and wills, even in a certain sense, into the bodies of men and women, infecting us all with egotism. What could this possibly mean?

What this aspect of the doctrine is forcing us to see is of central spiritual significance. Cosmologists and physicists remind us that every action of ours, even the tiniest movement of a finger, has implications for every other reality in the universe. There are no discrete events in a cosmos made up of things that are inextricably *connected* one to the other. It is wrong, they tell us, to imagine the universe as a theater in which self-contained "actors" move about and have only incidental contact with one another. Rather, the cosmos is a blur of energy fields, each "thing" but a concentration of energy whose boundaries and borders are virtually impossible to specify. All things and all events, therefore, "wash" into one another, affecting and shaping and determining one another.

This insight of the cosmologists was given sharp philosophical expression in the writings of Alfred North Whitehead, the Cambridge mathematician turned metaphysician. Critical of the naively premodern substance metaphysics of Aristotle and Aquinas, Whitehead proposed an ontology in line with the new cosmology, holding that the basic building blocks of the real are not the self-contained "substances" of old but rather what he called "actual entities." These entities are not things so much as events or moments, or what White-head will specify as "processes of feeling." An actual entity "prehends" or feels the universe that surrounds it, finding itself in the very act by which it encounters what is other. And this "other" is itself nothing but an actual entity involved in a similar act of feeling and prehen-sion. The upshot of this theory is that the universe is a tightly woven web of radical interdependence, a wash of mutual feeling, sensing, and tending. Interestingly, there are links between the metaphysics of Whitehead and the mystical insight at the heart of Buddhist enlight-enment, namely, the dependent cooorigination of all things, the mutual coming-to-be of all realities, symbolized in the "jewel net of Indra."

In light of this metaphysic of interdependence, at once both an-cient and modern, the teaching regarding the "infection" of all human beings with the originating sin seems perhaps less naive than its critics had suggested. For what is true at the most elemental level of reality is undoubtedly equally true at the psychological, social, and spiritual level: "no man is an island." There is no moral act or psychological attitude that does not, in one sense, affect the entire organism which is the human race, and there is therefore no warping or misuse of spiritual energy that does not adversely affect the whole "body" of the humanum. The abuse of freedom, from the earliest people down through the centuries, has set up a sort of negative field of force that, willy-nilly, affects every person on the planet today. Egotism exists as a kind of poisonous spiritual atmosphere that all of us breathe from the moment we enter into the human condition. The originating sin of fear moves into our institutions, our governments, our modes of social organization, our systems of education, our languages, our religions, our literature and philosophy, our mythic stories, our military estab-lishments, our styles of recreation, our economic structures. Through these systems and institutions, sin surrounds us, envelops us, almost determines us. Like the prisoners in Plato's cave, we find ourselves — despite our best efforts and intentions — held in place by the shackles of institutionalized sin.

Trent tells us that the negativity of Adam's sin is passed on "not by imitation but by propagation." Though this formulation was undoubtedly shaped by Augustine's peculiar theology of sin as a sexually transmitted disease, there is something inescapably correct about Trent's insistence that sin is carried by a process far more basic and subtle than mere imitation. Our brief look at Whitehead was meant to show that the poison of egotism creeps into our hearts and forms us long before we engage in something as conscious and self-reflective as "imitation." It is decidedly not the case that we simply notice the sinfulness of others, find their behavior attractive, and then resolve to mimic them. It is much closer to the truth to say that sin *finds us* and shapes us and so largely determines the sort of behavior that we will consider attractive in the first place. Perhaps the word *propagatione* (by propagation) is awkward, but I wonder whether it is, in the end, not the most appropriate term. We have indeed inherited the energy of sin; it is part of our instinctual make-up; it is, almost literally, in our bodies and nervous systems. Fear, in the basic sense, is not something that is simply learned or picked up through imitation; rather it is a pattern of human existence itself.

This entire discussion of sin has taken place under the rubric of soul-doctoring. The assumption is that looking at sin has a transformative and ultimately salvific purpose. Nowhere is this soul-doctoring quality more evident than here. One of the greatest dangers in the spiritual life is to fall into the trap of auto-salvation, the conviction that one can save oneself through heroic moral effort or mystical insight or flights of theoretical knowledge. The principal problem with such a strategy, of course, is that it simply results in the strengthening of the very egotism that one is hoping to overcome. What Jesus so consistently and vehemently critiqued in the Pharisees was just this kind of presumptuousness and subtle egotism: "You are whitewashed sepulchres, all clean on the outside, but on the inside filled with dead men's bones." Trent's claim that the originating sin is in us *propagatione et non imitatione* is meant to convict us of the impossibility of ever extricating ourselves from egotism through egotism. Sin is not simply a weakness that we can overcome but rather a condition from which we have to be saved. Again, this insight should not depress us. *Au contraire,* it should allow us, at an elemental psychological and spiritual level, *to relax*, to surrender, to let go. What happens so often in the hearts of sinners is a kind of clenching or tightening of the spirit as the mind and will strive to break out of the prison of fear. All of this stretching and straining serves only to throw the ego back on itself in a misery of failure and self-reproach.

The classic example in the Christian tradition of this obsessive attempt at auto-salvation is the herculean but finally fruitless striving of the young monk Martin Luther. "If ever a monk was saved by monkishness it was I," said the older Luther humorously acknowledging the utter hopelessness of his quest. What saved Luther, as we know, was the liberation of the tower experience, the moment when he realized that freedom from sin and guilt can come only from a God who breaks into our prison from the outside. It came, in short, only when he relaxed the tenacious grip of the ego and allowed himself to be caressed by the divine power. There is an interesting link between Luther's spiritual experience and the findings of psychologists dealing with obsessive-compulsive disorder (from which Luther possibly suffered). As long as the obsessive thinker dwells on the morbid and agonizing thoughts that bedevil him, he will never escape from their power. The harder he tries to dismiss them, the more he wrestles with and addresses them, the more obsessed he becomes. Researchers have discovered that the only way to break the grip of an obsession is actively to move outside of its sphere of influence and *do* something.[16] It is only through relaxing and surrendering to another aspect of the psyche that relief comes.

If I am in the soup of sin, as Trent teaches, the solution is not to thrash around, since that will only cause me to sink deeper. The answer instead is to accept the saving help that can come only from a power that stands outside of the mess that I am in. To state it more abstractly, if the energy of egotism is the problem, then more egotism is not the solution. Only something that breaks in from outside of the system invented and perpetuated by egotism can be a saving grace. In this context it is helpful to recall the effort of the sinful Dante to mount the shining hill at the very outset of the *Divine Comedy*. His ego was only momentarily checked by the power of his despair, only stunned as it were, but it quickly recovered and pushed him once more to achievement. But the road of ego was immediately blocked by the three beasts representing the darkness of the ego itself, and salvation came only when Dante surrendered and opened himself to grace. After a lifetime of breathing in, he learned how to breathe out.

We remember from the introductory chapter that Jesus' inaugural speech was, first and foremost, an invitation to see something that had occurred, to notice a new state of affairs. It was not, primarily, an exhortation to moral excellence or a humanistic call to ethical reform; rather, it was a summons to see what God has done in Jesus himself. As such, it was the announcement of a lightning bolt coming from outside the human condition, the intervention of a God who has arrived, not so much to teach as to save. Implicit in Jesus' words is the assumption that human beings are stuck in the mire of sin and cannot raise themselves out of it. As we saw, Christ urges his followers, not to reform society or even to reform themselves, but rather to have "faith," to trust in the power of the coming together of the divine and human that has taken place in him. In all of this, we see the antecedents of the teaching of the Council of Trent concerning the "passivity" of the human in the presence of God's saving grace. Without this frank acknowledgment of the sin of Adam living in all of us, we are destined to remain on the ever turning wheel of fear and egotism. The breakthrough of the Incarnation amounts to God's stopping of that wheel, that terrible and self-defeating cycle of terror and self-reproach. Insisting upon the inescapability and universality of the predicament is an essentially important act of soul-doctoring.

What Trent insinuates is that the human race is a dysfunctional family. When someone is born into a family dominated by alcohol or characterized by physical abuse, he is, willy-nilly, conditioned by the destructiveness of the family. He picks up the patterns of the group, learns to play its games and live by its perverse rules; it is probably difficult for him to imagine that there is another way of living a human life. A world of fear, threats, violence, and suspicion is the only world he knows. It is impossible, researchers tell us, for someone in a dysfunctional situation simply to lift himself out of it through his own efforts, precisely because every one of his thoughts and actions is inescapably infected by the dysfunction. What saves (and this is the only appropriate word) someone from such a family is inevitably the intervention of an outsider, one who bears the good news that there is another way to live. When the Council of Trent insists that we *as a human family* are all infected by the disease of sin, it similarly reminds us that we cannot save ourselves. Any achievement of ours — be it intellectual, moral, scientific, or political — is necessarily tainted by the disease. It states in more abstract language what both Dante and the author of Genesis say: only through "grace," that is to say, some intervention from a power beyond the dysfunctional human family, is salvation possible. We must see our darkness and then long for the amazing grace that alone can liberate if we are to move toward *metanoia*.

A narrative poem, an ancient story, a formal doctrinal statement: all salves for the soul. Dante, the author of Genesis, and the fathers of Trent are making a similar observation: our fear has sickened us, and we cannot save ourselves from it, for the harder we try, the more fearful we become. To *see* this fact, they feel, is however an indispensable first step toward solving the problem. The Buddhist spirit masters speak of inviting one's fears in for tea. They mean that we must face our spiritual anxieties and see them for what they are: fundamentally illusions, phantoms that do not finally threaten our existence. In dissociating ourselves from our fears, we realize that there is a dimension to our being that is deeper than those terrors, a place of real freedom. In looking at Dante's Hell, at the lost paradise of the author of Genesis, and at the universality and inescapability of sin presented by the Tridentine fathers, we are not overwhelmed but *liberated*. We contemplate our sin, in all of its power, and thereby rob it of its ultimate power. Awareness of sickness is the first step in soul-doctoring.

But, again, this is only half the story. For as the author of Genesis, Dante, and the fathers of Trent affirm, there is contained *in the very act of sin itself* a clear sign that we are not sheer darkness. In the very movement toward sin, there is a glimmer of the *imago Dei*, since sin is nothing but the corruption of what remains essentially good, namely, the awakening to freedom and responsibility. We fall from God only, paradoxically enough, through those powers that make us most god-like: freedom, intellect, will, spirit, and sense of self. We are helpless in our sin, but we are also, strange though it may sound, children of God precisely in that condition. We do indeed need a savior (and not simply a teacher), but there remains in us *something to be saved.* Finding that quality, that light, that divine spark is equally essential to the process of *metanoia,* change of consciousness. It is to the *imago Dei* that we now turn.

Chapter Four

THE MIND OF TRUST

Beginning with Merton

In his remarkable novel of the Civil War, *The Killer Angels,* Michael
Shaara presents a conversation between the young idealistic colonel,
Joshua Lawrence Chamberlain, and his grizzled Irish aide-de-camp,
Kilrain.[17] The exchange takes place on the eve of the second day
of the battle of Gettysburg, the bloodiest battle of the bloodiest war
in American history. The occasion for the conversation is the arrival in camp of an injured runaway slave, and the topic becomes
philosophical and theological: is this creature, so alien yet so familiar, in fact a man? Chamberlain recalls his admittedly few encounters
with blacks in Maine and he concludes, "To me there was never any
difference.... You looked in the eye and there was a *man.* There was
the divine spark, as my mother used to say. That was all there was
to it ... all there *is* to it." Kilrain loves Chamberlain and admires his
idealism, but he can't bring himself to agree, not so much that blacks
are not human, but that anyone, white or black, has this godlike quality: "The truth is, Colonel, that there's no divine spark, bless you.
There's many a man alive no more value than a dead dog." Conclud-
ing his gloomy assessment of the race, Kilrain reminds Chamberlain
sardonically: "They burned a Catholic church up your way not long
ago. With some nuns in it.... *There* was a divine spark."

Thus we see innocent idealism versus hard-boiled pessimism, a
one-sidedly positive and one-sidedly negative take on the human condition, just the sort of bifurcation that renders real *metanoia* extremely
difficult. Chamberlain sees the divine spark of intelligence, love, and
creativity, while Kilrain sees the demonic "spark" of hatred and violence, and if our analysis to this point has shown anything it is

that each man is right and each man is wrong. The young colonel is still, perhaps, in the realm of dreaming innocence, and the wizened sergeant is, perhaps, sinking in the sea of originating sin. And their one-sided and exclusive visions would render each ineffective at the level of soul-doctoring, for the young man does not see the need to change and the old man does not see the possibility of changing.

A much more accurate and spiritually dynamic account of the human situation is given a bit earlier in the novel. It emerges in the context of a laconic exchange between Chamberlain and his Yankee father several years before the war. The two men are clearing a field of boulders, and, during a pause in their labors, the son proudly recites the well-known speech from *Hamlet* that he had just committed to memory: "What a piece of work is man...in action how like an angel!" Smiling, the old man responded dryly: "Well, boy, if he's an angel, he's sure a murderin' angel." No bifurcation here between the angelic and the demonic; no easy resolution into either/or. Instead, the two facts — angel and murderer — are placed ironically but realistically side by side. And, of course, it is this description that provides the title for Shaara's book and a focus for his reflection on Gettysburg and the war in general: even in the midst of our greatest violence and stupidity, there is a hint of nobility, courage, and godlike compassion. This, as we have been arguing, is the proper vision of the soul-doctor and the mystagogue: yes, we are murderers, but we are killer angels.

Our task in this chapter is to find the angel that hides behind the guise of the killer or, to use St. Anselm's phrase, to uncover the diamond that has fallen into the muck, to spy the divine spark that is never wholly extinguished by the waves of sin. Once more we shall use a variety of sources: a spiritual autobiography, a theology of beauty, and a theology of radical dependence. Our purpose, as always, is soul-doctoring. By raising to the surface the godlike quality in us, by polishing off the diamond, we do what Jesus did: we appeal to and awaken the divinity that is implicitly at work in us. We stir up that longing for God that remains despite the dysfunction, and we thereby prepare the way for transformation of the soul, for *metanoia*.

⊁|⥽

The principal theme in the writings of Thomas Merton is, arguably, the tension between the true self and the false self. Merton felt in his bones that his own life constituted a battleground between conflicting interests, warring tendencies, mutually exclusive "selves." For him, the spiritual life could be defined as the awakening to the true "I," the Christ living in me, and the dying to the vaporous and destructive ego created by fear.

The motif of the inner battle is presented in gripping narrative form in the autobiography that Merton published in 1948, *The Seven Storey Mountain.*[18] Though Merton distanced himself from some of the youthful excesses of this work — its crude Catholic imperialism, its exaggerated moralizing, its sharp dichotomizing between natural and supernatural — *The Seven Storey Mountain* remains not only Merton's most popular book, but one of the literary and religious landmarks of the twentieth century, an effort sometimes compared to the *Confessions* of St. Augustine. It is the account of a young man slowly awakening to his deepest identity and mission, throwing off the disconcerting influence of egotism, discovering the image of God within himself, and thereby coming to peace. To walk through the sometimes jumbled, sometimes overheated, but always compelling narrative of *The Seven Storey Mountain* is to become immersed existentially in the reality of sin and in the even more overpowering reality of grace at work in the soul. We shall use Merton's autobiography as a route of access to the great theme of *imago Dei,* the divine spark that *metanoia* stirs to flame.

The struggle between two selves is announced on the opening page of *The Seven Storey Mountain:* "Free by nature, in the image of God, I was nevertheless the prisoner of my own violence and my own selfishness, in the image of the world into which I was born." Merton acknowledges the predicament, the morass of sin that we have already described: he is not simply attracted by sin; he is its "prisoner" and he is stamped, almost indelibly, with its image. But at the same time, there is something in him that is irreducibly positive, a "freedom" that is the mark of God at the depth of his being. Merton's autobiography is the story of how his soul learned to fly after many years of being weighed down, his wings of Satan giving way to the wings of angels.

But what are the signs of this freedom, the hints of grace that can be found even in the midst of sin? Merton gives us a clue in his description of his parents: "my father and mother were ... in the world and not of it — not because they were saints, but in a different way: because they were artists." The vision, skill, intuition, and sensibility of the artist remain, for Merton, clear signs that all is not lost in the human condition. His father, he tells us, "painted like Cézanne.... His vision of the world was sane, full of balance, full of veneration for structure ... and for all the circumstances that impress an individual identity on each created thing." Merton's father was able to see the *concordia,* the harmonious play of parts, in physical objects and landscapes. He could glimpse some of the *claritas,* or radiance, that shone from them making them unique, unrepeatable. In a word, he could see the beautiful, the stamp of the divine, and this artistic insight allowed his spirit to soar upward and outward toward the source of Beauty: "his vision was religious and clean."

An eye for the beautiful, a sense and taste for harmony and individuality, remains, for Merton, one of the clearest signs that the *imago,* the likeness to God, is at work, and the cultivation of this capacity in himself remains an essential element in his coming to faith. Like William James and Duns Scotus, Merton has a healthy dislike for the abstract, for the fanciful intellectual flight away from the particular. In fact he tells us that he developed an enthusiastic animosity toward Plato when he first came across the Socratic dialogues at Cambridge: "I do not know exactly why I hated Plato: but after the first ten pages of *The Republic* I decided that I could not stand Socrates and his friends ... I do have a kind of congenital distaste for philosophic idealism."[19] This is because his vision is that of the artist who reverences *this* apple or *this* smile and revels in a very particular play of light and texture, and not that of the metaphysician who longs to gather things under the most general categories of the mind. What will bear the divine for Thomas Merton is not so much ideas but things, events, friends, sights and sounds, the very particular forms in which the divine beauty is incarnated.

As he moves through his life story, Merton gives us numerous examples of this eye for sacred beauty. In his early childhood, when he and his father are living in the south of France, he is caught up out of himself by the sight of ruined monasteries whose contours and textures he describes with special care: "My mind goes back with great reverence to the thought of those clean, ancient stone cloisters, those low and mighty rounded arches hewn and set in place by monks who have perhaps prayed me where I now am."[20] And he recalls a moment of epiphany when he was, still as a young child, living in Douglaston outside of New York: "The sound of the churchbells came to us across the bright fields. I was playing in front of the house and stopped to listen. Suddenly all the birds began to sing in the trees above my head, and the sound of birds singing and churchbells ringing lifted up my heart with joy." In the wake of this simple yet ecstatic experience, young Tom Merton remarked to his father, "All the birds are in their church," and then asked, "Why don't we go to church?"[21] The rhythm in both cases is wonderful and typical: the sense of the beautiful — in sharp and defined images — stirs in the soul a feeling of aesthetic wonder which, in turn, awakens the longing for the divine source of beauty. The simple interrogation, "Why don't we go to church?" is an implicit recognition that the beautiful is a gift from a gracious God to whom worship is due, in whose presence awe and thanksgiving are the only proper responses.

One of the most striking examples of the aesthetic-sacramental process is in Merton's description of the town of St. Antonin, the tidy little French village in which he and his father lived in the 1920s. He shows us, indirectly, how his artist's eye — his share in the *imago Dei* — helped him to sense the sacramentality of the environment: "Here in this amazing, ancient town, the very pattern of the place, of the houses and streets and of nature itself, the circling hills, the cliffs and trees, all focused my attention upon the one, important central fact of the church and what it contained.... Every street pointed more or less inward to the center of the town, to the church. Every view of the town, from the exterior hills, centered upon the long grey building with its high spire."[22] The child Merton has the vision to grasp the town and its environs as something like a medieval rose window in which all medallions and pictures are linked harmoniously to a center from which they radiate. Like the cathedral roses, the town of St. Antonin itself becomes a sacrament or microcosm of the whole universe, a conglomeration of disparate elements that nevertheless center around and derive their meaning and purpose from a divine source. It was the French artist and restorer Viollet le Duc who, upon seeing the rose window at Notre Dame de Paris, exclaimed: "Écoute! C'est le rosace qui chante" (Listen! It is the rose that sings). Young Merton similarly hears the chanting of nature and architecture.

This aesthetic sacramentalism reaches its height, for Merton, during a visit to Rome in the 1930s. The remnants of the imperial city, which Merton found "pornographic," did not "sing"; they did not stir the soul of the young pilgrim as had the monasteries of France or even the birds in the trees at Douglaston. But something else did manage to evoke the transcendent: "I found myself," says Merton, "looking into churches rather than into ruined temples.... The effect of this discovery was tremendous. After all the vapid, boring, semi-pornographic statuary of the empire, what a thing it was to come upon the genius of an art full of spiritual vitality...an art that was tremendously serious and alive and eloquent and urgent in all that it had to say."[23] What was it that made the difference? Why did depictions of the cosmic Christ and Byzantine saints stir the young man's soul when the ruins of an ancient empire left him flat? "Its solemnity was made all the more astounding by its simplicity — and the obscurity of the places where it lay hid, and by its subservience to higher ends." What Merton saw in these mysterious and obscure works of art was the sacramentality that is the proper focus and raison d'être of any beautiful thing. When a beautiful object speaks beyond itself, when it effaces itself in deference to the grounding beauty of which it is a reflection, it is, paradoxically, most authentically itself and hence most beautiful. Hans Urs von Balthasar says that the slogan *ars gratia artis* (art for art's sake) is invalid because it discourages the very humility and other-orientation that is essential for the proper flowering of the work of art. A great painting or sculpture or building exists, not "for its own sake," but for the sake of the ultimate and unconditioned beauty that speaks through it. It is wonderful that Merton notices the "obscurity" and "hiddenness" of the frescoes that so moved him. These *objets d'art* are not in the full light of publicity, not drawing attention primarily to themselves; rather, like the great saints, they radiate the divine precisely by becoming silent and humble before God.

And in this they mimic the ultimate form of the beautiful which is Christ, the enfleshed divine. Thomas Merton comes to a living, existential knowledge of Christ for the first time through these dark and unprepossessing mosaics in the great churches of Rome: "These mosaics told me more than I had ever known of the doctrine of a God of infinite power, wisdom and love Who had yet become Man, and revealed in His Manhood the infinity of power, wisdom and love that was his Godhead."[24] Jesus is the physical beauty which, through its very humility and other-orientation, speaks most impressively of the transcendent Beauty of the divine. Christ is the prototype of all finite expressions of the beautiful, since in him the two "natures" of limited and unlimited beauty coinhere. What Merton saw in the mosaics of Rome was a clear reflection of this Christ-like coming together of the divine and the nondivine, and it was thus that these ancient pictures moved him to a felt knowledge of the sacred. The pictures, hidden in dark corners in cavernous churches, were like the God who humbled himself, accepting our human condition even to the point of death. "Soon I was no longer visiting them [the churches] merely for the art. There was something else that attracted me: a kind of interior peace. I loved to be in these holy places." Once again, the sacramental alchemy has worked: the Light appears in the lights, Beauty shines in the beautiful — and praise is the only possible response.

Merton's eye was artistic, attuned to the harmonious and radiant play of parts that is the aesthetically pleasing, and it was thus that he naturally saw the beautiful as a route of access to God. But there were other routes, other paths, that he rather spontaneously took to grace; there were other ways in which the *imago Dei* shone forth in him. One of them is what I could call a keen sense of dependency, his own emptiness in the presence of a sustaining power infinitely greater than he. Interestingly, this awareness of insufficiency was usually prompted by an experience of sickness or death, what theologians would later call a "limit experience." When Merton was in secondary school, his father fell mortally ill with a brain tumor. When Tom Merton saw his father in the hospital and came to grips for the first time with the gravity of the situation, he wept, unable to think of anything to say or do. And when his father, after a long period of suffering, finally succumbed, Merton was left empty and cold and felt no desire to pray.

Several months later, however, while he was on his aesthetically enlightening trip to Rome, Merton came to appreciate the religious meaning of his father's death. His account of this breakthrough is one of the most mysterious and compelling sections of the autobiography. Merton tells us that he was in his hotel room at night when suddenly, "... it seemed to me that Father, who had now been dead more than a year, was there with me. The sense of his presence was as vivid and as real and as startling as if he had touched my arm or spoken to me." In this flash of awareness, the young man saw into the darkness of his own soul and realized that he had to revolutionize his life. It was as though his father was speaking to him from another dimension and urging him to conversion. And in the wake of this encounter, Merton says, "I think for the first time in my whole life I really began to pray ... praying out of the very roots of my life and my being, and praying to the God I had never known." There is a fascinating play here of double limitation and double dependency. It is as though the reality of his father's death dawned on him for the first time in this encounter, the fact that his father was really gone. And this awareness of radical finitude allowed him to see another limitation, namely, that of his own spirit and inner life which had become corrupt and unfocused. In short, physical death (his father's) shocked him into an awareness of spiritual death (his own), and both of these radical limitations threw him back on the God who is without limitation and beyond death (he began to pray).

A second instance of this "limit experience" access to God is related at the end of the first major section of *The Seven Storey Mountain*. Merton had always found his maternal grandfather, nicknamed Pop, a source of both embarrassment and amusement. (The account of Pop's "invasion" of Europe as the ultimate ugly American tourist is the funniest and most charming section of the autobiography.) But during his college years at Columbia, Merton had grown quite close to his grandfather, finding in him a friend and professional confidant, and thus it was with great sadness that Merton learned of the old man's death. He hurried home from school and walked into Pop's room, which was filled with "cold November air" since all the windows were open. He gazed at the body lying under a sheet and then "a strange thing happened." Without thinking or debating, the normally areligious young man "closed the door and got on his knees by the bed and prayed."[25]

Something similar took place when, just a few months later, his grandmother passed away. Merton recalls that he spent hours by the old woman's bed "listening to the harsh gasp in her throat" and found himself, once more, moved to pray, though he wasn't the least bit sure whether he had any explicit faith. The prayer, he realized, meant that he was at least indirectly acknowledging "the supreme Principle of all life, the ultimate Reality, he Who is Pure Being, He Who is Life Itself, He Who simply is."[26] The language that Merton chooses here is worthy of attention: the radical *restriction* of being that is so dramatically evident in death opens him to that power whose being is *unrestricted*. God is *Life Itself*, and he sees this precisely when life is threatened; God is *ultimate Reality*, and he understands this when he confronts the harshest limits to the real; God is *pure Being*, and he knows this when the nonbeing of death is most in evidence. It is the play of contrast that brings about the sharpest awareness of the divine; it is dependency that signals Independence.

We have seen that Merton is not someone naturally given to abstract forms of thinking. Suspicious of platonic "ideas," Merton prefers the earthy and sensual, and it is just such concrete experiences that he tends to present in his life story. But there was a book, an extremely dense and abstract tome of scholastic philosophy, that was to have a profound impact on Merton's life and religious sensibility. In February of 1937, Merton found himself on Fifth Avenue in New York with "five or ten loose dollars burning a hole in his pocket." In the window of Scribner's bookstore he spied a volume entitled *The Spirit of Medieval Philosophy*, by Etienne Gilson, the noted Thomist scholar.

Because he had signed up for a course in medieval French literature, he bought the book, only to be horrified when, on the way home, he noticed the *imprimatur* and *nihil obstat,* the official approbation of the Catholic Church, on the frontispiece. Overcoming his native anti-Catholicism and post-Enlightenment suspicion of religion, he began to read Gilson's presentation of some of the major themes in Christian philosophy and metaphysics. What Merton discovered astounded him. He had always assumed that Christians had a naive and vaguely superstitious notion of God, conceiving of him as a "noisy and dramatic and passionate character...a jealous, hidden being, the objectification of all their own desires and strivings and subjective ideals."[27] But in Gilson's book, he found a deep and philosophically precise idea of God as that reality which simply is, as that being which alone possesses *aseitas,* "through-itself-ness." God is not *a* thing or *a* being, but rather the sheer act of Being itself, that which exists by reason of itself and in whom all other things exist, that which enjoys "complete independence not only as regards everything outside but also as regards everything within Himself."

It might strike us, at first, as surprising that Merton considers this idea of divine aseity as something which was to "revolutionize" his entire life. But our surprise gives way to understanding when we see that what Gilson expressed in technical philosophical language is none other than what Merton had felt and responded to in his limit experiences. His need to pray at the death-beds of his grandparents and during his mystical encounter with his father in Rome came from the same source as Gilson's metaphysical speculations: the keen awareness that our being is a dependent being relying finally on some reality which is not dependent, which exists *a se,* through itself. It seems clear that the reason Merton responded so readily to Gilson's Thomistic abstractions is that he *had lived them* first; he knew in his blood what Gilson was describing in more distant analytical language. That God is Being itself is what young Tom Merton *felt* when he got to his knees and prayed for his father, his grandparents, and himself, even before he had faith in any conventional sense. Gilson simply gave a precise intellectual framework for this experience of radical dependency and insufficiency.

Interestingly, in the wake of reading this book of Christian metaphysics, Merton is compelled to go to church, to acknowledge existentially the God whom he had discovered, to pray. And here we see the *imago Dei* with great clarity. In our very dependency and insufficiency, in our very fear and limitation, in the very threatened quality of our existence, we have within us an openness to the God who is neither dependent, nor insufficient, nor threatened. We carry about in our bodies the death of Christ, as Paul said, and in that very mortality we are oriented to the immortal source of being. When we sense how fragile and nonself-explanatory we are, we are forced, by a kind of inner compulsion, to kneel, to pray, to acknowledge the divine. This darkness that opens to light is another form of the *imago Dei* within us.

The events that we have been analyzing are described in the first half of Merton's autobiography. They have to do with the awakening to faith that is antecedent to the real integration of a religious vision and lifestyle. The second half of *The Seven Storey Mountain* is the account of the flowering of the *imago* into a life commitment, the full flight of the soul toward an existential union with God. Merton tells us how he allowed the God whom he had glimpsed through the positive experience of the beautiful and the negative experience of dependency to lure him toward baptism, then toward the Trappist monastery where he found his vocation as a contemplative monk and priest. Merton acknowledges what spiritual searchers have taught across the centuries: the *imago Dei*, once discovered and aroused, pushes the soul toward total surrender, total gift. Once the divine inscape has been uncovered, there is a relentless push in the direction of integration and concrete expression of that divinity. One cannot remain a bland spectator or "student" of the *imago*; one must allow it to grow and unfold like a seed in the soil of the soul. Once the buried treasure has been found, everything must be sold so that field can be bought; once the pearl of great price has been discovered, everything must be abandoned for its sake. It is as though the *imago* cannot bear to coexist with sin and therefore exercises an expulsive influence, pushing out all that compromises its own integrity. And this is the spiritual trajectory of Merton's life story: from sin to *imago* to election and vocation. The true self wins victory over the false self.

❊

There is a third and most powerful exploration of the *imago Dei* in the writings of Merton, one centering around the theme of the *point vierge* (the virgin point). This is the place of emptiness and purity which dwells at the deepest heart of the person, that point of contact between the soul and God, that place where, in the words of Meister Eckhart, there is no real distinction between Creator and creature. It is this "point," both nothing and everything, that sums up what we have seen so far: it is the sense and taste for divine beauty and it is the hunger and thirst for God. It is the way that the divine is stubbornly and unavoidably present even in the dysfunctional *pusilla anima*. We will explore this theme by looking at a classic text from *The Conjectures of a Guilty Bystander*, but to prepare ourselves for that analysis, we will dwell just a bit longer with *The Seven Storey Mountain*.

When Merton first went to Gethsemani Abbey for a retreat in the spring of 1941, he was overwhelmed. Everything impressed him, intoxicated him: the liturgy, the garb of the monks, the Gregorian chant, the rhythm of the life, the surrounding countryside. He was convinced that he had found the "real capital of America," the center around which the whole nation turned. It was a mountaintop experience par excellence. And when he descended from the mountain, returning to his ordinary life as a professor of English at St. Bonaventure's College, he found the world around him flat and banal, "slightly insipid and insane." Having experienced an enormous intensification of consciousness at Gethsemani, he, understandably enough, looked rather pityingly and condescendingly at the unenlightened around him. And when he returned definitively to the monastery some months later to become a monk, he happily closed the doors behind him, rejoicing that he had "shut out" the world in the great "fortress" of spirituality and prayer.

Something happened to Merton in the ensuing decades of his monastic life, something that changed this arrogant attitude concerning himself and the "world." He came to realize that the monk is not set apart from the benighted secular arena in an exalted spiritual realm; rather, the monk is one who is profoundly and compassionately aware of the sacrality, the sacredness, of all people and of the whole cosmos.

Accordingly, his task is not to bask in his difference, but, having awakened to his own *magna anima,* to bring others to this consciousness, to help them to see how sacred they are.

This shift of insight, though hinted at in some of Merton's writings in the 1950s, came explicitly to expression only after an extraordinary experience of revelation that occurred on the corner of Fourth and Walnut Streets, in the center of the Louisville shopping district. Merton was standing at this busiest intersection of the city, this place that in previous years he undoubtedly would have condemned as hopelessly redolent of the "world," when it suddenly occurred to him that he "loved all those people" who were bustling past him. They belonged to him and he to them in such a way that they could never be aliens, "even though they were total strangers." This stunning awareness of his connectedness to all people through God was like "waking from a dream of separateness," the illusion that his existence was uniquely "holy."[28] His monastic vocation, he saw in a sort of flash of insight, was not to run from the world to cultivate a special mode of being, but rather to step back from the ordinary run of things in order to see more clearly and in a more focused way. "We [monks] take a different attitude toward these things, for we belong to God. *Yet so does everybody else belong to God.* We just happen to be conscious of it and to make a profession out of this consciousness" (emphasis added).[29] The monk is unique, not in his being, but in his seeing. In some ways, Merton perceived, the decades of his monastic life had effectively prepared him for the deepening of consciousness that occurred at Fourth and Walnut; his stepping away was the proper preparation for stepping back with greater insight and compassion. How wonderful it was to realize that he didn't have to maintain the pretense of separateness, that he could revel in being, not so much a monk, but simply a member of the human race that God himself had deigned to join in Christ. "To think that such a commonplace realization should suddenly seem like news that one holds the winning ticket in a cosmic sweepstake." The account reaches a sort of emotional climax when Merton exclaims: "There is no way of telling people that they are all walking around shining like the sun."[30] This, of course, is a beautiful indication of the *imago Dei.* Human beings are vain and stupid, violent and self-absorbed, prone to sin and subject to unspeakable sorrows, but they are, despite all of that, "shining like the sun," filled with the radiance and *claritas* of the divine life. There is, in all of us, that stubborn spark that originating sin cannot finally put out.

But what is it, precisely, that Merton sees in this passage? What is it, exactly, that links us all to one another? It is, he says, that secret depth, that inner core, that ground of the soul "where neither sin nor desire nor self-knowledge can reach." This secret and silent place at the very center of all people is the *point vierge,* the virginal point, where we "belong entirely to God" for it is there that we are here and now being created by God. It is that "interior castle," the impregnable fortress that neither sin nor despair nor hatred can ultimately undermine. Though sin is a power of death and dissolution in us, a tendency toward nonbeing, and though this power is dreadful and practically all-encompassing, it *cannot have the final say,* since being is always more basic than nonbeing. As long as we exist, we are held up by the power of God; as long as we are, we are linked to the Creator by an indissoluble bond. And thus even the worst of us, even the most desperate and lonely and bored and hate-filled among us, is, despite himself, "shining like the sun." Merton sums up what he saw that day in Louisville: "It [the *point vierge*] is like a pure diamond, blazing with the invisible light of heaven. It is in everybody, and if we could see it we would see these billions of points of light coming together in the face and blaze of a sun that would make all the darkness and cruelty of life vanish completely. . . . I have no program for this seeing. It is only given. But the gate of heaven is everywhere."[31]

As we saw in our brief survey of themes from *The Seven Storey Mountain,* Thomas Merton knew all about sin and its soul-corroding power; there was nothing naive in his vision of the human condition. Indeed, when describing the inner state of the spirit, Merton most frequently employs the image of warfare. But in the passage just considered we see the flip side: if there is something surprisingly wrong with us, there is something even more surprisingly right about us, and it is upon this basic and indestructible godliness that the work of conversion and renovation can begin. Soul-doctoring is needed because of the *pusilla anima;* it is possible because of the seeds of the *magna anima.*

Chapter Five

THE IMAGO IN FULLNESS AND EMPTINESS
Balthasar, Schleiermacher, and Tillich

One does not have to look far to find theological treatments of the three themes hinted at in Merton's autobiographical writings. Many thinkers over the Christian centuries have sought to present the dynamics of the *imago* in terms of the human openness to beauty — Augustine, pseudo-Dionysius, Bonaventure, and Anselm come readily to mind — and many others, Aquinas and Rahner, for instance, have seen the *imago* as a hunger for wholeness of being. And many more — Juan de la Cruz, Teresa of Avila, Meister Eckhart — have developed the motif of the inner sanctuary, the point of contact with God at the root of the soul. In this chapter I will consider three theologians — one Catholic and two Protestant — who have given these motifs a more doctrinal expression. Our purpose remains constant: to uncover the Christ who is asleep in the boat, to find the divine spark and stir it to flame.

No contemporary theologian has reflected more profoundly on the beautiful as a route of access to God than the Swiss Catholic thinker Hans Urs von Balthasar. Unlike most theologians, Balthasar was trained, not primarily in the rational discipline of philosophy, but in the far more affective and intuitive arts of music and literature. In fact, as a young man, he seriously considered the possibility of pursuing a career as a concertizing pianist. When he decided to enter the Jesuits and study for the priesthood, he was deeply dissatisfied with the ossified and stale scholasticism that was the basic intellectual diet

of Catholic scholars of the time. In the smug and lifeless manuals of
the Thomists — so lacking in the daring and cultural confidence of
the works of Thomas himself — Balthasar found little that would en-
liven the soul. What saved him was the discovery of the Scriptures
and the fathers, for there he found a literature that spoke from the
standpoint of a lived encounter with the Spirit of God. And what
especially moved him was the dominant presence, in both the Bible
and patristic texts, of the category of the beautiful. It was only natural
that a musician and poet would respond readily and enthusiastically to
this category, discovering in it a vitality too often missing from more
philosophical discussions of the truth.

And so it was that when Balthasar began his own theological work
he chose as his methodological starting point, not the relatively familiar transcendentals of the good and the true, but rather the beautiful,
the "glorious" light so beloved by the authors of the Bible and the first
great pastor/theologians of the church. In his multivolumed *Glory of
the Lord*, Balthasar sets out to analyze the beautiful as a sacramental
manifestation of the divine presence.[32] He finds this theme throughout
the Scripture and in authors as diverse as Origen, Irenaeus, Augustine, Dante, Gerard Manley Hopkins, and G. K. Chesterton. All of
these figures witness, in different ways, to the beautiful as a force
that prompts a sort of alchemy in the soul, lifting it up, coalescing its
powers, and finally focusing it on the divine source of beauty. And all
agree that the ur-form of the beautiful is Christ himself, the coming-
together of divinity and humanity in an aesthetically compelling and
overwhelming manner. It is the form of Christ, Balthasar concludes,
that most dramatically prompts the spirit to an encounter with the
source of Beauty itself.

Our study of Balthasar will focus, not so much on the better-known
Glory of the Lord, but on the relatively overlooked second installment
of his trilogy, the *Theodramatik* (*Theo-Drama*).[33] In this five-volume
work, Balthasar develops his theological anthropology and his Christology, and it is in the second volume, *Dramatis Personae: Man in God*,
that he reflects most profoundly on the issue that preoccupies us in
this chapter, namely, the image of God in the soul. When he had
finished his early work on beauty in the *Glory of the Lord*, Balthasar

had been criticized by some for presenting an essentially elitist, effete, disengaged theology. He had turned the believer, some said, into a dispassionate museum-goer, blandly surveying the "icons" presented by the Scripture and tradition, and he had transformed Christ himself into an ahistorical "portrait," a beautiful form without density, a "pretty picture" that makes no demands on those who see it. Balthasar composed the *Theodramatik* to correct just such misinterpretations of his aesthetic perspective.

The beautiful — be it a rose, a strikingly handsome face, a Mozart symphony, or a Bernini statue — has, says Balthasar, the character of grace or "favor." It does not exist dully or indifferently, but rather it attests to itself, witnessing to its own perfection and attractiveness, inviting a response: "The beautiful presents a challenge to all that is mean and common. It does not stand turned in on itself but turned outward, facing all who can grasp it."[34] There is something provocative and disturbing about the truly beautiful; it cannot simply be admired blandly but must be *seen* and taken in, dealt with. One can grasp this arresting quality precisely in those "privileged moments and encounters, when something uniquely precious, felicitous . . . presents itself to us."[35] Notice how Balthasar speaks here of the beautiful "presenting" and "offering" itself to us, as a mystical guide offers us wisdom and direction. The proper response in the presence of such a vision is wonder — "that such things should exist!" — the wonder that is, according to Aristotle, the beginning of philosophy. And the graciousness of the particular object, the self-offering of the beautiful, raises the mind to an awareness of the graciousness of Being itself, the source from which all beauty is derived. When confronted by a truly beautiful "event," one realizes that the hidden ground of all is a challenging, provocative and inviting Beauty. To express this in more explicitly and classically religious terms one could speak of revelations and Revelation: the aesthetically arresting has a self-disclosing and summoning power, a "revealing" quality, which, in turn, mediates the self-disclosing of the ground of Being.

Another way to express this revealing power is to describe the "word" that comes from any beautiful object or event. "The thing of beauty 'speaks to us' from a region in which language operates

transcendentally.... Being reveals itself ... as the Good, the True and
the Beautiful and this very fact is language at a root level."[36] What
Balthasar means here is that beauty speaks and invites in the most elemental way and, in this very primordial speech, language, the desire
to speak to others of what one has seen, is born. Language itself, in
other words, emerges in the wonder evoked by beauty and is sustained
by the spiritual need to proselytize on its behalf. The self-disclosure
of being (the Word) opens us to self-disclosure in response (words of
praise and invitation).

And this give-and-take between the revealing beauty and the
aroused perceiver points to the "electing" or choosing that happens
in the aesthetic moment. An encounter with the deeply beautiful —
what is not merely entertaining or diverting — is a meeting that concerns and shakes and changes the subject. People sometimes speak of
the aesthetic experience as "enrapturing" or "transporting," signalling
that one is taken away (rapt), stolen, translated into a different realm
of existence. The beautiful cannot leave us indifferent, unaffected, but
rather it works its way into our bones, into the sinews of our life, indelibly marking us and setting us off. In Balthasar's language, the one
who sees the beautiful has, necessarily, been given a mission, or better, awakened to the mission the contours and *gravitas* of which have
always been present in that person but only dimly sensed. The power
of beauty sinks deeply into a soul and then bursts forth, the perceiver
becoming, like the Creator God himself, *diffisivum sui*, self-expressive:
"The spark of the *bonum diffisivum sui* enters into the man who is privileged to glimpse it and makes him, too, a person who is unreservedly
poured out."[37] The one who has been grasped by the beautiful is like
the woman in the Gospel who breaks open the alabaster jar at the feet
of Jesus and allows the aroma of the perfume to fill the entire house:
she is willing to break open her life in order to witness to what she
has seen and heard.

In light of Balthasar's clarifications, it is fascinating to review the
biblical accounts of encounters with the glory and beauty of God. In
a biblical perspective, "visions" of the divine are never given for the
sake of private edification or contemplation; on the contrary, there
is always a commission attached to the insight. It is never the case

that the "seeing" is an end in itself, as in some more straightforwardly mystical traditions. For the scriptural authors, the vision opens to mission: you have been given to see that others might see. Moses, for instance, goes up the mountain and is transported by his experience of the divine, marked so profoundly that his face and hair become radiant. But he does not stay on the mountaintop, content to bask in the glory of God; instead he comes back down filled with the mission to set his people free. The aesthetic arrest before the burning bush (a wonderful image of the beautiful!) is succeeded by action and liberating praxis; the "mark" that Moses bears is not so much that of contemplator as liberator. And when Saul of Tarsus is turned around on the road to Damascus, bathed in the light (the *claritas*) of God's glory, he does not stay in rapt wonder, satisfied with the depth of his insight. Instead, he is sent into Damascus where he is given a mission to carry the message of Jesus to the Gentiles. The beautiful became a fire within him, prompting him to a missionary life of proclamation. And Simon "sees" the glory of Jesus' messiahship ("no mere man has revealed this to you, but my Father in heaven"), and is immediately given the commission to anchor and ground the community which will proclaim what he has seen: "You are Peter and upon this rock I shall build my church." Finally Isaiah has the rapturous vision of the divine glory — smoke and heavenly throne and cascading angels — whereupon he hears the invitation, "Whom shall I send?" Once more, awareness is the prompt to mission.

In all of these cases, a human being is given a new identity and a new practical purpose precisely through the mediation of the beautiful, through the rapture that comes from the radiant form. God, it seems, refuses to disclose himself without a "price," without the ulterior motive of commissioning the visionary for service to the whole community. From God's perspective, art is not for "art's sake," but for the sake of the mission. The beautiful does indeed "speak" and its word is one of invitation, even coercion. There is something nearly unavoidable, almost violently compelling about the commission: to refuse it would be tantamount to refusing the best of oneself, to ignore it would be to ignore who one was meant to be. In one of the letters of his unforgettable *Letters to a Young Poet*, Rainer Maria Rilke counsels an aspiring writer that he should take up the dreadful career of the literary artist only if he senses within himself an inner necessity, a compulsion to write: "There is only one thing you should do. Go into yourself. Find out the reason that commands you to write; see whether it has spread its roots into the very depths of your heart; confess to yourself whether you would have to die if you were forbidden to write."[38] He is asking his young corespondent whether the beautiful has so possessed him that his very identity, his very person, *is* the mission to communicate beauty. He is searching out the deepest motivations of this young man in order to discover whether he has the "vocation" to write, the summons from God that is like the coal placed on the lips of Isaiah or the fire burning uncomfortably in the bones of Jeremiah. His young friend must feel a compulsion to write that is like the compulsion of St. Paul to proclaim the Gospel: "I am ruined if I do not preach it!"

Thus the beautiful seizes a person, orients her radically toward the transcendent source of beauty and then *sends* her outward as a missionary. There is an expansive, propulsive, centrifugal energy to the beautiful, causing an enlargement, a broadening of the powers of the soul. If Augustine is right in defining sin as *curvatus in se* (turned in upon oneself), then the beautiful is a sort of antidote to sin, since by its nature it turns the spirit away from itself in ecstasy and mission. Under the influence of the *claritas* and *concordia* of the beautiful, the soul stirs out of its self-complacency and boredom, finding itself in service to what transcends it. Dante's Satan is a perfect symbol of the soul stuck in the ice of self-absorption, so preoccupied by the sufferings of the past and present that it is incapable of even seeing the beautiful. We recall that all Satan does is weep from his six eyes. His tears, born of his frustrated egotism, blind him to the beautiful that could liberate him from his prison.

One of the most intriguing moves that Balthasar makes in his *Theo-Drama* is to connect this philosophy and psychology of the beautiful to a theology of freedom. Freedom, he feels, is one of the most misunderstood and misapplied notions in the marketplace of ideas, and the roots of this misunderstanding are in the nominalism and voluntarism of the late Middle Ages. By the end of the medieval period, thinkers began to identify freedom as a sort of absolute sovereignty, an indifference, a hovering above "yes" and "no." Thus for voluntarists such as William of Occam or René Descartes, the divine freedom is tantamount to a sheer and even frightening arbitrariness. For Descartes, 2+2 could equal something other than 4 if God but willed it in his unchallenged freedom. Consciously departing from the Thomistic view that God cannot do that which contradicts the structures of being, Occam and Descartes proclaim the divine sovereignty over the laws of existence that God himself in freedom has established. This same notion of freedom as radical liberty from outside constraint shapes the overbearing and unchallenged dictatorship of a Louis XIV or Stalin: the law becomes simply that which the ruler arbitrarily determines.

What Balthasar is at pains to show is that this typically modern idea of freedom has nothing to do with the notion of freedom that held sway through the Middle Ages. In authors as diverse as Augustine, Bernard, Anselm, and Aquinas, authentic freedom is tantamount, not to unrestrained indifference, but to expansiveness of spirit. For these figures, to be free means to be unrestricted by the terrible "no" to being which is the essence of sin. In the words of Anselm, true freedom is not the capacity to say "yes" or "no," but rather the capacity to say only "yes." When one can consistently say "yes" to the full range of existence, one is liberated from the icy constraints of egotism; one is able to fly out of the cocoon of self-absorption and inhabit through mind and will the whole of reality.

I can't help but see a link between this more classical Christian idea of freedom and the wonderfully rambling monologue of Molly Bloom at the close of Joyce's *Ulysses*. The word that returns like a mantra in Molly's stream of consciousness, that echoes almost comically through the entire speech, and that brings the monologue and the novel as a whole to a close is "yes": " . . . and I thought well as well him as another and then I asked him with my eyes to ask again yes and then he asked me would I yes to say yes my mountain flower and first I put my arms around him yes and drew him down to me so he could feel my breasts all perfume yes and his heart was going like mad and yes I said yes I will Yes."[39] As she ranges imaginatively around the whole of her experience and affirms all of it, Molly, though physically confined to her bed, is supremely free, since she is able to say only "yes," drawing to her breast the whole of life. In this she is like the God of Thomas Aquinas who is "unable" to sin, incapable of saying "no" to himself or to the universe that exists through him. God, for Aquinas, does not hover above affirmation and negation (like us sinners), but rather consistently, almost compulsively, affirms, drawing to her breasts the energy of existence.

Derivatively, human or finite freedom is this ecstatic embrace of one's own subjectivity and, more importantly, of all the being that environs and determines the "I." When we discover and affirm ourselves as an existing thing, says Balthasar, we implicitly discover and affirm the full range of being which, in a similar way, exists and calls out to us. To be freely ourselves, therefore, is not to be sovereignly alone in the universe, an isolated monad, unaffected by anything else; on the contrary, it is to *be with,* to exist in the presence of others. And in the ultimate sense, it is to be with the God, the Other who grounds and transcends our subjectivity. Balthasar reminds us that "this primal, secure self-possession [freedom] is not a self-intuition or grasp of one's essence; it articulates itself only in and with the universal opening to all being, leaving itself behind to embrace the knowledge and will of others and other things, particularly in shared being."[40] At the heart of the Fall, as we have already seen, is an affirmation of freedom through exclusion: Adam and Eve cling to themselves out of fear, setting up a barrier that blocks them from one another, from nature, and from God. Their voluntarist "freedom," hovering above yes and no, is a denial of the *Mitsein,* the "being with," that for Balthasar is the mark of true freedom. They tried to be like God in majesty and freedom, but they completely misconstrued the nature of divine liberty and hence became mirror images, photographic negatives of the divine being.

Here again is the great irony of the Fall: attempting to make themselves into God, Adam and Eve became a pathetic parody of God, something like the tri-headed Satan of Dante; hoping to find security in self-sufficiency, they found only greater terror. What Balthasar urges on us is the lesson of the whole Scripture, namely, that Godlike freedom, authority, and sufficiency are discovered, not by setting the rest of being off as a rival, but precisely by including it, embracing it in love, revelling in its beauty. *Mitsein* (being with), the risky acceptance of the other in compassion, is, ironically enough, the key to the security and peace we all crave, and it is the essence, strangely enough, of true freedom.

What then, for Hans Urs von Balthasar, is the *imago Dei* in us sinners? What is it that links us, almost despite ourselves, to the divine source? It is, first, this curious, surprising capacity to be enraptured by beauty. Despite our sins and violence and stupidity, we can still fall into aesthetic arrest, still be taken up beyond ourselves by the simple harmony and radiance of a rose or a stained-glass window or a graceful movement. We can still be surprised out of our self-absorption by the shocking graciousness of the beautiful. And this capacity for aesthetic amazement in turn awakens our hunger for the divine ground of all beauty; it excites the wonder which is the beginning, not only of philosophy, but of theology as well. This enchantment of the heart then stirs the missionary desire to proclaim the beautiful to all the world, and in this mission, true freedom of the spirit is unleashed. The *imago* therefore is an eye, a vision, a sense, a hunger, an openness to wonder and a passion for freedom in love. All of these interrelated powers are alive in the soul, but they lie dormant in most of us, stilled and pinned down by the dead weight of originating sin. But when the divine beauty shines on them, they reflect back, taking on some of the quality of that light; when the divine tone is heard, there is awakened in them a *vibration sympathique;* when the divine water is poured on them, the seeds come to life.

And is this Balthasarian *imago* not very close to what Thomas Merton describes in such compelling narrative form? Caught in the sin of the race, debilitated by concupiscence and fear, Merton nevertheless could be beguiled by the beauty of birdsong and architecture and ancient iconic painting. This stirring of the soul could, in turn, lead him to worship, to the acknowledgment of the infinite power of Being itself. And this acknowledgment could compel him to give his life to prayer and to writing, to the establishment of a powerful *Mitsein* with the world. And finally, in this "being with," in this surrender of his egotism and his fearful clinging to self, Merton could find freedom. As he entered the monastic enclosure, the place where the modern world would least look for liberty, he could say: "I entered the four walls of my new freedom."

And is the same pattern not discernible in Dante? We spent a good deal of time exploring the dynamics of sin and conversion in the *Inferno*, but Dante's journey continues through the purgation of the seven-storey mountain (Merton!) and upward through the heavenly spheres until he arrives, through the guidance of Beatrice and St. Bernard, at the very vision of God, the summit of beauty. And upon seeing this beauty, Dante is, in a sense, only beginning his career, because he realizes, in his very ecstasy, that his obligation is to return from this height with the message of God's justice and love. He must witness to what he has seen and experienced. In short, he contemplates the beautiful itself and then becomes a missionary on its behalf, the *imago* in him thereby coming to full expression.

Another Christian theologian deeply concerned with the issue of the *imago* was the nineteenth-century Protestant thinker Friedrich Schleiermacher. In his breathtaking originality and radicality, in the sheer capaciousness and discipline of his theological reflection, Schleiermacher deserves to be ranked with Augustine, Aquinas, and Calvin as one of the premier systematic theologians of the Christian tradition. Schleiermacher burst on the scene in 1799 with the publication of his youthful work *On Religion: Speeches to Its Cultured Despisers*. Moving about in the sophisticated circles of Enlightenment Berlin, Schleiermacher had become convinced that religion, in the authentic sense, was in danger of extinction. On the one hand, rationalist critics were chipping away at its supernaturalist foundations, calling into question the phenomena of miracles and revelation; and on the other hand, self-appointed defenders of religion were misconstruing the essence of the spiritual by translating it into a mode of metaphysics or morals. He felt that it was incumbent upon him to address this cultured audience of both despisers and defenders in order to preserve and re-present the heart of religion for his time. In doing so, he gives rise to a much-praised and much-disputed philosophy of religion, a perspective that will prove the subject of controversy throughout the nineteenth and twentieth centuries. For our purposes, it is enormously helpful to study Schleiermacher's conception of religion because it sheds light on the question of the "contact point" — what the Germans call the *Anknüpfungspunkt* — between God and human beings. This link-up between the divine and the human, this contact despite all sin, is, Schleiermacher implies, the *imago* that makes *metanoia* possible.

In the well-known second speech, Schleiermacher gently chides those who wish to reduce religion to either a form of knowing or a form of acting. There were, in his time, certain thinkers who maintained that religion had to do with a kind of metaphysical knowledge concerning the ultimate cause of the universe. One thinks, for instance, of the Deists who presented a rational case for the existence of a first principle of being and motion, a sort of first designer of the Newtonian machine which is the cosmos. But Schleiermacher is convinced that, however much religion has been translated into metaphysical terms over the centuries and however much final philosophical questions are related to religion, authentic piety (his word is *Frömmigkeit*) cannot be reduced to this type of knowing. He memorably comments that "quantity of knowledge is not quantity of piety."[41] The deepest essence of the religious is not, finally, an act of the discursive intellect.

Others in Schleiermacher's cultured circle argued, probably with Kant in mind, that religion is best understood as a mode of morality. But this too, for Schleiermacher, is inadequate. However much the religious attitude has been expressed in the language of morality, however much it gives rise to moral commitment, religion cannot be simply reduced to a discourse on human behavior. It has to do, he is convinced, with something more basic, more elemental, something inclusive of, yet beyond, both knowledge and behavior.

As he gropes toward the articulation of this phenomenon, he uses the language of "contemplation," but he immediately senses the danger of an intellectualist misconstrual of the term: "This contemplation is not turned, as your knowledge of nature is, to the existence of a finite thing, combined with and opposed to another finite thing. It has not even, like your knowledge of God . . . to do with the nature of the first cause." In other words, religious contemplation is not speculative or scientific knowledge of any particular being or combination of beings; it is not knowledge of the "supreme" reality alongside of others. Rather, "contemplation of the pious *is the immediate consciousness of the universal existence of all finite things in and through the infinite and of all temporal things in and through the eternal*" (emphasis added).[42] Religious people across the ages — prophets, seers, sages, saints, ordinary believers — share, he thinks, this basic intuitive awareness in common: all things exist in and through the power of the infinite reality, of that whole that he later calls the *universum.* This "consciousness," this contemplative sense, is deeper than any explicit, reflexive grasp of the mind. It is not an intellectual act of clear vision, categorization, or analysis, not a deeper awareness of the net of finite interdependency. It is, instead, an "immediate feeling" for the reality of God as the grounding and all-enveloping power of existence.

There is something basically passive in this properly religious or pious state of soul. Whereas metaphysical knowledge is aggressively analytical and moral consciousness is "self-controlling," piety for Schleiermacher "appears as a surrender, a submission to be moved by the whole that stands over and against man."[43] The religious person does not so much seek as allow himself to be found, not so much control as permit himself to be overwhelmed. In the religious context, it is the power of the *universum,* the influence of the infinite, that always has the upper hand, and it is the rational, manipulating consciousness that is quelled. Now this is not to imply that the religious has no impact in the realm of the scientific or the moral. On the contrary, Schleiermacher thinks that the greatest achievements of mind and heart are rooted in piety: "What can man accomplish that is worth speaking of, either in life or in art, that does not arise in his own self from the influence of this sense for the infinite?"[44] Pious consciousness, in short, precisely as the most precious and all-pervasive form of feeling, undergirds and inspires the best of human intellectual and moral effort.

In what is perhaps the most famous line from the *Speeches,* Schleiermacher holds that "true religion is sense and taste for the infinite."[45] One can hear some of the overtones of romanticism in the choice of language: sense and taste rather than knowledge or vision. The religious attitude is a contemplative "feel," an artistic intuition. Just as one's "taste" in painting is difficult to articulate clearly, so one's "taste" for the infinite is impossible to clarify or categorize rationally, since both take place at a level of soul deeper than discursive thought. And this feel is for the "infinite," for the unbounded totality, for the embracing fullness, the all "on whose bosom" the pious person rests.

It should be obvious that much of this rhetoric would prove offensive to Schleiermacher's more rational and "tough-minded" contemporaries. Is he not simply reducing religion to a vague emotion, and is he not confusing the saintly mind with a somewhat overheated adolescent enthusiasm? And is he not opting finally for an uncritical Spinozan pantheism, an easy identification of God and the cosmos as it is presented airily in the imagination? These questions would have remained unsatisfactorily answered had Schleiermacher left us with only the *Speeches*. But later, when he was ensconced at the University of Berlin and at the height of his popularity and critical powers, he produced the masterful *Glaubenslehre* (Teaching on Faith) in which he took up once more the issue of the pious consciousness and analyzed it with greater precision.

Early on in the *Glaubenslehre,* Schleiermacher studies the complex dynamics of human self-consciousness. Never, he tells us, does the ego know itself in splendid isolation as an island in the sea of reality. On the contrary, in every concrete act of self-possession there are two elements, active and passive. The subject knows and posits itself through its own power, *and* it feels the influence of another; it "causes itself" and it "allows itself to be caused."[46] One comes to know oneself, in short, as a play of freedom and dependence, bouncing oneself off of the myriad influences that impinge upon one. I truly assert myself — but precisely in my interaction with the powers of nature, politics, and society that condition me. Even in my most personal acts, I realize that I am largely marked and led by forces out of my control. Though free and self-determining to some degree, I am conditioned by the stubborn givenness of my body, my environment, my position in the web of finite things. This receptive or passive dimension of self-consciousness Schleiermacher refers to as a *feeling of dependence.* We notice that in using the word "feeling" (*Gefühl*), Schleiermacher is not restricting himself to an emotive or purely affective interpretation. To "feel" dependency is to experience in the broadest sense, through mind and heart and affect, the effect that the "other" has on oneself. It is to know, again in a rich and multivalent way, the determination of my being through powers external to the ego.

Now everything in the "world" upon which I depend is also, at the same time, something which depends upon me, something which can be conditioned by my freedom. Just as all things in the web of conditioned relations affect me, so I affect, at least in principle, all things in the web. Once more, the mutual play of freedom and dependence governs the relations of things in the finite realm. However, says Schleiermacher, amid all of the proximate dependencies that I feel, I also sense an "absolute dependency." There is, at the very center of the consciousness, an awareness that I am in relationship with a power that I in no way control and that, in turn, utterly determines me. The "whence" of this feeling, its origin and ground, can, obviously, be no thing or collectivity of things in the realm of finitude; it must, instead, be that infinite and immeasurable reality that Schleiermacher referred to in the *Speeches* as the "Universum." The energy of Being itself is the only possible "whence" of the feeling of total dependency, since only Being as such could be that which determines and causes a finite thing in every dimension of its reality.

Now Schleiermacher holds that "to feel oneself as totally dependent and to be conscious of being in relation with God are one and the same thing."[47] As in the *Speeches*, God has been discovered, not through metaphysical argumentation or scientific demonstration, but through introspection and intuition. But the "sense and taste" for the infinite of the *Speeches* has been specified and rendered more pointed in the *Glaubenslehre* as the "feeling of absolute dependency." Both are descriptions of the immediate intuition of the divine presence that can be found in human consciousness, but the second formula is more "existential" than the first, since it highlights the sensing of God precisely as the one who bears us up in our ontological insufficiency. God is felt, in accord with the *Glaubenslehre* formulation, as the steady ground, the rock, the anchor of our dramatically unsteady lives. In

relation to any other reality in the universe, we sense our relative limitation, dependency, and neediness, but in relation to God, we feel
the total dependency of our finite being, our sheer emptiness and insufficiency. God is discovered, in short, in the context of the ultimate
limit experience.

❖

It is only natural that when theologians of a Schleiermacherian per-
suasion began to do their work in a twentieth-century context they
would incorporate the findings of psychoanalysis in their articulation of this "feeling" of total dependency. Such is the case with Paul
Tillich. Tillich became especially convinced of the threatened quality
of human existence while serving as a *Feldprediger* (chaplain) during
the First World War. Picking up the bodies of his friends, presiding at
heartbreaking burial services, cowering in the trenches while the shells
fell around him, Tillich knew in his bones that human life is precarious. When he began to theologize just after the war, young Tillich
sought to express the insufficiency and neediness of the human condition in terms that were, at one and the same time, psychological
and ontological. He tried to translate the more detached language of
Schleiermacher into the engaged and vivid terminology of Kierkegaard
and Freud.

Accordingly, the dependency and finitude that Schleiermacher
spoke of are now described as frightening: "finitude in awareness is
anxiety."[48] To be conscious of one's ontological incompleteness is to
be afraid, is to tremble with that vague but dreadful *angst* that the
psychologists call, appropriately enough, "existential."

There are several modalities of this fundamental anxiety, each proceeding from our relationship to a defining characteristic of finitude.
Thus it is frightening to exist in time, since temporality signals our
"being toward death," the grim fact that we are hurtling toward dissolution and can do nothing to stop the process. Time eats away at our
beauty, our power, our wealth, leaving us, in the end, with nothing.
And when we become profoundly aware of this brutal truth, when our
carefully constructed defenses against it are either dropped or broken

through, we experience what Tillich calls the "shock of nonbeing," the clear sense of our ontological incompleteness, our proximity to the nothing.[49]

Similarly, we experience this shock in relation to our spatiality. All finite things dwell, necessarily, in space as well as in time. But no one's place is ultimately secure; no one's rootedness in space is guaranteed. A home can be destroyed by fire; a plot of land can be washed away in a flood; a homeland can be lost through political machinations or military invasion; an apartment can be taken away because one is unable to pay the rent. We all stand in some place and derive a certain security from that rootedness, but no place is finally safe, no ground is immune to earthquake. Tillich, of course, spoke from dreadful personal experience on this score, having endured exile from his native Germany at the hands of the Nazis. Also, all finite things are caused, that is to say, they come into being through the intervention of another. Following Heidegger's well-known analysis in *Being and Time,* Tillich reminds us that we are "thrown" into existence, emerging into the light without being consulted, and that we will one day be "thrown" out of existence, once more without being asked. There is a terrible precariousness to our lives precisely because we are not our own causes, our own ground. Since we come into being through another, we are beholden to forces that surround us, compelled to exist according to them. Thus the fact of causality signals our radical nonbeing and hence frightens us.

Finally, all finite realities, for Tillich, are substances, that is to say, particular things, existents. But, as Aristotle taught long ago, substances are susceptible to substantial change, i.e., a complete destruction, a radical loss of form. Thus a chair can be burned to ashes, and a living human being can be transformed into a corpse, a collection of chemicals. In short, substances, by their very nature, are, curiously, "insubstantial." When this fact enters into consciousness, we become painfully aware of how "unnecessary" we are, how fleeting and finally inconsequential is our being, how possible and thinkable is our nonexistence. Interestingly, Freud speculated that the real ground for the belief in the immortality of the soul is the psychological impossibility of thinking oneself as nonexistent. For Tillich, the very real possibility of just such a thought is what puts us shockingly in the presence of nonbeing.

To be temporal, spatial, caused, and substantial is to be radically insufficient and hence to be afraid. It is to know, better to feel, that we are, in the most radical sense possible, nonself-explanatory. What Tillich has done is to cast in more psychological and experiential language precisely what Schleiermacher means by "absolute dependency," for to feel dependent is to feel insecure. He has reminded us, in the stark language of ontology, that we are all like the disciples in the storm-tossed boat on the sea of Galilee: afraid, insecure, and looking for a savior. Now one response to this disquieting state of affairs is to conclude that human life, as such, is simply meaningless, that Bob Dylan's character is right when he says, "there are many here among us / who feel that life is but a joke," that we are like the man in Schopenhauer's parable barely keeping himself afloat on a raft that is hurtling inevitably for the ruin of the falls. This is the option of Sartrean existentialism: we must accept the "objective" meaninglessness of our lives and do our best to create meaning for ourselves subjectively, through imagination and freedom. Within the context of this option, frightened and threatened human finitude proves, if anything, the nonexistence of God, the anxious soul becoming a sort of anti-*imago Dei*.

But Tillich sees another more compelling option. He sees that, though we are hemmed in by temporality, spatiality, causality and substance, though we are nonself-explanatory, though we need not exist, nevertheless we exist. There is nothing necessary about us, but, strangely, uncannily, we are. This threatened but undeniably real existence of ours is, then, not a proof of our tragic aloneness in the cosmos, but rather a demonstration of our existence *through another*. Precisely because we are so dependent in our being, there must exist some independent power that accounts for us, that holds us up. Our precarious temporality orients us to a reality that is eternal, outside of the ravages of time; our threatened spatiality opens us to a reality that is ubiquitous, beyond, and inclusive of all space; our dire "thrownness" makes us aware of a reality that exists through the power of its own being; and our insubstantial substantiality clues us to the reality which

is infinite, outside of all the categories of being. In short, our very ontological anxiousness is itself an *imago Dei*. The psalmist recognized
this when he sang that our bodies "pine for God like dry weary land
without water," our very aridity and incompleteness orienting us to
the Source.

And is this Schleiermacherian/Tillichean analysis not close to Merton's narrative evocation of the limitation of his own being in *The
Seven Storey Mountain?* What drove the young Tom Merton to his
knees at the deathbed of his grandfather was the anxiety of which
Tillich speaks, and what prompted his fascination with the metaphysics of Gilson was the feeling of absolute dependency of which
Schleiermacher speaks. In his tears, in his neediness, in the painful
cry of his soul, Merton was oriented to that unshakeable power that
exists mysteriously *a se*, in a realm beyond the transitoriness of finitude. Both beauty and terror, both the light and the darkness, called
forth from Merton the *imago Dei*, the hint of the *magna anima*.

In the *Catechism of the Catholic Church*, we find the simple but
powerful affirmation that the human being is, by nature, a "religious
being."[50] This means that all people are oriented, from the depth
of their existence, to communion with the sacred; they have a *ca-
pax Dei*, a capacity for God. In his *Introduction to Christianity*, Joseph
Ratzinger specifies the complex structure of this orientation: "both
the poverty of human existence and its fullness point to God."[51] Bor-
rowing to some degree from the Protestant tradition, Ratzinger argues
that human incapacity, inadequacy, failure, and need serve "again and
again as a pointer to the quite other." At the same time, when human
beings experience "existence in its fullness, its wealth, its beauty, and
its greatness, they have always become aware that this existence is an
existence for which they owe thanks." The very richness and perfection of life point to the graced character of all existence: "Who am I
that such a thing should appear to me?"

What Balthasar helped us to see, in typically Catholic style, is this
positive dimension of the *imago*. There is in all of us an eye and taste
for the beautiful, a wonder that orients us to the open sea of the Beautiful itself. And what Schleiermacher and Tillich offered us, in more
typically Protestant style, is the negative aspect of that same *imago Dei*.

In our very hunger, our radical dependence, our existential neediness, in the terrible irresolution of our hearts, we are, paradoxically, directed to God and hence in the image of God. The desire for God, born of anxiety and need, is itself a sacred seal.

We are sinners, but, in the poverty and richness of our ordinary humanity we remain mirrors of the divine and hence "capable" of *metanoia*. How often physicians say that all they do is to awaken and focus the native healing powers of the body itself. Is there something similar at work here? Soul doctors such as Merton, Balthasar, Schleiermacher, and Tillich appeal to the dormant divinity within and hence salve the soul. They disclose the possibility of a *magna anima* that neither grasps nor hides, but rather opens itself in awe and gratitude to the ever greater, ever more alluring Mystery. Yes, we are sinners in a dysfunctional family of sinners; no, we are not capable of saving ourselves. But there is in all of us, almost despite ourselves, a sense of what we would look like "fully alive" and a hunger for the God who wants nothing more than to give us that fullness. We are all, whether we know it or not, "shining like the sun." To the source of that light, vaguely seen and passionately desired, we now turn.

Part II

The Uncanny God

Chapter Six

No Grasping, No Hiding

Beginning with Faulkner

It is the rock, the storm, the lion, the flood, the desert. It is the bear, the leviathan, the whirlwind, the barely audible whisper, the voice, the silence, the city strongly compact, the mother with abundant breasts, the tearful father. There is a mysterious reality, at the borders and at the heart of our ordinary experience, suffusing and yet transcending all that surrounds us, a reality that can be evoked with a thousand names and that cannot, finally, be caught by any name. This mystery judges us and energizes us, frightens us and gives us incomparable peace, overwhelms us and captivates us. Like Melville's white whale, it surges up from the depths and sinks our ships, and like Jonah's whale it draws us into itself and gives us protection. It is as high as the heavens are above the earth and as low as the caverns of Hell; it is as dark as a pillar of cloud and as luminous as a pillar of fire; it is the burning bush that is not consumed, and it is water from the rock. It is the sheer act of Being itself, and it is nothing at all; it is what is hardest to see, and it is what is most obvious.

Every great mystic, prophet, or theologian knows that this mystery cannot be spoken of adequately, that, like a wily fish, it escapes all the nets of thought and language that we set for it. Thomas Aquinas — the most talkative theologian in the tradition — simply stopped talking at the end of his life, convinced that all he had said of the mystery amounted to so much straw. And yet, as my catalogue of traditional names suggests, we talk, almost compulsively and manically, of this power, pushed by some inner drive of the spirit. We cannot speak of God, and we must speak of God. It is as simple and as strange as that.

We are compelled to theologize precisely because we are who we are: those strange beings already described in this book, sinners open to *metanoia,* change of mind. God must be spoken of because we are alienated from the Mystery that alone can give us life, and we know it; God must be engaged because we are wired for the Mystery and nothing short of the Mystery can give us peace. We are not so much rational animals (as Aristotle thought) or productive animals (as Marx would have it) as we are those animals who speak of God. Time and again, in the course of the centuries, various philosophers and social reformers have predicted that we would grow out of our debilitating and embarrassing tendency to engage in God-talk, but they have all faded away, and God-talk remains. The preoccupation with the Mystery is in us, and it can't ultimately be wished or thought or threatened away. All of this suggests, of course, that the naming of God is a vitally important spiritual exercise and not merely a game of the mind. To name the divine with something approaching adequacy is to foster a right relation with the Mystery, to undo, to some extent, the effects of the originating sin that has placed us at a remove from God.

And this might give us a clue why the biblical and theological and mystical traditions have described the divine in such wildly diverse ways, using remarkably multivalent and, sometimes, mutually exclusive symbols. Many are the subtle tricks of the *pusilla anima,* and hence many and subtle must be the correctives to these sinful ruses. We have already seen in some detail what the original sin of Adam and Eve produced in us, namely, the tendency to place ourselves at the center of the universe, to render ourselves unconditioned and absolute. This false move of the spirit, in its turn, resulted in the objectification of all things and people around us: the god-ego threatened by rivals on all sides. And the greatest rival of all became God, that supreme being who must, at all costs, be either attacked or avoided, defeated or hidden from. We remember vividly the two moves of our mythic first parents: to steal from God (as did Prometheus) and then, in shame, to hide from God. Both strategies are errant precisely because both involve the objectification of the divine: only a supreme being over and against the unconditioned ego can be either manipulated or avoided. What becomes clear as we read the Genesis account is that Adam and Eve suffer from bad theology, from a fundamentally illusory sense of who God is. God, the rivalrous ultimate reality, is an invention of the sinful ego, and the theology based upon or supporting this view is poison to the spirit. Luther knew that the mind is every bit as fallen (affected by originating sin) as the will and hence that the mind can produce elaborate systems in service of egotism.

It is my conviction that the God-talk of our tradition (though tainted by sin) is a consistent and largely successful attempt to undo the effects of the Fall by orienting us to the God who is really God and not the fantasy of the sinful soul. The theology, art, literature, architecture, drama of the Christian heritage constitute an attempt to name God, not as the pathetic rival to the ego's phantom unconditionality, but as the power in which the fearful ego can find itself through surrender. God is that reality which, thankfully, can be neither manipulated nor avoided, neither controlled nor hidden from, and, as such, God is that which effectively invites the ego to give up its fearful and finally illusory place at the center of the universe. In naming God in the wildly diverse ways that it does, the Christian tradition attempts to doctor the soul, to frustrate the myriad moves of the grasping or self-concealing ego.

I hope to show how our spirit masters have described the divine in this soul-doctoring way. Once more, we turn to a variety of sources: the fiction of a twentieth-century novelist, the spirituality of a biblical author, and the evocative theologies of the Christian tradition. As we name God, we stir to life the *magna anima*.

As usual, the poets say it best. In 1942, William Faulkner published a cycle of seven stories under the general title *Go Down, Moses*. The centerpiece of this set is the remarkable tale "The Bear," a narrative that speaks of the conflict between nature and civilization, the struggle between white and primal cultures, the psychological heritage of the Civil War, the coming-of-age of a young man, and, most captivatingly, of the mystical encounter with the alluring reality of God. Like so many other poets and spiritual writers, Faulkner cannily chooses an animal — at once beautiful, fierce, elusive, inviting — to speak of the ultimate power.

The story begins with an evocation of a boy and a bear. The boy, Ike McCaslin, is ten, and he has been invited for the first time to join the men as they go on a late fall hunting foray into the deep woods. They will shoot for quail and deer, but the ultimate goal of their quest is Old Ben, the legendary bear who roams an area one hundred miles square and who has, for years, terrorized the villages around the woods, ruining corn cribs, slaughtering pigs, and even carrying calves bodily into the forest. The bear has lived in the boy's dreams and imaginings for many years: this great beast "too big for the dogs which tried to bay it, for the horses which tried to ride it down, for the men and the bullets they fired into it."[52] Long captivated by the image of the bear, the boy is, at one and the same time, frightened and fascinated at the prospect of facing it.

When he arrives at camp, deep in the forest, Ike enters into an experience not unlike that of a novice in a religious community. He is met by Sam Fathers, part Indian, part black, who will be his mystagogue in the ways of the hunt. He becomes accustomed to the rude lifestyle of the hunter, to the simple and poorly prepared meals, to the damp and cold of the stands where he waits, through long hours, for the rush of deer through the woods. He learns that "patience and humility" are essential for survival in the forest, that the overeager or cocky hunter never lands a kill. Ike feels that he is "witnessing his own birth" as he follows Sam into a new realm of experience.[53]

Then one morning, during the second week of his novitiate, while he waits on his lonely hunting stand, Ike hears the unusually high-pitched yipping and barking of the dogs, and, with some trepidation, he readies his gun. Sam Fathers tells him, "It's Old Ben," and the boy stiffens in anticipation and excitement. The two listen and watch until finally Sam knows that the bear has slipped back into the woods. "He do it every year," Sam explains. "He come to see who's here, who's new in camp this year, whether he can shoot or not, can stay or not." The boy has been dreaming of the bear for years, reaching out to him in imagination and will, and now the bear has established contact with the boy, sizing him up and monitoring his readiness for a richer encounter, gazing mysteriously from the shadows of the woods, seeing without being seen. The hunted, Ike realizes, is himself a hunter.

Sam teaches the boy how to track the bear, and he manages to find a vestige of the beast, Old Ben's footprint in the mud, bigger and more fascinating than he had imagined. Then, sometime later, having moved deeper into the dark of the forest, stationed at another lonely stand, Ike listens carefully, and he hears no baying of the dogs, only the solitary drumming of a woodpecker. When even that sound stops, he knows that the bear is, once again, looking at him. He has no idea whether the animal is before or behind him, whether he is far or near, and he stands still, the useless gun at his side, the taste of fear like brass in his mouth. And then, just as abruptly, it is over, the bear is gone. When Sam emerges from the woods a few minutes later, the boy excitedly tells him of the encounter, but he adds, somewhat puzzled, "I didn't see him; I didn't, Sam." And the old man replies, "I know it; he done the looking."[54] Wisely and mysteriously, the bear has, once more, sought out the young man and watched him, but this *being seen* awakens in Ike the even more intense desire to see: "So I will have to see him; I will have to look at him."[55]

And so the next June he returned to camp, this time with his own rifle. While the men hunted, Ike ranged out into the woods, using his compass as Sam had taught him, identifying landmarks, tracking animals, even finding, once more, Old Ben's crooked footprint, but the bear himself he did not encounter. He spent hours and hours every day exploring the woods with increasing confidence, returning later and later to camp, amazing the men who had roamed the forest for years and had never attained the boy's level of competence. When he tells Sam Fathers of his exploits and of his frustration at not having seen the bear, the old man knowingly responds, "You ain't looked right yet."[56] When the boy protests that he has been following all the recommendations of his mentor, Sam cuts him off: "I reckon that was all right. Likely he's been watching you."[57] But the reason, he explains, that the bear has not come out into the open is the gun that the young man carries: "You will have to choose," Sam explains, between the safety the gun provides and the experience of seeing the bear close up.

The next morning, before light, the boy set out into the woods, consumed by the desire to commune with Old Ben. Purposely he left behind his weapon and entered the woods armed only with a stick to ward off snakes and a compass to find his way back. He remembered that Sam had told him to "be scared but not afraid" since nothing in the woods would hurt him unless it was cornered or smelled fear. By noon, he had wandered further into alien country than he had ever gone, and he knew that he would make it back to camp only after dark had fallen. Still there was no sign of the bear. He stopped to wipe his brow and to glance at the compass. Perhaps, he thought, the surrendering of the gun was not enough; perhaps the bear demanded that he leave behind everything, all weapons of defense and all instruments of direction. And so he hung the compass on a nearby bush and he leaned the simple snake stick against it, and, stripped of any of the accoutrements of civilization, he entered deeper into the forest.

Before he knew it, he was lost, enveloped by the woods. But he did not panic, for Sam Fathers had taught him ancient Indian techniques for tracking in the woods. While he was without the aid of his compass, executing one of Sam's maneuvers, he saw the familiar crooked and enormous footprint, but this time it was not old; as he looked at it, it was still filling with water, proving that Old Ben had just been there. Frightened but fascinated, Ike followed the prints, though he knew the reckless decision to follow Old Ben into the trackless woods, hours from his home camp, would leave him either dead or hopelessly lost. Still he pressed on, "tireless, eager, without doubt or dread," following the prints to a lovely open space, a glade deep, deep in the woodland. And then he saw the bear. "It did not emerge, appear; it was just there, immobile, fixed in the green and windless noon's hot dappling, not as big as he had dreamed it but big as he had expected, bigger, dimensionless against the dappled obscurity, looking at him."[58] Next the animal moved across the glade, pausing ever so briefly in the direct light of the sun and then, as it passed into the obscurity of the woods, it glanced once over its shoulder and spied the boy. Finally, it sank into the deep darkness of the forest just as a great bass sinks, almost motionlessly, into the depths of a pool.

The sketchy summary that we have provided here can only begin to hint at the richness and mysterious beauty of Faulkner's account. Like Ike himself, the reader is lured by Faulkner's snaky prose, gradually and achingly, into the arcana, the technique, and the mystique of the hunt. He too is being disciplined, readied for the encounter. And the very elegance and solemnity of the story show that we are being drawn into a sacred space, a confrontation with the deep things of God. Therefore let us now view this lovely tale through the interpretive lens of a religious consciousness.

We begin with a hunt, a quest to find and to kill. The great old bear is a menace to life and property, and something must be done to stop it. But beneath this practical concern, there is, among the hunters, something of an aesthetic fascination, a desire simply to commune with the bear, to revel in its size and strength, to return and tell stories of it. This ambiguity in the intentionality of the hunters corresponds to the ambiguity in the feelings of sinful human beings vis-à-vis the mystery of God, the split in consciousness that we have already referred to. To the sinner who has made herself the unconditioned center of the universe, God is, necessarily, experienced as a threat, as the one who plunders and carries off the goods of her realm. Like the bear, God, the authentically unconditioned, breaks into her sinful soul with awesome and disquieting power, unsettling her complacency, stirring her to fear and violent response. This rivalrous God must, accordingly, be either hidden from or ruthlessly hunted down and eliminated. The hunting down of God is, of course, in a Christian context, of enormous importance, since, when the divine appeared in human flesh, he was pursued and eventually killed by the power of sin. The crucified and hunted Christ reveals, as it were, how the sinful ego responds in the presence of the sacred.

But, as Faulkner suggests, this is only half the story. Even the boy knows that the hunters really never intend to kill Old Ben, that, at least with regard to the bear, the hunt is more of a pilgrimage, an attempt to commune. Though they are frightened of the beast, they are, even more, compelled by it, captivated. Rudolf Otto, of course, taught us long ago that trembling and fascination were the twin poles of the natural human response to the divine, a fearful awe in the presence of that which judges and a dazzled awe in the presence of that which overwhelms and lures. The fascination before the divine — the pull toward the wonder of God despite all fearful pushing away — is a function of what we have been calling the *imago Dei*. We are afraid of God, but we are also irresistibly drawn to God, our sense of beauty stirred. And so, like the hunter/pilgrims of Faulkner's tale, we all go out, with split souls, to meet the sacred.

Now Faulkner purposely orients his reader to the perspective of the boy, Ike McCaslin, as he is introduced into the ways of the hunter, and he uses the evocative language of monastic novitiate or shamanic initiation to describe the process. As the boy endeavors to join the party of hunter/worshipers, there is a disciplining of consciousness required, an entry onto the path of "humility and patience." Like most children, Ike probably wants to leap into the fray, to encounter the bear quickly and effortlessly, and this childlike enthusiasm, left unchecked, would have been his undoing. In some ways, he is like Dante at the beginning of the *Divine Comedy*, desirous of a quick ascent of the mountain and in fact in need of a chastening discipline. And so his Virgil arrives, the half-black, half-native American Sam Fathers, the wisdom figure who will be his spiritual guide, fathering him into the mystery of God.

Just as there are disciplines and techniques that enable a person to survive in the trackless wood, so there are disciplines and techniques in the spiritual life, that is to say, ways of orienting oneself in the dark wood of the divine reality. Accordingly, Bonaventure gives us his *Itinerarium mentis in Deum* (The Mind's Journey into God), and Ignatius offers us Spiritual Exercises and Juan de la Cruz guides our Ascent of Mount Carmel. All of these — ascetic disciplines, practices of prayer, focusings of consciousness, moral endeavors, etc. — are attempts by some of the shamans of Christianity to tame the often erratic spirit of the sinner and to give direction to its quest. And at the heart of so many of these shamanic disciplines of the Christian tradition are the twin virtues that young Ike McCaslin learns: patience and humility. Though we are ravenously hungry for God, the divine is not something that responds to our demands and on our timetable. God appears when he appears, and for his own reasons. Thus we must be humble and docile in his presence, ready to wait, if necessary, through long hours, days and years, prepared to hear the rush of God through the woods when it comes. As all spiritual searchers attest, there is a healthy tediousness to the religious life, a settling into routine that is necessary if one is to be ready when the divine chooses to show itself. We think here of the novice in a Benedictine monastery being put to the tasks of setting tables or cleaning toilets and being compelled to stand, with his brothers, through long hours of chanting and silence every day. Perhaps, our tradition wagers, God will not appear until the fallen ego is ready to see.

After considerable waiting, Ike finally hears the overexcited barking of the dogs, and he knows that the bear is close, but the great animal itself he does not see. When the ego has been chastened and readied, the divine deigns to come closer, perhaps knowing that its presence will be properly appreciated. But it is still known only through signs, hints, indications. If God appeared unambiguously to a consciousness at this still primitive level of development, God would devastate it: no one sees the face of God and lives. It is only analogously and elusively through his creatures that God first speaks. Thomas Aquinas compares the initial experience of the divine to a man who approaches a house and concludes that it is burning though he never sees the fire.[59] What he feels is the ever increasing heat as he moves from porch to foyer to drawing-room. So the patient and humble spiritual seeker begins to receive signs of God in his created effects.

But most interestingly, Sam Fathers tells Ike that it is the bear who has been doing the seeing. This is the great reversal that is usually shocking to the sinful ego: the divine one whom I have been seeking (or hunting) is in fact seeking and hunting me. The psalmist knew this experience both uplifting and deeply troubling: "Lord, you search me and you know me; you know my resting and my rising, you discern my purpose from afar" (Ps. 139). The sinner is convinced that the spiritual life is his game and that God is a prey to be stalked, a prize to be won. The unsettling fact is that we are mastered, we are stalked, and the very condition for the possibility of our finding is that we have already been found. While we desperately seek after God, God is already even more desperately seeking after us, and what most spiritual writers eventually urge on us is a surrender to the divine hunt. The Curé of Ars once described his liturgical spirituality in these words:

"I look at Him and He looks at me." So while Ike peers through the woods to see Old Ben, the bear is already and much more successfully peering through those same woods to see the boy.

Excited by his first contacts with the world of the hunt and by his mystic encounter with the power of the bear, Ike returns the next summer, supplied with compass, woodsman's skill, and a shiny gun. He stands now for the spiritual apprentice sure of his game, the seeker who has been touched by the sacred and is ready for fullness of contact. His grace and skill in the forest evoke the growing adeptness in the ways of the spirit. Ranging deep into the woods, he is the mystic confidently moving in the black forest of the divine presence, finding hints of the sacred (the footprint of Old Ben) through prayer and fasting and study. Chastened, humbled, disciplined, he is relatively successful in the ways of the spirit, far more so than his older contemporaries. But the decisive moment is reached only when his mystagogue tells him of the choice, the decision he must make between the safety of the gun and the ecstasy of the vision of the bear. The bear will not show itself as long as the boy carries with him the instruments of guidance and violence, in other words, those things that contribute to his mastery of the situation. With his compass and rifle, he is in control, he is doing the seeing, and he can determine the quality of his encounter with Old Ben.

These tools are evocative of the frightened and grasping consciousness of Adam and Eve, the fearful and God-hunting state of mind. Both Sam Fathers and Ike realize that letting go of these accoutrements of egotism is dangerous — the boy could easily be lost or killed — but absolutely necessary if the bear is to be encountered close up. The ego must drop the aggressiveness and defensiveness that flow from its self-elevation; it must abandon all those descendants of the loincloths of Eden, those instruments of protection. It must realize that any semblance of the hunting of God must be eradicated. Alone, naked, unafraid (as Sam pointedly reminds Ike), the soul must present itself to the Mystery.

And so the boy lets go of the compass, the stick, and the gun, and, with fear just beginning to rise in him, he enters the deepest part of the woods. And it is there, in that place and in that state of soul, that he sees: in a glade, a small clearing in the forest, the bear is simply there. Intriguingly, the animal first appears in the "dappling," the playful mixture of dark and light so characteristic of forest scenery. God is always seen and not seen, visible but ever more invisible, available but ever elusive, epistemologically and metaphysically in the dappling; the power of Being itself cannot be unambiguously understood by the rationality of the ego, forced into the glaring light of science and analysis. The implicit goal of Enlightenment science — the mastery of nature through knowledge — is, quite simply, irreconcilable with the goal of spiritual knowing, namely, the experience of being grasped by the very ground of reason. The bear moves across the glade and only for an instant is in the direct light of the sun before fading once more into the half-light. This momentary illumination signifies the passing, fleeting quality of the vision of God available in this life: occasionally we see, with frightening clarity, but before we can even begin to reflect on such a vision of the divine, it fades, receding into the dark. How often in *Moby Dick* (a book to which Faulkner's "The Bear" has a more than passing resemblance) the white whale tantalizes the sailors, rising just for a moment above the roiled surface of the ocean, only to sound once more into the murky depths. So with the God who passionately seeks us, but refuses to be mastered by us.

Just before disappearing into the woods, Old Ben pauses, ever so briefly, and looks at the boy once more "across one shoulder." When, in the book of Exodus, Moses asked to see Yahweh, God placed his servant in the cleft of a rock and then told him to close his eyes as the divine presence passed (Exod. 33:18–23). Only when God had gone by was Moses permitted to look and see the hindquarters of the sacred. When we are ready, when we have divested ourselves of the tools of hunting and manipulating, when our egos have been sufficiently humbled and disciplined, God sometimes appears, looking at us across one shoulder, allowing us to see something of his being, tantalizing and seducing us to deeper vision and more thoroughgoing surrender. Hence, control and evasion — the twin strategies of sinful Eden — are foiled by the odd mode of God's self-offering. The Bear is neither trapped nor avoided.

❖

Faulkner's story gives expression, as we have seen, to some of the elemental dynamics of the spiritual life as it has been experienced and described by the Christian tradition. And this should not surprise us, since this mid-twentieth-century American writer from the deep South had, obviously, been profoundly shaped by a biblical vision of the world. The deepest roots of Faulkner's mystical narrative are in the scriptural descriptions of the always strange and always life-changing encounters with the mystery of God. With "The Bear" very much in mind, let us turn now to one of the most celebrated biblical accounts of a divine self-disclosure, the manifestation to Moses of the divine presence in the burning bush.

The context for this well-known story is terribly important, but it has, too often, been overlooked. The child Moses, placed in a basket and floated among the reeds along the Nile, is found by the daughter of the pharaoh who raises him as her own son. Without necessarily succumbing to the imaginative excess of Cecil B. DeMille, we can still fairly assume that the Egyptian career of Moses was a glorious one. Raised at least in the pharaonic milieu, the fortunate adoptee would have been exposed to the advantages of a sophisticated education and a relatively advanced culture. It is probably safe to assume that the author of Exodus wants us to know that Moses led a pampered, princely life and that he was, like most members of a privileged class, accustomed to having things his way.

And the admittedly few narrative details we have only confirm this reading. Seeing an Egyptian strike a Hebrew slave, Moses promptly kills the aggressor and hurriedly buries him, betraying thereby his lack of both prudence and proportionality (Exod. 2:11–14). There is, it seems hard to deny, something arrogant and self-absorbed in this violent outburst. And then, some days later, when Moses intervenes to break up a fight between two Hebrews, the aggressor retorts, "Who appointed you to be prince over us and judge?" The man brings to light a certain willfulness and self-righteousness in Moses' character, and then he turns up the heat by reminding Moses of his poorly concealed act of violence: "Do you intend to kill me as you killed the

Egyptian?" The Scripture tells us that Moses fled the country in fear, realizing that the pharaoh would kill him for this transgression, but I wonder whether there was not a deeper reason for his flight. As is so often the case with the heroes of biblical narratives — Abraham, Jacob, Joseph, Paul — there is a process of purgation and cleansing that must unfold before the real confrontation with God and the acceptance of mission can take place. Is it possible that Moses came to realize his shallowness and egocentrism and accordingly fled in spiritual fear into the desert, into a foreign land, a place of exile in order to purify himself?

On this reading, of course, the time in the land of Midian with Jethro and his daughters is of enormous spiritual significance. Moses leaves behind the sophisticated courts of the pharaoh and takes up residence in the tents of simple shepherds, going about the ordinary tasks of watering and tending flocks. Like Jacob and Joseph before him, and like Dante after him, Moses learns to curb the violence and imperiousness of his ego through the adoption of a humble, servile lifestyle, in exile from all that he had come to know and value. It is significant that he names his son Gershom because he is "a stranger in a foreign land." There are few acts more solemn and more revelatory of the soul than the naming of a child, and here Moses celebrates the birth of his firstborn with a name evocative of exile.

It is only after years of this desert time that Moses is summoned to an encounter. While tending his flocks on the slopes of Horeb, the sacred mountain, he sees the remarkable sight of a bush that, though on fire, is not consumed. Filled with wonder and curiosity, he approaches: "I must go and look at this strange sight and see why the bush is not burned" (Exod. 3:3). Can we hear something of Moses' lingering willfulness and egotism in this statement? *He* must go and examine and understand; *he* must bring this unusual sight into his purview and its mystery into the categories of his intelligence. Thus when he draws near, the God who has summoned him calls out only to warn him: "Come no nearer; take off your shoes, for the place on which you stand is holy ground." God's alluring beauty has called him, but now God's transcendent majesty has limited him: the characteristic divine rhythm of invitation and distantiation has commenced. Moses

is drawn by the sacred immanence, but the sacred transcendence pre-
vents him from coming too close, from examining too intrusively, from
imposing his ego too boldly. What the author of Exodus implies here
is that the hunting tools of willfulness and intellect must be put down,
and even the shoes that allow one to walk too confidently on strange
ground must be taken off if the holy one is to be felt.

Then the voice speaks, identifying itself as the God of Abraham,
Isaac, and Jacob, that is to say, as the friend and protector of very
particular individuals. God is a person who knows the names of those
he has chosen for intimacy. Furthermore, he tells Moses that he has
heard the cries of his people in Egypt, the groaning of some of the
most forgotten people on the face of the earth, slaves laboring in
despair for despotic masters. This one who speaks from the burning
bush is the God, not of kings and princes, not of those at the top
of the societal ladder, but rather of the lowliest and most miserable
people imaginable. And God's purpose vis-à-vis these lowly ones is
salvific and liberating: "I mean to deliver them out of the hands of
the Egyptians . . . and I send you to Pharaoh to bring the sons of Israel, my people, out of Egypt." This surprising God of the fiery bush
is a power of scandalous, even slightly comical, condescension. What
kind of God is this that would waste his time on a people as forgotten
and insignificant as Hebrew slaves in Egypt? Moses must have begun
to wonder, with some disappointment, whether he was dealing with a
rather insignificant desert deity, one of the lesser gods of the region.

And so he poses his famous question concerning this God: "But
if they [the Israelites] ask me what his name is, what am I to tell
them?" Moses is commonsensically inquiring about which of the myriad immanent gods this one might be and which particular name he
might bear. Since this god knows Moses' name and since he is on intimate terms with one people, he is obviously a familiar deity, one god
among the many worshiped in this region, and he must therefore have
a defining identity. Having lured Moses with intimations of his intimacy, this God of the burning bush now overwhelms him with a taste
of his transcendent inapproachability: "And God said to Moses, 'I am
who I am'" (Exod. 3:14). In one sense, what God says here is "stop
asking such stupid questions!" God is not a particular being, not one

god among many, not a reality that can be facilely named, described, defined, delimited. Moses wants God to fit into one of the linguistic or religious categories that he is accustomed to, and God adamantly refuses. The divine spirit is not this or that kind of being, not here rather than there, not great rather than small, not up rather than down; instead, God simply is: "I am who I am." And thus his answer is a sort of nonanswer, a refusal to be drawn into the net of the mind that Moses spreads out before him.

Once again, we face a paradox. Once again the back-and-forth rhythm of immanence and transcendence has set in. God is so low as to be present in saving grace to slaves in Egypt, and God is so high as to be uncatchable by any name, even the most exalted; God is in the mud with the poorest of the poor, and God is in the realm beyond the clouds. "I am the God of Abraham, Isaac, and Jacob," and "I am who I am." In a word, God is that uncanny reality that can be neither set aside nor controlled, neither escaped from nor manipulated. God is that strange power that both resists our attempts to hunt and confounds our attempts to hide. Through the ages religious people have spoken of gods who were tied to particular places and tribes, and from ancient times philosophers have spoken of the God in the transcendent realm beyond the world, but the author of Exodus speaks of the divine power who is, at the same time, both unspeakably close and unspeakably far. The two easy options of pure immanence or pure transcendence are the choices that appeal to us sinners, to us descendants of Adam and Eve. We want the "supreme being" who is either so familiar that he is contemptible or so distant that he is irrelevant; Exodus gives us the God who is so familiar he cannot be ignored *and* so distant he cannot be controlled. It offers us the bear that lures, hides, and then, only through grace, allows itself to be seen. It gives us, in short, the undoing of original sin.

Chapter Seven

THE SERENITY AND
THE CREATIVITY OF GOD

It is intriguing that the Bible never offers anything even approaching a "proof" for the existence of God. The various biblical authors, writing across several centuries, never felt it incumbent upon themselves to demonstrate that the God of the burning bush exists. Like Faulkner's Old Ben, God, whether hunted or feared, whether sought after or fled from, is simply there. The psalmist recognized this inescapability of the divine when he sang:

> Where can I run from your love?
> If I climb the heavens you are there.
> There too if I lie in Sheol. (Ps. 139)

The insight of the biblical tradition seems to be that the human condition itself — whether in its sinful mode or in its graced mode — witnesses to the inevitability of the divine. When we are in rebellion (lying in Sheol), God is the power that hounds and pursues us, and when we are in touch with our soul (climbing the heavens), God is the power that captivates and enlivens us. The scriptural tradition feels that we can never finally stand outside the experience of God and pose the disinterested rational question whether God exists. We can be entranced by God or frightened of God; we can be at home in the courts of the Lord or in desert exile from the divine presence, but we can never really doubt whether there is a God. As both the psalmist and St. Anselm remind us: "Only the fool says in his heart that there is no God."

Paul Tillich gives expression to this biblical conviction when he says that God is the origin of our feeling of "ultimate concern." Every person is hemmed in by proximate concerns — for food, money, family security, pleasure, etc. — but each of these can be put aside or relativized. None of these presses on us with unrelenting power. But amid all of the proximate, relative concerns of our lives, there is some preoccupation that cannot be marginalized, put aside, thought away; at the root of the thousand particular concerns that demand our attention, there is a final and ultimate concern that determines all we think and all we do. Now the origin of the feeling of ultimate concern cannot be a particular thing or principle or political party or even a supreme being, since such a reality could be ignored or relativized vis-à-vis other things. In order to capture something of the all-embracing and unconditioned quality of the source of this concern, Tillich refers to it as "Being itself." This unconditioned reality — both high and low, both transcendent and immanent, both frightening and fascinating — is, whether we like it or not, inescapably *there*, affecting us, willy-nilly, in every way. To seek to "prove" its existence is to acknowledge that one has already been grasped by it.

To be sure, this reality can be given names other than "Being itself." Those standing in the Merton/von Balthasar tradition might call it "Beauty itself"; those at home with the Thomist approach might call it "Truth itself"; and those identifying with the thought-world of Augustine might call it "the Good itself." No matter: whatever presses on the soul with ultimate, inescapable power, whatever stands at the center and core of the spirit, is this mysterious and unconditioned reality that religious people usually call "God." Now what we find when we seek to name and know this reality more thoroughly is precisely what we found in our analysis of both Faulkner and Exodus: that unnerving and compelling *complexio oppositorum* (coming together of opposites). Being itself — and not some supreme being — is obviously that which transcends any particular existent, that whose mode of existence is utterly unique, transcendent to the categories of the finite realm. And Being itself — the sheer energy of existence — must be that which grounds every particular thing in the universe, that which works its way into every nook and cranny of finitude, that which is unsurpassably immanent to creation. Beauty itself is the alluring *telos* of every artistic quest and thus that which goes beyond

any particular beautiful thing; and Beauty itself is that which undergirds and informs every artistic aspiration, act and accomplishment. It
is, once more, unspeakably different and inexpressibly close. Similarly,
Truth itself is the ever elusive, ever retreating goal of all intellectual
questing, the "horizon" always approached but never reached; and
Truth itself is that which energizes the mind in its every act and
that which marks every particular expression of truth. Once more,
the unconditioned is simultaneously utterly mysterious and utterly
obvious.

When attempting to name the source of our ultimate concern, in
short, we are a bit like a trainer trying to get hold of two horses
galloping in precisely opposite directions. Accordingly, almost every
theologian and spiritual writer in the Great Tradition has realized that
scientific knowing of the divine reality through clear and distinct ideas
is out of the question. The only naming possible is in the poetic mode
of symbol, myth, or metaphor, that style of speech characterized by
odd juxtapositions and creative, unlikely alignments. The only legitimate theological speech is that which leaves the speakers and hearers
strangely off balance, unsure of themselves, that which says "yes" just
when they have become accustomed to "no," that which insists on
"no" just when "yes" seems the only possible response. And, as we
have seen, this circus act is not merely of theoretical interest. Rather,
its deepest purpose is to disorient the psyche that wants the easy solution of grasping or hiding. Proper theological speech is like incense
that stings the eyes and clouds the vision, rendering straightforward
seeing impossible. We are, of course, in the midst of a paradox here.
What seems to be "clear" seeing (the grasp of the sinful mind) is in
fact illusory, and what seems to be foggy (the anti-vision of the theologian) is really crystal clarity. The eyes of sin, which produce the
illusion of clarity, must be salved by the stinging balm of theological language. And thus the fundamental project of theology — the
naming of the divine — is in service of what we have been calling
soul-doctoring. In the very act of calling God by relatively adequate
names, we realign the sinful energies of the soul, cajoling them into
right order. Let us now embark on this paradoxical soul-doctoring
process.

✦

In his *Dogmatik* of 1925, Paul Tillich speaks of the *Klarheit* (clarity) possessed by God; in his *Summa theologiae*, Thomas Aquinas speaks of God's characteristic attribute of simplicity; in his *Church Dogmatics*, Karl Barth insists upon the *Gottheit Gottes* (the Godliness of God). All three theologians are describing what I have chosen to call the serenity of the divine reality. In one sense, God is like the clear unbroken surface of an unroiled sea, or like a single Doric column rising into a cloudless sky, or like a pure soprano voice singing the simplest of melodies. There is a peaceful untrammeled serenity to the divine being, since God is the sheer act of existence. As the sacred name "I am who I am" suggests, God is not this or that kind of being, not this or that particular deity, but rather the act of Being itself. There is therefore something clean, pure, untroubled, and uncomplicated about the divine reality.

For Thomas Aquinas, this simplicity is tantamount to the identity of essence and existence in God. All finite things, argues Thomas, are hybrids of essence and existence. This means that their act of being is received and limited according to an essential principle which defines the type of thing they are. Thus, a tree is the act of to-be "poured into" the receptacle of treeness, and a human being is the act of existence received according to the delimiting principle of humanity. But God is the act of existence unreceived, unlimited, undefined; God is not a type of being, but rather the sheer energy of to-be itself. Interestingly, what renders finite things describable for Thomas is precisely their ontological complexity, the fact that they are composed of whatness and the act of to-be. The play in a thing between its act of being and what delimits it is what enables a philosopher or poet or scientist to categorize or capture it as "this" rather than "that." As the unreceived act of existence, God is, frustratingly, indescribable, a bit like a great unrelieved expanse of snow.

And thus, just as the wanderer becomes easily disoriented in a whited-out landscape, so the theological explorer becomes quickly lost in the trackless country of the divine simplicity. When mystics from John of the Cross to Thomas Merton speak of the highest attainments of the life of prayer, they describe an area of experience beyond words, speech, imagery, and conceptuality, a silence deeper than the mind. They are describing, in a necessarily halting way, something of the divine serenity, the simplicity beyond differentiation.

As usual, the mystics help us to see the spiritual power behind theological statements. One of the basic tricks of the self-elevating ego is to control God through the mind. The ego, naturally enough, goes about the business of knowing and manipulating the things of the world, organizing and categorizing them confidently, but then it makes the terrible mistake of trying the same with God. With images, concepts, ideas, traditions, customs, prejudices, it hems God around, defining and corralling him. We claim to know how God thinks and how God acts and why God does what he does; on the basis of our rational theologizing we even make bold to predict what God will do and how he will deal with us. But over and again, the Bible shows us how surprising God is, how strange and elusive are his ways. Just when the people of Israel expect deliverance, they get exile; just when they expect punishment, they are met with mercy; just as they await an avenging Messiah, they get the crucified God. All of this biblical playfulness is in service of the divine simplicity, that is to say, the essentially unknowable and hence uncontrollable majesty of the sacred. The soul that wants too much to cling to the tree of knowledge must be doctored by the salve of this simplicity.

Another implication of God's serenity is God's infinity. Since the sheer act of existence itself is not received or limited by any essential principle, since it is not definable as a type of being, it must, necessarily, be without restriction or border. God is the limitless, always open-ended power of existence. It is intriguing that, for many of the ancient philosophers, infinity is an imperfection, since it implies incompleteness, inchoate unformedness. The truly divine, they thought, is that which is utterly complete, pristine, and definitive. Christian theologians have consistently maintained, on the other hand, that God's boundlessness is not an imperfection but rather the expression of the inexhaustibility and endless *fascination* of God. St. Bernard of Clairvaux says that the saints in heaven drink from the divine source and then, in the very satiation of their thirst, they become thirsty for

more. Heaven, accordingly, is a delightfully endless process of exploration into the infinite God. Thomas Aquinas says something similar
when he asserts that the blessed in heaven, witnessing the beatific
vision, are seeing for the first time just how *incomprehensible* God is.
What they see in short is not a finite supreme being whose beauty,
however stunning, would eventually become stale, but rather the end-
lessly captivating Black Forest of the divine infinity, a field in which
they can play for an eternity. The very indefiniteness that frustrated
the ancient philosophers is what calls out to Christian thinkers. Once
more we see the salving of the soul. One of the greatest temptations
of the self-absorbed ego is to be bored by God. We sinners convince
ourselves that the divine is a relatively comprehensible dimension of
reality, a realm that we perhaps have to deal with from time to time,
but one of decidedly limited interest. Indeed, it becomes a commonplace of the sinful imagination that almost anything — sex, career,
relationship, pleasure — is more diverting, more entertaining than the
things of God. We have eaten of the fruit of that tree, and we move on
to other trees and other fruits, assured that they will be more appealing than the first. The doctrine of God's infinity is meant to persuade
us that nothing is more captivating, inexhaustible, compelling than
the divine reality, that grounding and endless power in which all other
existents inhere. All other joys are finite; God's joy is limitless. All
other journeys come, disappointingly, to an end; the journey into God
never ends.

An elemental affirmation of both the Bible and the great tradition
is that God is one. The Shema ("Hear, O Israel, the Lord your God
is God alone") is, for the Old Testament authors, the fundamental
statement, not only of their belief in God, but of their commitment to
God. And the Christian churches certainly imitate the Shema in their
great creedal proclamation *credo in unum Deum* (I believe in one God).
What I want to make clear is how this conviction concerning the
unity of God flows from the divine infinity. If God is infinite, that is
to say, containing within himself the fullness of existential perfection,
then God cannot be divided against himself, split into opposing deities.
If there were two infinites, one would *not be* the other, but the infinite
is that which contains nothing of nonbeing. Therefore, the properly

infinite must be one. Now this might strike us as nothing more than logic-chopping, but the insistence on the divine unity — found at the very start of the Creed and at the heart of the Jewish tradition — is of crucial spiritual and moral significance. Since Yahweh alone is divine, no other reality — country, political institution, king, rival deity — can hold the ultimate loyalty of the people. When we say *credo in unum Deum* we make the similarly provocative claim that nothing else proposed for our worship is worthy of it. Since God is one, in short, all idols must be smashed.

And the chief idol, of course, is the self-elevating ego. When Adam and Eve tumbled from the garden, they made themselves into gods, accepting the illusion that they exist as rivals to the all-embracing, all-surrounding unity of the divine. But the infinite power of Being itself has no rivals, brooks no opposition, accepts no competition. Yahweh tells his people in the very first commandment to have no other gods beside him (not to deny his unity), and he informs them why he makes this demand: "for I the Lord your God am a jealous God." This should not be interpreted as though God had fallen into an envious snit vis-à-vis other gods; rather it should be read as a statement of metaphysical and spiritual fact: there are no real gods alongside of Yahweh, and accordingly Yahweh is displeased with our illusions on this score. What the Bible seems to imply is that all false gods are finally projections of *the* false god which is the sinful ego. To affirm the serene, unrivaled unity of God is, accordingly, to break the idolatry of egotism and thereby to perform an elemental act of soul-doctoring.

All of the names of God that we have considered under the heading of the divine serenity are meant to frustrate the grasping tendency of the sinner, the reach for the fruit in the garden. They are meant to calm the Promethean obsession that fire must and can be stolen from God. In a sense, the divine names of simplicity, infinity, and unity lure the sinner into a wasteland, a literally endless tract, a place where all methods of coping break down, where there is finally nothing to see or control, a land where the divine ego is not at home and where it is compelled therefore to surrender. Or in a more positive sense, they are meant to draw us sinners into the awe-filled conviction that there is something infinitely more appealing and beautiful than the puny ego.

Now the names that we have just considered are, in themselves, perfectly valid descriptions of God, but, as we suggested earlier, they become idolatrous and spiritually problematic unless they are held in tension with a set of contrary names. Many theologians, especially in our century, have expressed dissatisfaction with just this sort of one-sidedness in the naming of God. If the divine is *only* serene, *only* simple, infinite, and unique, it becomes a distant, self-absorbed, intimidating, and finally irrelevant reality. If God is only the pure and pristine act of existence, he has nothing to do with the roiled, complex, and anything but pristine realm of being that we inhabit. If God is only the *actus purus* (pure act) that Aquinas spoke of, how can God impinge upon and be affected by the altogether changeable universe? In a word the problem is this: in one-sidedly solving the problem of grasping, we have perhaps opened ourselves to the opposite spiritual problem of hiding from God. Accordingly, another set of names must be placed in tension with the set we have just considered, symbols that point, not to the ungraspable transcendence of God, but to God's unavoidable immanence.

I choose to group these titles under the general heading of the divine *creativity*. As that which *ultimately* concerns us, God is serene, but as that which ultimately *concerns* us, God is creative, that is to say, intimately involved with all expressions of finitude, reaching down, insinuating himself into the roots and seeds of being. If in his serenity, God is like the unbroken surface of the calm sea, in his creativity, he is like the waves on a storm-tossed ocean; if in his serenity God is like a single elegant column, in his creativity he is like the jumbled complexity of a Gothic cathedral. As creative, God is, in Augustine's phrase, *intimior intimo meo* (closer to me than I am to myself), and is found, in Tillich's phrase, at the *Ich-wurzel des Ich* (the very root of the self).[60]

In this creative dimension of his being, God is something like the "Will" that Schopenhauer speaks of or even like the "Id" that Freud posits. God is the dark and mysterious "ground" that informs and undergirds the structures of the world and the psyche, the fundamental energy that pushes all things from within. There was a powerful

debate that raged throughout the Middle Ages between the proponents of mind and the advocates of will, the former arguing that God
is the object of an intellectual contemplation and the latter that God
is "known" only in the darkness of love. Perhaps the mind camp was
more in touch with what we have been calling the serenity of God,
and the will camp was insisting on the divine creativity, the energy
that is felt through participation rather than known through speculation. For Schopenhauer, one senses the "Will" that courses through
all being precisely by surrendering to it and joining it through action.
And so we sense the creativity of God through allowing ourselves to
be grasped by it.

Creation is one of the most important but misunderstood themes in
Christian theology. Interestingly, the affirmation of God's creativity is
situated at the very beginning of the creed — "I believe in God, the
Father Almighty, *maker of heaven and earth*" — but the implications of
this claim, for us and for God, are rarely spelled out adequately. For
most believers, creation describes an activity that God performed at
the "beginning of time," the bringing all things into existence from
nothing. On such a reading, the divine creativity has little or nothing to do with the world as it is presently constituted: having given
rise to the cosmos, the Creator God could easily have slipped into a
benign neglect of what he had made, retreating into an indifferent
transcendence. But such a deist interpretation of creation is far from
the minds of our best theologians and spiritual writers. Thus Thomas
Aquinas speaks of God's *creatio continua* (continual creation) of the
world, that is to say, God's ongoing and ever present bringing of the
universe into being.[61] And Karl Rahner says that creation designates
the here-and-now relationship between the infinite mystery of Being
itself and the beings that exist through that mystery.[62] In short, creation is not a once-and-for-all act of the essentially transcendent God,
but rather the ever present and ever new gift of being poured out
from the divine source. Thomas describes creation in an unusually
poetic way as *quaedam relatio ad Creatorem cum novitate essendi* (a kind
of relationship to the Creator with freshness of being).[63] What he implies is that the creature *is a relationship* to the energy of God which is
continually drawing it from nonbeing to being, making it new. When

Jesus speaks to the Samaritan woman at the well and promises her "water bubbling up to eternal life," he evokes what Aquinas means by creation: the presence of God always at work at the very roots of our being. Meister Eckhart, a Dominican disciple of Thomas Aquinas, tells us that we must sink into God, discovering the Creator in the "inner wine cellar" of the soul, and Teresa of Avila finds the Creator in the "interior castle" at the center of her psyche. Thomas Merton, as we saw, insists that the essence of contemplative prayer is finding that *point vierge* (virginal point), that place of nothingness, where one is here and now being created by God. All of these mystics and theologians are witnessing to the existential reality of creation and hence to the startling intimacy of God felt in the soul. This divine insinuation is what I mean by God's creativity.

Now from this basic affirmation, many of the classical names of God flow. If God is the continual creative ground of all existence, then God must be described as *omnipresent*. The Creator God cannot be isolated at the top of some hierarchy of being, at a distant remove from creation; rather, he is in all things, present intimately to all aspects of the world. Many of the ancient philosophers maintained that the serene and perfect God cannot be in direct contact with something as mutable, material, and imperfect as the cosmos. Accordingly, they held that there is a buffer zone between God and the world, various levels of being through which God's involvement is mediated. The Christian insistence that God is omnipresent is irreconcilable with any such schema. God, Christians hold, is just as close to a simple stone as to an archangel, just as intimate with a forgotten corner of the most unimpressive wasteland as with the grandest of the planets. There is no place where the grounding power of Being itself is not at work, not displayed. And hence there is no place to run from the Creator. We remember that Adam and Eve tried to conceal themselves from God after their sin, retreating into the underbrush of Eden, presumably far away from the press and attention of God. God's effortless discovery of his errant children is an expression of the divine omnipresence that we have been analyzing. We sinners, convinced that sin itself provides a ground where we can stand free of the divine, are confounded by the inescapability of God, lured by this doctrine into surrender.

Another implication of the divine omnipresence is a sacramental view of the universe. Since God is the creative energy at work in and through all things, all existents, even the least significant, even the most vile and repugnant, are signals of God, reminders of God's presence. The omnipresent God has marked all beings with his seal, and hence all things announce him in a sacramental way. Now a sacramental cosmos — a world charged with the grandeur of God — is a delight for someone in right relationship with the divine, but for the sinner, it is a somewhat harrowing place. When all the sinner wants to do is get far away from God, he is a bit unnerved by a world that clearly announces the hopelessness of such a strategy. The inescapability of the divine is, once more, stinging salve for the soul that is stubbornly on the run.

One of the great sufferers of the omnipresence of God is the biblical character Jonah. God summons Jonah to prophetic witness in Nineveh, but Jonah refuses to accept this call, fleeing in the opposite direction by boat, apparently convinced that God is but a local deity whose jurisdiction he can avoid. But the omnipresent Creator is not so easily given the slip. Lord of sky and sea, God sends a terrible storm to rock Jonah's boat and then, when the reluctant prophet is thrown overboard, God instructs a whale to swallow him and carry him to the shore near Nineveh. What this marvelous comic tale communicates is just how annoying a sacramental view of the cosmos can be! It is not exactly reassuring to someone who wants to flee from God that even the whales in the depths of the ocean are divine accomplices, agents of the sacred. The point, of course, is to stop fleeing and to allow the world to be what it is: a theater for the glory of God.

Another attribute of God that fits under the heading of the divine creativity is God's omniscience. It is a commonplace of both Scripture and tradition that God knows everything that can be known, that nothing escapes his purview. This confidence in God's knowledge flows from the experience of being created. If God is the ground of the being of the entire universe, if God is intimately present to all expressions of finitude, then God most certainly *knows* everything in the world. If God is here and now creating every aspect of the cosmos, there is nothing in the cosmos that could possibly escape his view.

Prior to Descartes's speculations, knowledge was always appreciated, not so much as cognitive insight, as a type of experiential contact. The ideal knower was not the dispassionate analytical observer but the one who *felt with* that which she sought to know. It is in this pre-Cartesian sense that our tradition affirms omniscience of God. God is not a spectacularly brilliant analyst who stands at a certain remove from the world and happens to have data in his mind about all things in the cosmos; rather, he is the one who naturally knows all things that he makes by the most startling and immediate contact. God does indeed "search and know" the cosmos the way a potter knows the clay that she is kneading or the way a mother knows every mark and wrinkle of her infant's skin. Isaiah gives voice to God's omniscience when he puts in the mouth of Yahweh the unforgettable claim: "I have carved you on the palm of my hand."

Again, this omniscience is, depending on one's perspective, either worthy of celebration or deeply unnerving. For the sinner in flight from the divine, the universality of the divine knowledge is a source of great anxiety. God necessarily sees all that we do and appreciates all that we think and imagine, and hence there is no hiding from the moral press of God. There is no movement of the heart, body, or soul that is so small or insignificant that it escapes the notice of God. If Jonah is the reluctant witness to God's omnipresence, then King David is the unwilling witness to God's omniscience. We recall the powerful account of David's lustful and narcissistic conspiracy to acquire the wife of Uriah (2 Sam. 11). He sends the trusting Uriah into the thick of the battle, effectively murdering him, and then takes the fallen soldier's widow, Bathsheba, to himself. Presumably convinced that God has not noticed this subtle and private sin, David goes about his business until he is confronted in one of the most devastating scenes in the Scripture with proof of the divine omniscience. Nathan the prophet comes to King David and tells the pathetic story of a poor man who owned but one sheep, an animal that was so dear to him that he cared for it as a child. A wealthy man, who owned many sheep, nevertheless took the poor man's pet and slaughtered it to entertain some friends who had come to visit. Moved profoundly by this story of cruelty and self-absorption, David cries out: "The man who did this

deserves to die." Nathan replies laconically: "You are the man." David
learns through Nathan's narrative that nothing, even the quiet movements of the heart, escapes the vision of the omniscient God. In some
ways, of course, the accusation of Nathan is but the externalization of
the self-reproach that David undoubtedly felt in his own conscience. It
was John Henry Newman who speculated that the elemental and unavoidable religious experience, the sense of the sacred that all people
share in common, is the moral sense that flows from the voice of the
conscience. Interestingly, he says, the conscience is typically referred
to, not as a principle or a moral sensibility, but precisely as a *voice*,
that is to say, the communication of a person.[64] In short, implies Newman, the doctrine concerning an omnipresent and omniscient God is
not a bit of fanciful philosophical speculation, but rather a conviction
that flows from direct and basic religious experience. And once more
we see how this doctrine effectively doctors the soul that labors under
the illusion that it can hide in the underbrush of Eden. The bear sees
the boy long before the boy sees the bear.

Chapter Eight

THE SELF-SUFFICIENCY AND
THE FAITHFULNESS OF GOD

"You have no need of our praise, yet our desire to thank you is itself your gift. Our prayer of thanksgiving adds nothing to your greatness but makes us grow in your grace." This beautiful excerpt from one of the weekday Eucharistic prefaces in the Roman rite expresses richly the tension that I wish to communicate in the next symbolic pair. On the one hand, God is utterly self-contained, self-sufficient, in no *need* of anything outside of himself, and on the other hand, he is passionate to share his being, to communicate, to overflow. These two characteristics — mutually exclusive in the sinful creature — are mutually implicative in the ground of being.

✧

Let us look first at the set of symbols that cluster around the divine *self-sufficiency*. As Being itself, God is, quite obviously, beholden to no reality outside of himself. As the sheer and all-inclusive energy of existence, God cannot depend upon, or be substantially affected by, another reality. The divine is not one being among many, not one more thing caught in the net of creaturely interdependency, but is rather that upon which everything in the cosmos unilaterally depends. Tillich speaks, in this context, of the "closedness of God,"[65] and the First Vatican Council affirms that God is utterly happy in himself and stands therefore in no need of creation. Thomas Aquinas makes a similar point when he remarks, famously and controversially, that though the world is really related to God, God is not really related to the world.

In his classic anti-definition of God, St. Anselm similarly insists upon the divine self-sufficiency. In the *Proslogion,* Anselm states what appears to be a rather straightforward, banal description of God as "that than which no greater can be thought."[66] But upon closer examination, this formula discloses its strangeness and power. If God is truly that than which no greater can be conceived, then it follows that God plus the universe is not greater than God alone. If the perfection of the cosmos could add something to the perfection of God, then God, in himself, would not be the unsurpassable limit of perfection. Hence what Anselm implies in his description is precisely what the above-cited excerpt from the Preface hints at, namely, that nothing in the created realm could possibly augment the fullness of the divine reality. As Robert Sokolowski points out, "After creation there are more beings, but not more perfection of Being."[67] What all these authors see is the radical *difference* between the divine and the nondivine, the ontological separation between the power of Being itself and those things existing in the web of contingent relations. They signal what has traditionally been called the absolute or self-sufficient character of the divine reality.

Though many theologians and philosophers across the centuries have expressed impatience with this symbol, it remains of enormous spiritual importance. The God who has no need of our praise — indeed no need of our being at all — is a God who cannot be manipulated or drawn into our egotistic games. If we felt for a moment that God needs us in the same way that our other relationship partners do, we would become impudent and presumptuous in our religious life, toying with the divine through the offer and the withdrawal of our affection. The needy God would quickly take on the characteristics of mythological deities, those brassy but finally insecure supreme beings who look eagerly to the worship and acknowledgment of their earthly inferiors. One of the particularly painful qualities of our psychological life is precisely the interdependency that we feel with all things and all people around us. Because all of us are interdependent (even the king to some degree depends upon his subjects), we are all susceptible to games of manipulation and control. Because in even the best relationship, each partner needs the other to some degree, neither partner is finally secure in the love that he or she gives or receives. The absolute God is the one reality whose love cannot be bought, manipulated, or cynically withdrawn. And hence the symbol of the divine self-sufficiency both tames the controlling tendency of the ego and, paradoxically, gives the ego firm ground on which to stand.

Perhaps the classical way to express God's self-sufficiency is the symbol of the divine freedom. It is a commonplace of both the Scripture and the tradition that God is supremely free, sovereign in his majesty, uncoerced in his decision and action. The biblical authors affirm, again and again, that, in creating, in covenant making, in judging, in redeeming, God acts unilaterally out of the mystery and power of his own will. And indeed this must be the case if, as we have been arguing, God is the sheer and unreceived act of existence, for what reality outside of that act could possibly influence it or shape it? Freedom is constrained or limited only over and against some being, force, or person that conditions it, that presses on it with its own power of existence. But what is there "outside of" or "beside" He Who Is? Who or what is it that could, in the strict sense, compel the grounding reality of the universe to act or be in a particular way?

G. W. F. Hegel opined that, just as a creature needs the other to come to full self-possession, so God needs the "other" which is the world in order fully to understand himself, the infinite and eternal God knowing himself as such only in contradistinction to what is finite and temporal. But the mainstream of the Christian tradition has rejected the Hegelian option precisely because it so dramatically compromises the freedom of God vis-à-vis the world, and hence renders God less than divine. Were God in need of creation in Hegel's sense, the world — and especially the rational creatures who are at the summit of creation — would enter into a rapport of interdependent intimacy with God. It would have something that God desperately needs and hence would be in a position, once more, to control the destiny of God. Adam and Prometheus would reign.

To speak of the freedom and sovereignty of God is therefore to employ a powerful salve for the sinful soul. It compels the self-elevating ego to realize that it is not on the same playing field as the divine, that it is incapable of dictating terms to God or forcing God's hand.

In a word, it opens the sinner to the awareness that there is but one absolute freedom and that it belongs, not to him, but to God. We have seen that a basic form of sinfulness is the tendency to make of oneself the unconditioned power (think again of Dante's Satan) and hence to consider oneself as sovereignly free. In its most dramatic form this tendency appears as the demonically arbitrary freedom of Hitler or Pol Pot, an unrestrained, and therefore necessarily evil, will to power. To proclaim that God alone is sheer freedom is thus to force a reorientation of the disordered psyche, turning it from itself and to the bearing ground of its being. It is to shrink its imperially expanding boundaries and to call forth its surrender.

Undoubtedly the most evocative biblical image for this process is the tale of the Tower of Babel (Gen. 11:1–9). In their hybris and excessive freedom, the builders of the tower seek to reach up to heaven, that is to say, to construct through their own efforts a bridge linking creation and the Creator. They wanted to establish, through their decision, imagination, and action, a coequality in freedom with God. But, as we know, the tower comes tumbling down through the angry intervention of the God who is so sovereignly free that he can tolerate no such creaturely rivalry. Interestingly, in the wake of the disaster, the people of the town no longer speak the same language and hence are scattered in confusion. I think it is most important to see this, not as an arbitrary divine punishment, but as a necessary and finally salutary outcome of God's judgment. In the wake of the terrible outrages that have flowed from totalitarian and imperialist regimes in this century, I find it difficult to be edified by the city of Babel and its one great language. The uniformity of speech and action (they are all in on the project) strikes me as an expression of the all-embracing and overreaching will to power characteristic of empires. So the imperial will, the sovereign *voluntas* of the sinner, speaks in one uncompromising voice and usually seeks to draw all the powers of the world into its range of influence. How beautiful then that the truly sovereign God breaks up the evil empire, scattering the peoples of Babel and introducing a life-giving pluralism at both the linguistic and political level. So the salve of the divine freedom works on the infection of creaturely hybris.

Another symbol that can be arranged under the general heading of the divine self-sufficiency is God's *inscrutability* or *incomprehensibility*. Isaiah speaks the mystery of Yahweh: "As high as the heavens are above the earth, so high are my thoughts above your thoughts and my ways above your ways, says the Lord" (Isa. 55:9). The mind, intentions, and very being of God are unsearchable; his purposes and designs unfathomable. Isaiah reminds us accordingly that our God is always in principle a hidden God. Occult matters — visions, apparitions, locutions, etc. — are those that remain provisionally strange, for the moment inexplicable. The incomprehensible God must never be confused with such phenomena, since God remains essentially unknowable. We could imagine a time in which, given the advance of philosophy, science, and tools of measurement, the occult would effectively disappear, but we could never imagine a time in which the Mystery of God would disappear. God is that which, by its very nature, is outside of the realm of measurement and explanation through cause and effect.

This inescapable mysteriousness of God flows, again, from God's nature as the sheer and infinite act of existence. Whatever can be known — put into categories, compared with other realities, comprehended — is necessarily finite, and therefore the properly infinite is that which mocks all attempts to know it. Every grasp of God is thus inadequate, provisional, even basically misleading. This is why some of our greatest theologians and spiritual masters plant little verbal explosives in their writings, vivid reminders that even (perhaps especially) the most impressive theological systems remain hopelessly inadequate to that of which they attempt to speak. Augustine says *si comprehendis non est Deus* (if you understand, it is not God that you understand); and Thomas Aquinas insists that *quidquid potest intelligi vel cogitari minus est ipso Deo* (whatever can be known or thought is less than God himself). These are Christian versions of the Buddhist dictum "If you see the Buddha on the road, kill him" or of the Taoist motto "If you understand, it is not the Tao that you understand." All of these spiritual warnings are placed, as it were, in the sanctuary itself, in the sacred space of religion and religious thinking, just as the mocking gargoyle is placed on the facades and spires of the cathedrals. The clear implication is that it is especially in that realm of confident theological speech and liturgical action that we are in greatest danger of domesticating the whirlwind which is God. Intriguingly, the first demon that Jesus confronts in Mark's Gospel is in the synagogue, the sacred space.

On the spiritual plane, the doctrine of God's inscrutability is meant to correct this very distortion which many Protestant thinkers have termed "religion." In his early commentary on Paul's letter to the Romans, Karl Barth unleashes a steady polemic against the pretensions of religion to know and control God, and in his *Dogmatik* of 1925, Paul Tillich says that religion, in its self-absorption and domestication of the divine, is the height of the demonic. What these Protestant writers legitimately score is the Babel-like hybris which is the shadow side of any religious enterprise. Bob Dylan says: "The enemy I see / wears the cloak of decency." The properly inscrutable God is, once more, the smasher of religion in its grasping and manipulating form.

One of the most powerful biblical witnesses to the inscrutability of God and the danger of religion is the book of Job. We know the story well. Job, the most upright and God-fearing man on earth, is tested at the prompting of Satan. He is made to suffer every kind of agony to see whether he will turn from God and lose his righteousness. Despite the evil that befalls him, he does not curse God, but he does engage in some of the most penetrating and soul-wrenching theological speculation in the biblical tradition. Protesting his innocence, Job falls into disagreement with the three theologically minded friends who have come to comfort him. Reflecting the common religious conceptions of their time, the three friends argue in various ways that Job must have done something to provoke the terrible wrath of God, that he must have sinned in order to suffer so egregiously. But Job insists that the categories invoked by the three are inapplicable in his case, since he had always remained upright before God. The argument rages back and forth for most of the book of Job, each discussant basically remaining within the framework of the religious assumption that we human beings know how and why God acts.

And then the breaker of religion speaks. Called into the dock by Job, compelled by his creature to justify himself, God talks out of the desert whirlwind. "Where were you when I laid the earth's foundations?...Have you ever in your life given orders to the morning or sent the dawn to its post...? Have you ever visited the place where the snow is kept or seen where the hail is stored up?" (Job 38:4, 12, 22). God broadens the horizons of Job's mind, convincing him that there is a colossal mysteriousness even to the created realm. Whatever Job can grasp of the workings of nature is trumped immediately by the infinite expanse of what he does not know. And if Job has no capacity to master even the mysteries of creation, how much more ignorant is he with regard to the mysteries of the Creator? The burden of God's speech is this: how dare a creature imagine that he can understand the ways of God through the pathetic categories of religion and morality. How dare he think that he can predict how and why and whether God should reward or punish. What Job is reaching for — and what God is, as always, forbidding — is the fruit of the tree of the knowledge of good and evil, the grasp of the ultimate perspective. His intimidating speech is designed, not to frighten Job, but to force him to put down the gun and the compass of his moralizing mind and to accept alluring Mystery.

Thus Job's pretentiousness in baiting God is critiqued, but even more powerfully is the "theology" of the three friends put into question: "I burn with anger against you and your two friends," Yahweh says to Eliphaz, one of the theologians, "for not speaking truthfully about me" (Job 42:7). Those who think that they know precisely the ways of the divine are like the grasping Adam and Eve or like Prometheus stealing the fire of God's wisdom. The desert storm out of which God speaks to these practitioners of religion is wonderfully evocative of what we have been calling the divine inscrutability. Its very darkness is the incense salvifically obscuring the hunting vision of the sinner.

But now the pendulum swings. Having made all of these clarifications regarding the freedom, sovereignty, and incomprehensibility of God, we face, once more, a spiritual danger. A God who is one-sidedly free and inscrutable becomes a monster of arbitrariness and unpredictability. If God is nothing but sovereign and mysterious power, then we remain, unavoidably, anxious in his presence, and our perfectly understandable response is to run from him. Indeed, the desert whirlwind of incomprehensible freedom could decide that, having loved the world for a time, he now hates it, or having established certain ethical demands, he now suspends them, or having made a covenant with his people, he now breaks it. Some of the voluntarist philosophers of the late Middle Ages backed themselves into just such a position, arguing that moral and metaphysical laws are simply the result of God's arbitrary and hence altogether changeable decision. And it was John Calvin who, in his doctrine of double predestination, gave most pointed (and most terrible) theological expression to this one-sided notion of God. According to this doctrine, God saves some and damns others, and the reason for this discrimination can be found only in the sheer darkness and inscrutability of the divine will. Is it any wonder that so many Christians under the sway of such an understanding fell into a stance of terrified and finally resentful silence before the divine? Is it surprising that those shaped by this teaching in its various forms finally, like Adam and Eve, simply hid from such a divine beast or spent their lives defying him? How can one, in the end, have any confidence in a God who is *only* free and *only* inscrutable?

Once more balance must be sought; once more another set of names must be invoked. Thus God, we hold, is not only self-sufficient but also faithful. If the Scripture clearly emphasizes the freedom and awesome majesty of God, it even more clearly focuses on God's passionate love for the world that flows forth from him. From the very beginning of the book of Genesis, God is portrayed as a covenant maker, a faithful promise-keeper. With Noah, with Abraham, with Jacob, with Joseph, with Moses, Yahweh makes an agreement, a blood pact, a covenant. He has chosen the people Israel, and he will not abandon them, even if they sin, even if they reject him. Again and again, this covenant is alluded to by the great prophets Isaiah, Jeremiah, and Ezekiel who tirelessly remind the people that all they must do is return to the Lord to receive his benefits. That God is a rock, a place of safety, a sure stronghold of faithful love is perhaps the central affirmation of the biblical tradition. Therefore God's freedom and inscrutability must never be construed in such a way as to imply a divine arbitrariness, a cavalier indifference on the part of God. God's self-sufficiency expresses itself precisely as faithfulness.

How can we make sense of this tension? If we recall God's sacred name as Being itself, we see that God cannot be said not to be. If being is not simply an accidental modification of God but rather what God essentially is, then God cannot, strictly speaking, not be. Hence God cannot undermine or contradict the structures of his own reality; he cannot be in tension with himself or undo who he is. Thomas Aquinas raises the interesting question whether the all-powerful and supremely free God can sin, and he answers clearly in the negative: to sin is to be alienated from the divine love, and it would be a contradiction to say that God is alienated from himself.[68] But does this not limit the divine freedom? Aquinas — and with him most of the great figures of the tradition — says that authentic freedom is faithfulness to one's own self and hence that the God incapable of being untrue to himself is, in fact, eminently free. God, the sheer energy of existence, knows himself and loves himself — and cannot do otherwise, compelled as it were by the power of his own reality, and this very compulsion is his liberty.

Now God is not the only reality; rather, as we have seen, God pours out from himself the sheer gift of created being, establishing the universe. But this universe is, in every detail, a reflection of the divine being, since it participates in God the Creator. Accordingly, God knows, loves, and wills the world even as he knows, loves, and wills himself. But this means, in turn, that just as God is faithful to himself, God is faithful to all that he has made. Just as God cannot say "no" to his own being, so he cannot, in the end, say "no" to that which exists through him. Is God obliged to create? Must God make a world outside of himself? We have already seen that such a claim would indeed compromise the divine freedom and inscrutability and would open us to a fundamentally Hegelian view of the God/world relationship. No, God is not compelled to create. But, having made the world, is God tied to it, faithful to it, committed to it in love? The answer here must be "yes." Thus God does not toy with the universe, undermining its independence and the structures of its being. God does not arbitrarily change the laws of logic and morality; God certainly does not change his own mind or heart vis-à-vis the universe, now determining to hate it as fiercely as he once loved it. In a word, God cannot sin, either against himself or against the world that reflects him.

And this is why we can say, with a sigh of relief, that God is a rock, a stronghold, a firm place to stand. The God who is not one more shifting and indefinite creature but rather the ground of Being itself is a power upon whom we can rely, a covenant-maker whose word we can trust. In his very freedom and sovereignty as our Creator, God is a parent in whose lap we can serenely find our rest. Undoubtedly what has made religious belief such an indispensable part of human consciousness and behavior is just this assurance of safety that it brings. There is literally nothing in the cosmos that will not, finally, disappoint us. There is no place in the universe that will not, finally, be shaken. But God, the self-sufficient ground of existence itself, can be trusted not to disappoint and not to betray. "No storm can shake my inmost calm while to that rock I'm clinging," says the author of the Shaker hymn, witnessing ecstatically to this divine faithfulness.

I just used the term "parent" to describe the faithful God, and there is no better or more traditionally revered symbol for the divine fidelity. Isaiah puts into the mouth of Yahweh one of the most achingly beautiful evocations of God's relentless and ferocious devotion: "Could a mother forget her child . . . even if she forgets, I will never forget you." Is there any love, among animals or human beings, that is more powerful and passionate than that of a mother for her children? A mother jealously guards her young, violently defends them against attackers, and, if necessary, gives her life for them. Even this fierce and uncompromising love, Isaiah insinuates, is as nothing compared to the compassion of God the mother of the cosmos.

Let us linger a while with this especially helpful metaphor of God's maternity. A mother is linked to her children through a passion that transcends reason, a feeling that, in one sense, is beyond her control. Almost despite herself, a mother gives to and nurtures and loves the children she has engendered. If we were to ask a mother whether she cares for her children out of necessity, she would probably respond in the affirmative. Or to turn the question around, if asked whether she had a choice in the matter of loving them, she would most likely respond in the negative. I believe that our tradition implies that there is something even more compelling and irrational in the love that God the mother has for the universe. It would certainly be incorrect to say that God, in the strict sense, *needs* the world, but it would be equally incorrect to say that God is sovereignly indifferent to it. No, God *needs* the world in the same way that a mother *needs* to love her family: by an inner compulsion of the heart.

And thus some of the mystics and poets of the tradition can make bold to say that God "could not live one moment without creation," or Abraham can dicker with God on the eve of the destruction of Sodom and Gomorrah, confident that he can awaken the divine compassion; or the psalmist can tease and cajole the Creator of the cosmos, secure in the knowledge that God will never finally abandon those he loves. What keeps all of these dialogue partners in check is, of course, a clear sense of the divine self-sufficiency: they all know that they are not dealing with an ontological equal when they enter the lists with God. On the other hand, their serene, almost kidding, confidence is inspired by an equally clear sense of God's passion and maternal love. In light of the clarifications just made, I would suggest a terminological shift: instead of speaking of God's "neediness" with regard to the world, let us begin to speak of God's "connectedness" to or "compassion" for the world. It is just this link of the heart that so many of the critics of classical conceptions of God's freedom and self-sufficiency want, with legitimacy, to emphasize. In one sense, God is certainly "above" the universe, but in another sense, God is foolishly in love with and thus, if anything, "below" the world he has fashioned.

It is in this connection that I choose to speak of another much controverted attribute of God, namely, immutability. It is a commonplace in most of the great figures of the theological tradition (Origen is the exception) that God is unchanging. For both Augustine and Aquinas, for instance, God, as the sheer act of existence, is above the vagaries and changeability of the created realm. As the summit of perfection, God cannot achieve any more fullness of being and hence cannot "get any better" than he is. Nor can God, in any way, cease to be God, and thus he cannot diminish in goodness. Consequently,

God is immutable, absolute and unchanging in his ontological status. As should be obvious, this claim has excited enormous opposition especially in recent years. Theologians rooted in Scripture object that such a metaphysical absolute, divorced from the changeableness of the finite realm, is irreconcilable with the God disclosed in the Old and New Testaments as a passionate lover, revealer, punisher, and, finally, as incarnating presence. The immutable one might be Aristotle's first mover but he is certainly not the Yahweh of Genesis and Exodus or the God and Father of our Lord Jesus Christ. I would like to turn the tables a bit and suggest that immutability is a quality, not of God's self-sufficiency, but precisely of God's fidelity and hence is a divine attribute that should be positively embraced by the critics mentioned above.

It is interesting that when Thomas Aquinas discusses the divine unchangeableness in the *Summa theologiae*, he cites a passage from the prophet Zechariah: "I am Yahweh and I change not."[69] If we consult the context of this citation, we find that the prophet is affirming God's *covenant fidelity:* even though you, the people of Israel, change, I, the Lord God, do not change. The statement is not so much metaphysical, in the strict sense, as contractual. God is that power — alone among all the powers of the cosmos — that can be relied upon not to disappoint. When the theologians of the tradition, such as Thomas and Augustine, sought to express this utterly trustworthy character of the divine love, they adapted the language of the philosophers and spoke of God's immutability. They never wanted to imply thereby that God is incapable of real involvement with the world; indeed both Augustine and Thomas hold that God is intimately present at the very roots of creaturely being, and both think that God knows every thought of ours and every movement of our wills. More to the point, both these great defenders of God's immutability think that, in Jesus, God became a creature and identified himself with the universe in an act of stunning intimacy. Therefore, the critics notwithstanding, I hold that the unchangeableness of God is to be affirmed, precisely by those who feel that God is like a mother who could never forget her children. God is immutably passionate; unchangingly devoted, undeviatingly faithful to the universe he brings into being.

Now if the attributes situated under the heading of the divine self-sufficiency are meant to reorient the sinner who seeks too much to grasp at God, then the attributes just analyzed under the heading of the divine fidelity are meant to correct the opposite danger, hiding from God. The sinner who wants to flee from God would formulate a one-sided theology of the divine self-sufficiency, freedom, and inscrutability. A God who is in no need of the world, whose ways are utterly unpredictable, and whose freedom is absolute is a power that can be easily, or at least happily, avoided. If God is not really connected to the cosmos, the sinner can find a place of refuge in the confines of his own consciousness and moral freedom; if God is an arbitrary and unreliable distant reality, then a certain indifference or even defiance is justified in his creature. The God who is construed one-sidedly as self-sufficient is, I would argue, quickly brushed aside by the sinful psyche, and a great secular space is opened up, a realm in which God is absent, a field in which the autonomous ego can play unrestrainedly. If religion — the manipulation of God — is the fundamental problem for those who underemphasize God's self-sufficiency, then secularism — the conscious dismissal of the sacred — is the basic danger for those who underemphasize God's fidelity.

It is quite interesting that modern secularism flowed, at least in part, from certain themes developed during the Reformation. Luther was so concerned to protect the Godliness of God that he frowned upon any type of mysticism or metaphysics or spirituality that would focus on God's presence to the world or to consciousness. This thoroughgoing iconoclasm effectively desacralized the cosmos, nature, the psyche and the marketplace, all of these coming under judgment as places of sin and rebellion. But once the smoke had cleared from the wars of religion that followed the Reformation, and once the threat of judgment had become less pressing, many scholars, thinkers, and searchers walked through the "bare ruined choirs" of Luther's disenchanted universe and found appealing the very absence of God. The aggressive secularism of the Enlightenment, which has perdured in many quarters up until our time, is but the full flowering of this divorce of God and the world. Paul Tillich, one of the most important advocates of Luther's reforming theology in our century, nevertheless saw the spiritual danger inherent in Luther's program of desacralization and called for a return to "Catholic substance," a clear sense of God's availability in, and connectedness to, the realms of nature, psyche, and culture.[70] It was the much maligned First Vatican Council that saw a connection between Protestantism and the rationalist atheisms that grew up in the nineteenth century. Once the reformers had banished the sacred from the secular realm, it was only a matter of time, thought the Vatican I fathers, until the secular would come to believe in its own self-sufficiency. Once God became a distant reality, only vaguely connected to the world, it was only a short step to dismissing God altogether as an unnecessary postulate. And thus Ludwig Feuerbach could claim that God is nothing but a projection of frustrated human desire, and Freud could argue that religion is only an infantile wish-fulfilling fantasy. Both of these great atheists are, interestingly enough, correct inasmuch as they criticize a God who had come to be one-sidedly construed as self-sufficient, arbitrary power and hence as a rival to human well-being and full flourishing. Like Prometheus, they legitimately challenge such an idol.

But the ground of Being itself is not the idol smashed by Feuerbach and Freud and is not the distant holy one defended by Luther. As we have seen, it is that which, while remaining utterly free, is utterly faithful, that which, while inscrutable, is reliable in love, that which, though modally different from the world, is the world's own deepest foundation. The divine names grouped under the heading of fidelity are meant to lure the secularist and autonomous ego back into an enchanted universe. They are designed to convince us sinners that God is not the self-absorbed and insecure rival criticized by the atheists, but precisely the friend in whom we and the whole cosmos find our own identity and purpose.

There is, in the end, a wonderful coming-together of the two sets of names we have been considering. The God who is self-sufficient and faithful is disconnected enough from us to be playful and connected enough to us to be compassionate. God is reliable in his love *and* delightfully unpredictable in the way he demonstrates it. If God were only surprising, he would be a monster of unpredictability, and if God were only reliable, he would be a manipulative bore. The God who is both surprising and reliable is like a playwright or an artist, purposive but inventive, or like a lover or a parent, always involved in a gleeful give-and-take of love. Those who cannot relate to this God need the soul-salve of the divine self-sufficiency *and* the divine fidelity.

Chapter Nine

THE LORDLINESS AND
THE LOWLINESS OF GOD

At the very end of the Gospel of John, the dazzled and repentant Thomas kneels before the risen Christ and says, "My Lord and my God" (John 20:28). At the beginning of the Gospel of Matthew, magi from the East humbly kneel before the infant Jesus and break open their coffers in quiet homage. Thomas explicitly acknowledges the sublimity and awesome power of the sacred, disclosed in the resurrected Jesus, and the magi acknowledge the puzzling and moving humility of God, disclosed in the helpless child of Bethlehem. Framing the Gospel narrative, these two icons speak of what I choose to call the lordliness and the lowliness of the sacred. Our tradition consistently places the height and the depth, the majesty and the unpretentiousness of God side by side, refusing to resolve the tension. God is that than which no greater can be thought and, it is equally true, that than which no humbler can be thought. Go as high as you can, and God will be higher; go as low as you can, and God will be lower. Again, the twin strategies of Eden are foiled.

❧❧❧

Let us look first at God's lordliness. One of the commonest names for God in the Old Testament is *Adonai* (Lord). When the sublimely sacred name of "Yahweh" could not be spoken, one would say *Adonai* to designate the holy one. There is a political sense to this term. The Lord is the one who commands, directs, and oversees, and who, accordingly, demands obedience. The Lord is the king, the prince, the first in the chain of command, the one to whom the entire army and nation listen. For a military tribe such as the ancient Hebrews this term had, to be sure, an especially powerful resonance. This desert people, whose promised homeland had to be won through bitter warfare and whose nation had to be continually defended against stubborn enemies, certainly appreciated the importance of a strong and decisive king. Indeed, throughout the Scriptures, powerful leaders, especially of the military sort — Moses, Joshua, David, the Maccabees — served as vivid symbols of righteousness, while vacillating pusillanimous leaders — Saul, Absolom, or Ahab — were held up as counterexamples. And God himself, in the Old Testament, is frequently portrayed as a warrior desperately struggling with the enemies of Israel.

This kingliness of God, it should be clear, is related to the serenity and self-sufficiency of the divine. Being itself, the pure energy of existence, is simple, self-explanatory, and supremely *first*. There is obviously nothing greater, nothing more expansive and powerful than the ground of being. There is no reality beyond it or before it, nothing that could command greater attention. Being itself must be situated first in any hierarchy of existence; it must be given the highest status in the great chain of being. To express it in terms closer perhaps to a biblical consciousness, "I am who I am" must be the king and all other existents merely courtiers or servants.

One of the most traditional names of God — and one that I would group under the heading of kingliness — is all-powerfulness. In the very first article of the Nicene Creed we find the affirmation "We believe in one God the Father *almighty....*" It is elemental to a Christian conception of God that God is limitless in his power, that he is the Lord of both heaven and earth, commander of what is visible and invisible. This means that nothing — in this or any dimension of existence — escapes his press, his authority, and that no material thing, no soul, spirit, or angel compels God or overwhelms him. On the contrary, all things other than God owe their existence, their movement, their life to God.

Now what is the spiritual importance of this overwhelming divine power? Why has it been so consistently proclaimed by believers? Too often, unscrupulous or less than competent theologians have interpreted the divine power crudely, treating the almighty God as a sort of supreme circus freak, able to do anything at all, or as a mythological deity, capable of a capricious manipulation of nations and events. Thomas Aquinas comes much closer to the heart of the tradition when he articulates the meaning of the divine might. In the *Summa theologiae,* Thomas introduces his discussion of God's omnipotence with a scriptural citation, the word of the angel to Mary at the Annunciation: "Nothing is impossible with God."[71] What Thomas implies is that God's power has to do, not with arbitrary and bullying display, but with salvation. Nothing will finally stand in the way of God's salvific design for the cosmos because God is the Lord of all that exists, and his intention will be accomplished. There is no power of evil that can finally resist the divine press in the direction of salvation.

It is important to situate Thomas's description of God as first mover or first cause in this context. In his famous demonstrations from the beginning of the *Summa,* Aquinas shows that all change and coming-to-be in the universe must be traced back through a series of causes to some primal energy that explains and sustains them. Thus the movement of my fingers now typing these words is dependent upon a chain of causes stretching up through my muscular and nervous system to my brain; and my brain's activity is here and now dependent upon the influence of the oxygen that I am breathing, which is in turn dependent upon the gravitational attraction of the earth that keeps it in the atmosphere, which is dependent upon the spin of the planet, which is dependent upon the pull of the sun, etc. If we continued in this vein, says Thomas, we would inevitably arrive at God as the first or grounding element in the causal series, an unenergized energizer of all that becomes and grows and moves. What is interesting for our purposes is that this kind of reflection reveals the quality and extent of God's power. God is the force that pushes and pulls, causes and attracts, every entity in the universe; God's energy reaches out to move, change, and shape all things in the cosmos without exception.

Now we saw earlier that God is omniscient, that is to say, he knows and cherishes all finite things from within according to the deepest kind of intimacy. When we combine this insight with that concerning the limitless extent of God's power, we see that the universe cannot be conceived of as either as a place of chaos or as an arena of iron necessity. Rather, the world is a theater where the drama of salvation is being played out under the direction of an artist. God's power is this ultimately irresistible influence, designing and shaping the universe in the direction of salvation, that is to say, union with himself. Behind and before all of the happenings in the cosmos is not a blind force but a Will, that is to say, the desire of a person.

It is here, in the context of this discussion of God's power, that we must confront the most difficult question that a theologian faces, namely, the problem of evil. Having followed our discussion to this point, a critic is altogether justified in wondering why, given this universal and irresistible power of God pushing and pulling the universe in the direction of the light, there is so much darkness, so much suffering, so much unexplainable evil. If God is the director of this theater of glory, then he seems, at best, rather incompetent. This is, as I implied above, the most important objection to belief in God and the greatest obstacle to the adoption of a religious viewpoint and hence it must be considered carefully. There have been many classical approaches to this dilemma of reconciling the good and powerful God with the existence of evil; I will examine it, for soul-doctoring purposes, from a particular angle.

Both Augustine and Thomas Aquinas say that God permits evil so as to bring out of it a greater good. They imply thereby that evil is allowed and "worked with" as part of God's providential plan. Especially in light of the dreadful evils of this century — that litany of terrors rehearsed at the beginning of chapter 1 — many have questioned the legitimacy of this explanation. What possible commensurate good, they wonder, has come out of the Holocaust or out of the mass murder in the Cambodian killing fields? Or, to shift focus a bit, what "greater" good could possibly come out of the suffering and death of a five-year-old from leukemia? To get at these objections, we have to step back and examine how we ever came to the conclusion that a greater good has come out of evil. When we are enduring suffering, it can only appear to us as dumb and pointless. In the grip, even of a minor illness, all we can appreciate is the pain we are in, and this is precisely because evil has a tendency to narrow one's horizon and perspective.

We discover the greater good that has emerged from evil only after the suffering, to some degree, has passed and therefore only after we have allowed broader horizons to open up and to offer richer context. Thus it is only long after the death of a father that we can appreciate how a family deepened in intimacy and interdependence through their wrestling with the father's suffering and dying. It is only when we allow new political, social, psychological, and religious dimensions to emerge that we can possibly begin to see the undoubted "goods" that came from the cataclysm of the Second World War. The condition for the possibility of appreciating the meaning of suffering is, in a word, distance and perspective, and usually the greater the distance and the richer the perspective, the fuller the appreciation.

Now though we can see a certain meaningfulness to some evils, there are still, without doubt, evils that remain opaque, sufferings that, no matter how richly we contextualize them, remain mute to us. And it is here that the observation of Thomas and Augustine takes on its greatest importance. It is ultimately *God* who allows evil in order to bring about a greater good. It is the infinite, grounding, and creative mind that is here and now bringing the cosmos in all its details into existence, that is "permitting" the evils that we encounter. But this means that the broadest and richest possible horizon of meaning is being invoked, a dimension that can only be vaguely hinted at and never, in principle, understood. God has, as it were, an incomparable distance from the events of the world and an unsurpassably grand perspective from which to survey them. Thus it is not the least bit surprising that there are evils the purpose of which we cannot fathom, for how could we possibly attain the perspective that the Creator Lord of the cosmos has. Since God understands the intricacies of the chess game in a way that mocks our understanding, it is not unusual that he makes, from time to time, inexplicable moves, that he occasionally seems to surrender the key piece, radically compromising the match from our perspective. We are but beginners in the presence of the ultimate master. And, frustratingly, this master could never in principle give us a full account of why he makes the moves he does.

It is here that the book of Job is, once more, extremely helpful. We saw the strategy of Yahweh in the presence of the challenge of Job: to open up to Job the broader, richer, and deeper horizons that a human being can only begin to glimpse. Was Job's suffering inexplicable from the standpoint of Job and his friends? Absolutely. But does this mean that it is ultimately or finally inexplicable? The answer from the whirlwind is "no": there is a "why" to the agony of Job, but the deepest ground of that "why" is unavailable to the necessarily limited mind of a human being.

An analogy might be helpful at this point. Suppose a parent must take his three-year-old child to the hospital for serious surgery. Tragically, the child is old enough to sense the shock, the loneliness, the fear, and the pain of the experience but far too young to understand why he must suffer in such a way. And what makes it even more wrenching to the child is that, inexplicably, his father, whom he had always implicitly trusted to protect him, is now, it seems, presiding over and approving of all of this mayhem. He must wonder, in the depths of his being, why his benevolent father could be permitting all of this. And what is perhaps most wrenching of all is the father's unavoidable inability to make his son understand. Due to the relative capaciousness of his mind and the breadth of his experience, the father has a perspective on the boy's agony that makes it bearable, that allows him to see the agony itself as conducive to the child's ultimate good, but he cannot in principle offer that perspective to his suffering son. In a word, the considerable difference in mind between the father and the son sets up this heartrending tension on both sides. And to push the analogy to the end, all the father can probably do is to ask his son to trust, though it appears there is no ground for trust. Now if such is true between two human beings, how much truer between God and us. If the relatively minuscule psychological and intellectual difference between father and son sets up this desperate problematic, how much more does the literally infinite psychological and intellectual gap between God and us establish a tension. When we suffer, we are like the tiny child, sadly and angrily incapable of grasping the reason for our pain, and God is like the father whose only recourse is the invitation to trust.

This brief reflection on Job shows that, for our tradition, the presence of evil in the cosmos does not compromise the power or goodness

of God, but in fact invites us to consider more profoundly the properly
inscrutable working out of that power and that goodness. God is King
and Lord, drawing precisely this roiled and tragic universe according
to the unfathomable designs of his mind toward salvation.

Now how is the soul doctored in the presence of the kingliness
of God? The proper response to a king is obedience. The king commands, and the servant responds, simply, promptly, unhesitatingly. A
courtier or a messenger might not understand the rationale for, or consequences of, what the king has told him to do, but he does it, trusting
in the wisdom and power of the one who sends him. The word "obey"
is derived from the Latin *obedire,* to listen attentively, to heed. In the
presence of God the Lord, we his servants should listen, bending our
ears and our wills to his word. One way to characterize the sin of
Adam and Eve is as a refusal to obey, a failure to listen to the command of God, a stubborn preference for the voice of the ego. In sin,
the self-elevating psyche makes itself the center of the universe and
assumes that it knows best how to think and behave. Taking the place
of God the Lord, it becomes autonomous, that is to say, strictly self-
governing, self-regarding, self-absorbed. Refusing to listen, the sinful
ego becomes the commander of all that surrounds it; it seeks to order
(in the double sense) the cosmos according to its needs and plans.
When, as is inevitable, the universe does not obey, the sinner commands all the more imperiously and comically, sometimes surrounding
herself with titles and honors and weapons of violence. She shouts and
threatens and postures and, all the while, her kingdom shrinks and
shrinks until it closes around her like a trap. (Dante's Satan again!)
All of this takes place, of course, because we are not and can never
be the center of the universe; we are built ultimately for listening and
not commanding.

Here I am reminded of Richard Rohr's work on the initiation rituals
in the cultures of many of the primal peoples. In these rites we find a
dramatic challenge to the native autonomy and self-regard of the child
and an introduction of ever broader horizons of being and meaning.
Through terror, scarification, careful mystagogic instruction, and the
"vision quest," a young man is taken, physically and psychologically,
out of the cocoon of childhood and challenged to see that there is

infinitely more at stake in his life than he had imagined. He glimpses the "worlds" in which he exists and to which he must be related. Rohr sums up the spiritual teaching communicated through initiation rituals like the one outlined above: "Your life is not about you."[72] The young man is compelled to leave the garden of dreaming innocence where he is the center of things and to learn that he exists in the context of many and exhilarating horizons: the tribe and its history and tradition, nature whose powers are beyond his own, and finally the sacred which envelops and defines everything else. Only when he sees that the world of the ego is very small indeed and that he is but a tiny part of a much more fascinating and demanding universe is he ready to assume adult responsibilities and savor adult joys.

Our lives are not, finally, about us, and thanks be to God for it. We are part of what Urs von Balthasar calls the "theo-drama," the theater of God's glory. We are not the directors of the great play; we are but actors in it, struggling to follow the stage directions of the Spirit. We find ourselves precisely by surrendering to the momentum and meaning of the drama whose ultimate contours and final resolution can be only dimly glimpsed. In any well-written play, even the minor characters have an essential purpose, and sometimes those players who seem least significant for the bulk of the drama emerge, by the end, as the decisive figures. So it is in the theo-drama. Every human being has been created, our faith wagers, for participation in the play that God writes, and no one's role is unimportant. In fact, those people who seem most weighty in the ordinary judgment of the world — presidents, epic poets, generals, business moguls — might be, in the context of the theo-drama, only bit players, while, on the contrary, those who seem least significant to the world might, in the end, be the stars of God's production. The essential task for those in any drama is to listen to the director and to trust in his vision. When one player attempts to upstage another or to reinterpret her role, he upsets the delicate balance that the director wants to achieve. So in the theo-drama, we must obey the promptings of the *spiritus rector* and accept the role that his love holds out to us, even if it seems less than satisfying from our perspective. Since we cannot see the whole of the stage or grasp the complexity of the script, we must surrender to the goodness and wisdom of the director who sees and grasps both.

There is a wonderful scene in Robert Bolt's *A Man for All Seasons* in which Richard Rich, a promising and ambitious young man, petitions the saintly Thomas More for a position among the glitterati at the court of Henry VIII. More tells Rich that he can offer him a position, not as a courtier, but as a simple teacher. The young man is crest-fallen, and More tries to cheer him up: "You'd be a good teacher." Rich fires back: "And if I were, who would know it?"[73] The patient More explains: "Yourself, your friends, your pupils, God; pretty good public that!" What More assumes is that the only audience worth playing for in the end is the divine audience, and the only drama worth acting in — even in the smallest role — is God's. Interestingly, Rich's life takes a terribly wrong turn when he refuses to accept More's offer and instead compromises, schemes, and worms his way into the political prominence at court. To obtain the position of Collector of Revenues for Wales, he perjures himself and betrays Thomas More, effectively sending the saint to the gallows. As Rich passes the con-demned man on the way out of court, More sees the insignia of office around his neck and then remarks devastatingly: "You know, Rich, it profits a man nothing to give his soul for the whole world...but for Wales?" It profits a person nothing to achieve the greatest success in the ego-scripted drama if he loses his role in the theo-drama.

Our lives are not about us; they are about the King. We are built, not for command, but for obedience. In the presence of the awesome lordliness of God, that mind and will whose grandeur we can barely fathom, we bow, we listen, we surrender. And is this not precisely what was at stake in the garden? The originating sin, whose effects ring down through the centuries and poison the human condition, is none other than this refusal to surrender to the mysterious intentions of the Dramatist. God wants us to participate in his life — which is why the drama exists in the first place — but he wants us to do it through listening, following, obeying.

But by now we should be accustomed to the rhythm. Having made these bold and uncompromising claims about the kingliness of God and having adjusted our souls accordingly, we begin to feel a bit uncomfortable. The God who is only the Lord, only the all-knowing director of the play, only the commanding King can become, in short order, the object of resentment on the part of his overwhelmed creature. The God who cannot be grasped becomes, once more, a God whom we would like to hide from, and therefore we need another balancing name. In creative tension with the lordliness of God is what I choose to call the *humility of God*. God is not only lordly; he is also lowly, unobtrusive, quiet and self-effacing. God is that whose circumference is nowhere (infinity, lordly self-sufficiency), and he is that whose center is everywhere, that is to say, even in the smallest and meanest things. To be humble is, literally, to be close to the *humus*, the dirt of the earth. So, in his lordliness, God soars with the eagles and, in his humility, he crawls with the worms.

Paul Tillich, among others, often refers to God, interestingly enough, as the *Grund des Seins* (the ground of being), implying thereby that God is the underlying and sustaining source of all that is: God is like the rich dark earth that nurtures the foliage of the garden. But this must mean that God is lower than all things, indeed, in the most dramatic way possible, at the service of them all. God the Creator is not simply a valet who cares for the superficial needs of a master; he is the meanest slave who cares, every moment, for the very existence of the ones he creates. If the slave is the one who exists completely for the good of the other, then God is the slave of slaves, since his being is to be, in the most radical sense, a gift to the world.

It is so important to note that God *lets the universe be*. Though he does not need it, he continually creates it. Aristotle could not imagine that the prime mover would be the least bit interested in a world outside of himself; Christians hold that God is not only interested in the universe; he spends himself, gives himself away in its service. And this world that he makes is not some mode of his own being, not some necessary outgrowth of his divine nature; rather it is a realm that exists in its own independence and integrity: Being itself is not the same as any particular being or collectivity of beings. In this anyway Hegel was correct: God wants, through his creation, a dialogue partner that is feisty, free, able to stand on its own. It is the divine humility that permits such a conversation. In a certain sense, God says of the universe what John the Baptist said of Christ: "He must increase and I must decrease." Almost every philosopher, theologian, and mystic remarks that God's existence is hidden, that it is, at best, hinted at, vaguely seen behind the veil of creation. This insistence on God's hiddenness is, to some degree, in homage to God's simplicity and self-sufficiency, but I wonder whether it is not also a tribute to the divine humility. The divine reality allows the beauty and splendor of creation to shine forth first, to take, as it were, center stage. God demurely conceals himself, preferring, like a proud parent, to show off his children.

And this creative humility expresses itself clearly in the history of salvation. The lordly God who has no need of the human race nevertheless becomes our covenant partner, deigning to be beholden to us. By entering into a saving relationship with us, God decides humbly to follow the usually errant moves of our wills and patiently, kindly, persistently to run around us, luring us by his grace. The God of the Old Testament, even in his more lordly blustering, is essentially the heartbroken father who just cannot finally let his children be lost. Again and again, he forgets his own offended honor and, in fierce love, seeks out those who have broken faith with him. In the parable of the Prodigal Son, in the father's immoderate, almost embarrassing forgiveness, we see something of the humility of God the savior. Yes, God is lordly and commanding justice, "but his mercy mocks his justice."

In a preface to his novel *Brideshead Revisited*, Evelyn Waugh says that the principal theme of the book is the working out of the divine grace in the lives of a set of friends. And the English Catholic writer David Lodge says that what makes his novels uniquely Catholic is the consistent motif of God's relentless pursuit of the errant sinner. That the Lord of the cosmos should bother to insinuate himself in the everyday comings and goings of ordinary people is a startling indication of God's humility. And what is even more indicative of the divine self-effacement is the *way* that God goes about his work. Though the tradition celebrates examples of what could be called God's direct involvement in the created realm, it customarily signals God's indirect interventions, his tendency to use secondary causes. The divine ground of existence delights, it seems, in using trees, flowers, rivers, animals, automobiles, friends, enemies, church buildings, paintings in order to announce his presence or to work out his purposes. God normally channels his grace through the created realm, rejoicing in his own indirection and clandestinity and in the lifting up his creatures to a participation in his work. And this is precisely what Catholic writers like Waugh and Lodge chronicle: the divine director's use of numerous actors in the accomplishment of his purpose. Once again, it is the humility of God that makes the unfolding of the drama through a myriad of players that much more delicious. There is something crude in the depiction of God intervening directly in the play, the clumsy *deus ex machina* interrupting the speeches of the other actors and upsetting the stage. How much more tantalizing the God who hints and lurks and cajoles hiddenly *through and around* the actors, even unbeknownst to them. It is the humble God who chooses so to act.

How is the soul doctored by this lowliness of God? We have seen frequently that the twin moves of the sinful ego are to grasp and to hide; it is the hiding that is undone by God's ever more surprising hiddenness. No matter where the sinner conceals himself, God is there; no matter how cleverly the sinner dissembles, God can unmask him. God is lowly and humble enough to go into the dark and unsavory places in pursuit of the lost sheep. The hiding soul is the one that whispers to himself, "I am unworthy of love," and it is the humble God who whispers back "not if I have sought you in your very unworthiness." Since there is no place to hide, the fearful sinner ought simply to relax and allow himself to be found. In a sense, the illusory and excessive humility of the sinner is undone by the authentic lowliness of God, by the divine condescension that effectively raises it up and heals it. If the proper response to the divine lordliness is obedience, the proper response to the divine humility is a surprised confidence, a rejoicing in the fact of being loved.

God's lowliness also heals the soul by reintroducing an enchanted universe, a place where the divine is at play. The soul that is in hiding from God is convinced that God would never bother with the world, that he remains, at best, sequestered in his realm of angry transcendence. But the humble God, who uses even the meanest and least likely secondary causes in the accomplishment of his salvific purposes, delights in undermining this attitude. The universe is not a coldly secular place, but is rather the playground of God, a realm in which the divine magician is at large. In the 1950s Thomas Merton composed a prayer that has become enormously popular. He begins, "My Lord God, I have no idea where I am going; I do not see the road ahead of me," and he continues by emphasizing his complete incapacity to know whether he is following the will of God.[74] He begins, in short, in a stance of perhaps exaggerated humility: he is far from God and unable to discern his intentions. But then he acknowledges that the *desire* to please God does in fact please God, and he hopes that he has this desire in all that he does. If he does, "God will lead [him] by the right path, though [he] may know nothing about it." Now we are back in an enchanted, sacramental cosmos. And the excessive (finally self-indulgent) humility is overcome. Merton knows that the director of the play will have his way, even if he and his fellow actors "know nothing about it." The key is simply to surrender to the divine will, to trust in God's hound-like pursuit of the wandering sinner. It is the very humbleness of God that has awakened in Merton this properly acquiescent confidence.

Chapter Ten

LOVE

God's Deepest Name

To this point we have been drawing out the bipolar implications of one of God's principal names, namely, Being itself, "I am who I am." Because God is not a being but the very energy of existence, God must be described, we have seen, in a stubbornly both/and manner: both serene and creative, both self-sufficient and faithful, both lordly and humble. And we have seen how this tensive naming serves a soul-doctoring function, eliminating the two classic routes of escape from God: grasping and hiding. The God who is the sheer act of Being itself should be neither controlled nor run from but rather surrendered to in the blithe confidence that this surrender amounts to the finding of oneself.

Now all of this remains true and spiritually vital. However a problem emerges when we recall, with St. Bonaventure, that Being itself, though a valid Old Testament name for God, is not the ultimate title for the divine reality.[75] In his first letter, St. John tells us, with disarming simplicity, that God's simplest and highest name is not being but love: "God is love, and anyone who lives in love lives in God, and God lives in him" (1 John 4:16). Is there an insurmountable difficulty here? Are we forced to abandon the way of being that we have followed to this point? I think not. It is part of the genius of the great tradition always to have emphasized the continuity between the Old Testament and the New, and, more specifically, between these two ways of naming God: being and love. The rationale for this continuity becomes clear when we pay close attention to the very bipolarity of the being dynamic.

If God were only serene, self-sufficient, and lordly vis-à-vis the

147

world, he could hardly be described as loving. He would instead be, at best, indifferent to the universe and, at worst, hostile to it. He would be the coldly transcendent God of Aristotelian metaphysics or one of the brutally capricious gods of Greek mythology. And by the same token, if God were merely creative, faithful, and lowly, he could hardly be the God of love. Instead he would be the excessively needy Absolute of Hegelian metaphysics or the manipulable "force" of New Age fantasy. The God who is utterly transcendent *and* nevertheless unspeakably immanent, who is completely self-sufficient *and* nevertheless thoroughly faithful, who is sovereignly beyond need *and* nevertheless humbly passionate for creation — that God can best be described the way St. John describes him, as love.

If a man is completely indifferent to a woman, if he has absolutely no vital connection to her, if he is self-satisfied without her, we would hardly describe him as being in love with her. By the same token, if a man needs a woman so desperately that he manipulates her or allows himself to be manipulated, the two are in a pathological or neurotic relationship, hardly one of love. But if a man, while retaining his own independence and integrity, gives himself with abandon to a woman, and if she, while never losing her freedom and self-respect, gives herself with complete trust to him, then the two of them can be fairly described as being in love. Love, in short, is neither indifference nor neediness, neither distantiation nor manipulation, but rather a play between independence and self-gift. It is, accordingly, a strange, poetic, and elusive quality, a balance, in fact, that is exceedingly difficult to realize and maintain. What we have been analyzing is precisely this odd and compelling *complexio oppositorum* that exists in the very heart of the divine reality, this love that *God is*.

The last phrase is most important: love is not simply a quality of God, not only an activity of God in relation to the world; rather, love is the very being of God, the dynamic that describes his deepest core and identity. To be sure, we discover this fact in and through God's dealing with us, but God's love exists independently of his outreach to us; it is his very life. And this is why Christianity insists upon naming God as Trinity. I realize that this last claim might seem a bit of a leap. How do we get from something as warm and evocative as the statement that God is love to something as cold and abstract as the doctrine of the Trinity? It was G. K. Chesterton who observed that, though this link seems anomalous, in point of fact, the latter is simply the logical implication of the former.[76] If God *is* love, then there must be, within the very nature of God, a play between lover, beloved, and the love they share. There must be, in short, a Triune quality to the love-determined unity of the divine. The Trinity has, for too long, been seen as a sort of puzzle or conundrum of interest, perhaps, to theologians but of no relevance to the spiritual life. What I want to show is that, precisely as an expression of the love that God is, the Trinity is the *fons et origo* as well as the culminating goal of the spiritual journey. We sinners are called to let go of our awful self-absorption (*curvatus in se*) and surrender to the dance which is the Triune divine. In a word, the Trinity is everything. Let us begin to search this out by turning to the tradition.

In his classic work *De trinitate* (On the Trinity), St. Augustine seeks to understand the Trinity more thoroughly by seeking out analogies for it in our experience. He is confident that he can find them in all of creation since the Trinitarian God is the Creator and must therefore have left *vestigia* (vestiges) of himself everywhere. But nowhere is a hint of God's reality more apparent than in the one whom the Scripture calls the image of God, namely, the human being. Therefore Augustine turns his analytic eye on human interiority, hoping to discover there the clearest indication of the meaning of Trinity. What he explores is an analogy between the dynamics of consciousness in us and the Trinitarian dynamic which is the divine being.[77]

When we turn our introspective gaze on our own psychological functioning, we encounter, first, what Augustine calls *mens*. Normally rendered in English as "mind," *mens* is better translated as "spirit," for it is, not only the analytical or rational power, but the grounding psychological and spiritual energy of consciousness. It is the font and source of all intellectual activity, the spirit as such. Now *mens*, Augustine found, is capable of being present to itself, of forming an image of itself: it has the capacity of what he calls *notitia sui* (self-knowledge). Mind can be, in a remarkably complete way, a mirror to itself. And having come to self-reflection, *mens* can, finally, love itself, returning to itself through the affection and unitive embrace of the will. This activity he calls *amor sui* (self-love). It is most important not to fall into the trap of reification when interpreting Augustine's terms: *mens, notitia sui,* and *amor sui* are not so much things as acts, dynamisms of the soul. Thus *mens* is the activity of immediate psychological self-presence, *notitia sui* is the activity of self-presence mediated through consciousness, and *amor sui* is the activity of self-presence mediated through will.

As such, they are modally different, though they do not constitute different things; rather each *is* the mind, though each can be distinguished from the others through the uniqueness of its *way* of presence. In a word, the mind is, mysteriously, one and three.

Now the application of this analogy is obvious: *mens* corresponds, says Augustine, to the Father, the grounding energy of the divine being; *notitia sui* corresponds to the Son, the Logos by which the Father comes to self-consciousness; and *amor sui* corresponds to the Holy Spirit, the act by which the Father returns to himself in love. All three are the same divine reality, but each can be differentiated from the others modally. The Father is unbegotten, originating divine energy; the Son is begotten or derived divine energy, and the Spirit is the divine energy of love, linking the Father and the Son. This Trinitarian God is a blur of activity, a wheel constantly turning, an endless play of othering and returning. Just as the mind can never sit still, so the divine being never stays anchored in one place; rather it goes out from itself and comes back in an ecstatic rhythm. There is a constant "looking to the other" that characterizes the Trinitarian persons in this Augustinian perspective: the Father's whole existence is to generate the Son, the Son's whole being is to be generated by the Father, and the entire reality of the Spirit is to be the love between the Father and the Son.

In articulating his Trinitarian theology, Thomas Aquinas remains within a basically Augustinian framework, but he makes certain precisions of his own. For Thomas, the Son is the "interior word" of the

Father, the act by which the Father can, in a perfect and utterly interior way, make an image of himself. This inner word is, from all eternity, generated by the Father, and the Father and the Son, from all eternity, in their mutual love, "spirate" or breathe forth the Holy Spirit.[78] Hence, for Aquinas, there is an intriguing play in God between action and passivity: the Father's relation to the Son is one of active generation (speaking), while the Son's relation to the Father is one of passive generation (being spoken); and the relation of the Father and the Son to the Holy Spirit is one of active spiration (breathing), while the relation of the Spirit to the Father and the Son is one of passive spiration (being breathed out). Furthermore, because they are essentially connected, the three persons never operate in isolation from one another; rather they "sit together" (*circumincessio*), one always conditioning and accompanying the other two. Though the Son comes from the Father and the Spirit from the Father and the Son, there is no ontological hierarchy among the Trinitarian persons. It is not the case that the Father ranks higher than the Son or that the Son lords it over the Spirit. All three exist in a play of coequal love.

As was hinted above, this oddly playful God is the source of all being, the Creator of heaven and earth. And it is in the image of none other than this God that we human beings were made. Hence it should not be surprising that spiritual pain and dissolution follow from the rejection of the Trinitarian pattern of being. Sin, as we have seen, is a placing of the self-elevating ego at the center of one's life, the turning in of one's life in fear. The key to our joyfulness (and here is the spiritual power of the doctrine of the Trinity) is the awakening to a Trinitarian mode of existence in ourselves, a conscious imitation of the God who adamantly refuses to cling to himself. When we look and act like the Trinity, we harmonize with the energy of the ground of being. The University of Chicago psychologist Mihaly Csikszentmihalyi wrote a book entitled *Flow* in which he presented the findings of years of intensive research into what makes people happy.[79] What he found is that people are content when they are "in the flow," that is to say, when they have forgotten about themselves and have become lost in an activity, a person, a game. And they are discontented when, either through understimulation or through fear they lose the flow and fall back onto themselves. None of this should be surprising to us. We have been arguing throughout this book that our souls become sick when they fall out of similitude with God and that they are doctored precisely when they begin to resemble the divine. What Augustine and Thomas say, quite simply, is that God is always in the flow, that he is a constant rhythm of self-forgetting love. And what they imply is that we find our joy inasmuch as we imitate the divine dance.

What the Trinity shows us is that the real meaning of existence is not substantiality but relationality. It has become a commonplace in Western philosophy since Aristotle to maintain that the purest and truest instance of being is the substance, the self-contained individual thing, "that which is neither present in nor predicable of another." The Christian sense of God undermines this Aristotelian prejudice, revealing it finally as an expression of the sinful consciousness. It is the self-elevating ego that wants to believe that being is tantamount to substantiality or radical unrelatedness. It is the sinful soul that pretends that it exists in isolation from others and from nature (think of the game of blaming that goes on after the discovery of the Fall). What is extraordinary in the theology of the Trinity that we have just outlined is this: God is not a substance; God is a play of relationality. The persons within the unity of the God are altogether "present in" one another, influencing and flowing into one another. The Father looks, not to himself and his prerogatives, but to the Son, and the Son clings, not to his will and mind, but to those of the Father, and the Spirit is nothing but the breathing out of the love between the Father and the Son; one might even say she *is* the rapport between Father and Son. The implication for us is simple and extraordinarily important: we are most ourselves when, like the Trinitarian persons, we are least ourselves. We find our identity most assuredly when we look to another in love and self-forgetfulness. Our sinful world thinks that we become God-like when we cling and defend; the irony is that this cramping of the soul is what makes us most dramatically unlike God.

We saw that, for Aquinas, the Triune God is a rhythm of action and passion, commanding and obeying, giving and receiving. Once more this bipolarity is of decisive importance for our spiritual health. Our culture teaches us that the mature, accomplished, and self-possessed

person is one who is in control, in command, powerful in the exercise
of his faculties. And, consequently, the weak person is the one who
is passive, ordered about. We glory, in short, in the active, imperial,
virtuous (literally manly) qualities of soul, and we denigrate whatever smacks of subordination and passivity. Again, the Trinity calls
this one-sidedness into question. God actively generates and actively
spirates, but God also is passively generated and passively spirated.
God gives and God receives — all in the confines of his inner life.
And this reality is the ground of being, the summit of perfection. Real
goodness of soul accordingly consists, not in the imperious exercise of
power alone, but in the capacity to command *and* obey, to give life
and to receive it. God is like a heart that both pumps blood and takes
it in, or like a set of lungs that breathe in and out. Were the heart
or lungs to perform only one or the other of their essential functions,
they would collapse; it is the complementary back and forth movement of the two that renders them efficacious. So we sinners must
learn not only to breathe in, not only to take, but to exult as well in
the ecstasy of breathing out, letting go, letting be. The sinner is convinced that if he, even for a moment, relaxes his grip on life, he would
collapse. The Trinity teaches that precisely the opposite is the case: it
is the one-sided and excessive grasping that closes off the give-and-
take which alone makes life possible. And is the Trinity not therefore
precisely the soul-doctoring antidote to Eden? Adam and Eve had dominion over the garden; they could accomplish to the full extent of
their capacities, breathing in, as it were. What they were incapable of
doing was surrendering, breathing out, mimicking the passivity of God.

Finally we can consider the importance of *circumincessio*. The divine persons sit together in a choir, a community of coequal love,
no one person superior to any other. So much of sinful human life
is dedicated to the quest for superiority. From the playground to the
corporate headquarters, we strive to be on top, to realize ourselves by
subordinating others. Socially, politically, culturally, economically, we
rejoice in games of domination and subordination, continually wondering who is best or highest or most influential. If there is a hierarchy
in place, we struggle to get to the summit of it, and if there is no hierarchy, we battle to create one. The divine life, on the other hand, is

a community of persons in which there is no hierarchy and no subordination, no better or worse, no more powerful or less powerful. The Trinity refuses to play the games that so amuse the self-elevating ego; the divine persons refuse to jockey for position or seek pride of place. Instead they operate in mutual respect and mutual letting-be, each sharing in the activity and dynamism of the others. What the sinner learns at the school of the Trinity is the futility of competitiveness and hierarchization. He discovers that the highest position is the low place of cooperation and love.

My hope is that this analysis of God has confused the reader a bit, pushed him or her off balance. I would be pleased if he or she found my approach a tad inconsistent, even annoying. It would delight me if my reader is wondering why I cannot simply make up my mind about God and use some straightforward, unambiguous theological language.

I have tried to imitate the Great Tradition in its stubborn and sometimes disconcerting unwillingness to say "either/or" when it comes to God. Christian theology and spirituality come together in affirming that "either/or" tends to be the language of sin and "both/and" the language of grace. When things of the spirit appear to be too clear, when God is too neatly described, when we are too confident in our spiritual stance, we are, most likely, in the Kingdom of the supreme being, that place of grasping and hiding. The Great Tradition wants less clarity, less confidence, precisely because it sees theological murkiness and spiritual imbalance as conducive to the surrender that we in the dysfunctional family of Adam and Eve find so difficult. It is as though the bipolar language of our theology — summed up in the names of Being and Love — compels us to put down the gun and the compass and to give ourselves to the alluring darkness of the woods. Under the influence of proper theological language, the *pusilla anima* cracks and, in the language of Chesterton, lets some light into its cramped space.

Now who is it exactly that has prompted us to speak in this odd way? It is no philosopher, no poet, no mythmaker, no scientist, no social reformer, no dreamer. Any of those would share in the dysfunction of sin and hence give us false information about God. We know how to speak, with at least relative adequacy, because someone has come, we Christians believe, from the very heart of God bearing a divine word. Someone has come from outside of the dysfunction and shown us a new world. To this stranger, this unexpected emissary, this Misfit we now turn.

Part III

The Healing

Chapter Eleven

JESUS THE JUDGE
Beginning with Flannery O'Connor

He is the Son of God and the Son of Man; he is the running water for which we yearn. He is the servant, the Lamb, the suffering Messiah, salve for our wounds. He is the helpless child under the night sky, and he is the *Pantocrator,* the ruler of the cosmos. He is the prophet, the poet, the proclaimer of God's Kingdom; he is the agitator, the troublemaker, the one who annoys everybody. He is food for a world that is starving, and he is light for a world that has wandered from the straight path. He is the shepherd who feeds and leads and searches out; he is the vine on whom we are grafted. He is scourge of the demons and the harrower of Hell; and he is the pathway that leads up to the stars. Like finest wine, he is intoxication; like best of bread, he fills us up. Through the locked doors of our despair, he passes effortlessly, and across the roiled seas of our fear he walks. He is the transfiguration of our frail humanity and he is the manifestation of God's frail divinity. He is the heartbroken God who heals the heartbreak of humankind. Jesus of Nazareth is the coming-together for which we have longed since Eden, the embrace of God's relentless love and our hope against hope.

And the spirit of this Jesus animates the letters of Paul and the Gospels, the irrational self-sacrifice of the first martyrs, the deliberations of the great councils, the radical lifestyle of the desert monks, and the majestic liturgies of Constantinople and Rome. The vision of this Jesus inspires the missions to Ireland, England, Germany, and the East, and it directs the civilizing work of the medieval monasteries. Jesus' message catches fire in the minds of Dominic and Francis, Clare and Hildegard, Ignatius of Loyola and Catherine of Siena. Jesus' heart beats in the suffering mysticism of John of the Cross and in the ec-static mysticism of Teresa of Avila. The revolutionary quality of Jesus' preaching can be discerned even in the political reforms of the eigh-teenth century and in the social upheavals and liberation theologies of our time. Jesus is lovingly depicted by the Byzantine iconographers, by the artists of the catacombs, by the sculptors of the Middle Ages, by Giotto, Leonardo, Michelangelo, Caravaggio, Rubens, Rembrandt, Manet, Picasso, and Chagall. His shadow falls on the works of Dosto-evski, Melville, Hemingway, Eliot, and Graham Greene. His cross — that strange and disturbing reminder of his terrible death — is the dominant and most recognizable symbol in the West. Jesus is, quite simply, unavoidable. Our language, behavior, attitude, perspective, our aspirations, our fears, our moral sensibility have all been indelibly marked by his mind and heart. Even in rejecting him — as Nietzsche and Freud did — we remain beholden to him.

The dominance and centrality of Jesus is what I have assumed throughout this book. Though it appears as though much naming of ourselves and God has gone on independently of Christ, all of it in fact has been implicitly determined by him. At the outset, we heard the call from Jesus to *metanoia*, to move from a mind of fear to a mind of trust. Then we looked at the *pusilla anima*, the small soul produced by egotism. With the help of Dante, the author of Genesis, and the fathers of Trent, we dragged that cramped mind out into the light, exposing its illusory quality. What was not stated but what in part 3 comes to clarity of expression is that it is Jesus in his capacity as judge who allows us fully to see the dimensions of the *pusilla anima*. The very perfection and beauty of his mind is what enables us to see, by way of contrast, what is so terrible about the fallen mind. Next we looked, with the help of Merton, Balthasar, Schleiermacher, and Tillich, at the *imago Dei*, that spark of divinity in each of us, that beauty which remains despite the distortions of sin. What will now be made explicit is that the contours of the *imago* — the full flowering of who we ought to be — appear only in the light of Christ. It is the coming-together of divinity and humanity that properly reveals what our humanity at its best looks like. Then, in part 2, we examined the bipolar nature of God, that power that can be neither grasped nor hidden from, that en-

ergy of being which is best described as love. Our consideration of the
Lord Jesus will reach its high point when we meditate upon his cross
and resurrection, the event that reveals the full extent of the divine
love that reaches even to the limits of godforsakenness. Again, it is
Jesus — and not primarily philosophy or mythology — who reveals the
meaning of divinity to us. Our problem, our destiny, and the God who
saves us are all disclosed in Christ. He is, accordingly, judge, paradigm
of the new humanity, and the manifestation of the God who is love.
As such, he is the supreme doctor of the soul, and the holding up of
his icon in all of its complexity and multivalence is the surest means
to *metanoia*.

As is our custom, we will examine this "coming-together" from a
number of aspects and with a variety of sources. We will show the
soul-doctoring power of Christ as it is played out in the fiction of an
American writer, in the still surprising, still radical texts of the New
Testament, and in the sober doctrine of a fifth-century council.

❧❦

One of the strangest and most disturbing of contemporary writers
of fiction is Flannery O'Connor. Like her fellow Southerner William
Faulkner, O'Connor has a gothic imagination, a gift for dramatic
storytelling, and a biblical sensibility. But there is something else at
work in her writing, something at the same time unnerving and grace-
filled, a peculiarity of vision that flows from her Catholic Christianity.
The first impression that one has on reading almost anything by Flannery O'Connor is its terrible, macabre, or, to use her word, "grotesque"
quality. Her characters are the crippled, the deformed, the retarded,
ruthless killers, evangelists without faith, charlatans, racists, and the
just plain obnoxious. And her tales involve betrayals, exposures, cor-
ruptions, and, more often than not, violent death. But her stories are
meant, not to depress us or convince us of the hopeless depravity
of the human race, quite the contrary. O'Connor can tell the awful
black truth about human beings full out precisely because she knows
that this is not the whole story. She herself said that at the heart
of every one of her novels or stories is the offer of grace; the real

drama she presents is that of God gracing us fallen, frail, and seemingly hopeless human beings, with an opportunity for transformation.
She knows that the human condition is worse than we have imagined and, at the same time, incomparably better than we could have
hoped. And she realizes both of these truths in light of the awful
revelation that occurred in Jesus Christ, God come into our tragedy
and sin bearing a light that overwhelms the darkness. Nowhere is this
Christological perspective clearer than in the short story that many
consider Flannery O'Connor's masterpiece, "A Good Man Is Hard
to Find."[80]

The story begins with a warning. The grandmother tells her son,
Bailey, and his family that they oughtn't to go on a trip to Florida
because the paper says that an escaped convict, called the "Misfit,"
is heading there and that he has done terrible things to people he
has encountered. They ignore her — as it seems they usually do —
and set out on their vacation. The grandmother dressed carefully for
the trip, donning a jaunty hat and an elegant navy blue dress with a
spray of violets pinned to the collar. O'Connor tells us that "in case of
an accident, anyone seeing her dead on the highway would know at
once that she was a lady."[81] On the way, the self-consciously proper
grandmother mildly corrects her grandchildren when they say or do
inappropriate things, and she bemoans the general loss of respect in
the world. The little group arrives at an eating establishment called
"The Tower" run by a certain Red Sammy Butts. When June Star, the
granddaughter, says something rude to Red Sammy's wife, the grandmother hisses, "Aren't you ashamed?" Then she commiserates with
Red Sam when he complains that there is no one you can trust any-
more. "People are certainly not nice like they used to be," she wearily
explains. He concludes their dialogue, summing up his own worldview
and that of the grandmother: "A good man is hard to find."[82] In the
course of this homely narrative we have seen emerging the contours
of the grandmother's character and moral sensibility: she is careful,
proper, convinced of her own goodness and of the general dangerous-
ness and depravity of the world around her. The human race for her
does seem to be carefully divided between the very few who are, like
herself, good and all the rest.

As they continue on their journey to Florida, the grandmother re-members a lovely house she had known in her youth, situated not far off the road on which they are traveling. As she describes it, including tantalizing details such as the family silver hidden in a secret com-partment, she stirs up in herself and the children an intense desire to see it. The father does not want to waste any time searching for an old house, but when the children begin to kick and scream, urging him to take the detour, he gives in. On the way down the winding and bumpy side road, the grandmother, to her horror, remembers that the house in question is in another state; she has sent them on a wild-goose chase. Alarmed, she kicks her valise which upsets a bas-ket at her feet in which her cat was sleeping. The animal leaps up onto Bailey's shoulder and he loses control of the car, sending it into a somersault and landing them in a gulch by the side of the road.

This entire drama had been witnessed from a distance. A car soon arrives and out of it step three men who had seen the accident and who have come, presumably, to help. When the grandmother studies the bespectacled man with no shirt or undershirt and the ill-fitting blue jeans, she is convinced she knows him, but can't quite place him. And then it occurs to her in a flash and, before she could control herself, she blurts out, "You're the Misfit. I recognized you at once!"[83]

After this terrible *faux pas*, the tragedy moves quickly to its resolu-tion. "It would have been better for all of you, lady, if you hadn't of reckernized me," says the Misfit with a dreadful matter-of-factness. As his colleagues systematically usher father, mother, and children into the woods to be shot, the Misfit and the grandmother engage in a deadly serious conversation. Realizing what is happening, the old lady first tries to convince the criminal that he is a good man. He flatly denies the charge. And then she, with a certain desperation, urges him to call upon God: "Looking down on him, she asked, 'Do you ever pray?'" We notice, of course, that she "looks down on him," as she does upon most people she meets. His response is a simple shake of the head. Then when he tells her of his terrible years in the peni-tentiary, in solitary confinement for the killing of his father, she says, "That's when you should have started to pray.... If you would pray, Jesus would help you." He agrees with her but then adds decisively, "I don't want no hep. I'm doing alright by myself." At this point, we can see the remarkable similarity between the grandmother and the Misfit: both remain secure in their conviction of self-sufficiency. Despite their enormous differences at the surface level, both are in the same spiritual space. She, in her self-conscious elegance and moral superiority, and he, in his violent and hardened self-reliance, are equally unaware of their need for salvation. Neither needs any help. She in her superficial piety and he in his murderous indifference to human life are both trapped in the solitary confinement of the *pusilla anima*.

At this point, their conversation takes a decisive and finally salvific Christological turn. Having heard the gunshots in the woods, knowing that her family is dead, the grandmother sits in the ditch muttering "Jesus . . . Jesus." And the Misfit takes the cue: "Yes'm, Jesus thrown everything off balance."[84] This is the profoundest theological remark in the story and the hinge upon which it turns. The Misfit is acknowledging something that the Christian tradition has always held to be of central significance, namely, that Jesus is judge of the sinful world, that is to say, the one who, through the power of his life and witness, throws off balance the imbalance caused by sin. Christ is the Misfit whose very strangeness points up the disorder of the *pusilla anima*. And O'Connor's character amplifies his Christological vision: "Jesus was the only One that ever raised the dead, and He shouldn't have done it. He thrown everything off balance." The Misfit knows that Jesus' disturbing, unnerving work had to do with the raising of the dead, with going into the realm of hopelessness and bringing hope. With stunning theological acuity, he sees that the essence of Jesus' ministry was to bring the divine power into all the realms of death and thereby to call into question the finality of death. Light in the darkness, the mocker of the grave, divine love in the most godforsaken places, Jesus throws off balance the whole world of the small soul. Anxiety, depression, failure, sin, disease, death itself are no longer places where the *pusilla anima* can stake out its independence, establish its realm. They have all been invaded and conquered by Jesus, the one who raises the dead.

Displaying even more impressive theological insight, the Misfit continues, "He shouldn't have done that. . . . If He did what He said, then it's nothing for you to do but throw away everything and follow Him, and if He didn't, then it's nothing for you to do but enjoy the few minutes you got left the best way you can — by killing somebody or burning down his house or doing some other meanness to him. No pleasure but meanness."[85] The stark option is impressively presented. If God in Christ has really gone into the darkest places of the human condition and brought from them hope, then the only viable move is to follow him with a reckless abandon; if God's love is really stronger than death, then *metanoia*, real change of heart, is possible, even necessary. However, if Christ is a charlatan, if he is not the liberator from the power of death, then the *pusilla anima*, in all of its defensiveness and violence and self-absorption, remains the best psychological space to inhabit, and the "pleasure of meanness" is all that we can hope for. The Misfit knows that, precisely as "judge," Jesus is the one who provokes a *krisis*, a judgment or decision: "He who is not with me is against me."

Then, in her shock and confusion, the old lady says, "Maybe He didn't raise the dead," and the killer pounces on this suggestion with enthusiasm: "I wasn't there so I can't say He didn't. I wisht I had of been there. It ain't right I wasn't there because if I had of been there I would have known . . . and I wouldn't be like I am now." And in uttering those words, the Misfit signals a major spiritual transformation, for the one who just a few moments before had stated that he needed no help now acknowledges that all is far from right in him. And he furthermore knows that it is Jesus' conquest of death that would make all of the difference in his life, changing him from a person who finds pleasure in cruelty to someone who is able to throw everything away and follow Christ. He is not the self-sufficient and self-satisfied sinner he had imagined himself to be. In the presence and under the influence of the icon of Christ — God gone into godforsakenness — the Misfit can see his radical need for grace as well as the possibility of an entirely new life.

When he spoke those words, "his voice seemed about to crack," and in that moment "the Grandmother's head cleared for an instant." The spiritual/emotional breakthrough in the Misfit prompts a similar clarification in the mind of the old lady: "She saw the man's face twisted close to her own as if he were going to cry and she murmured, 'Why you're one of my babies. You're one of my own children!' "[86] Just a few moments before, the grandmother had been "looking down" on the criminal, and now they are face to face, the shift in physical attitude signaling a major shift in psychological and spiritual attitude. She knows, in the depths of her soul, that this horrible killer, this murderer of her family, is one of her own children, her flesh and blood; she realizes that in his anguished need for salvation, he is in essentially the same spiritual condition as she: both are sinners requiring mercy. At the outset of the story, the Misfit is a demon whom the proper grandmother simply condemns without hesitation. And now, through the terror of imminent death and the transforming power of the icon of Jesus, she has been brought to an acknowledgment of her solidarity in need and compassion with him. Both are in the soup of sin, and both are incapable of autosalvation. In the ecstasy of this realization, the grandmother reaches out to the Misfit in compassion, touching his shoulder. She has moved from condescension to personal identification.

But the killer reacts violently to this touch, springing back "as if a snake had bitten him," and shooting the old lady three times through the chest. Though he has begun to glimpse the way out, his instincts are still those of the *pusilla anima:* the compassionate outreach of the grandmother is perceived as an invasion of the ego-fortress.

This climactic resolution of the conversation is not, all indications to the contrary, one-sidedly tragic. In Flannery O'Connor's universe, death is hardly the worst of fates; in fact, it can be the bridge to fullness of life. Having seen what she needed to see — her solidarity in sin with even the worst of sinners — and having thereby opened herself to grace, the grandmother was ready for heaven. In death she sits "in a puddle of blood with her legs crossed under her like a child's and her face smiling up at the cloudless sky." She has recovered her innocence and has found her joy. And having shot the old woman, the Misfit "put his gun down on the ground and took off his glasses and began to clean them." Just as the grandmother's head had cleared in her moment of identification with her killer, so the Misfit's vision is clarified in the very act of killing her (he cleans his glasses). He has begun to

see something, or better, to see the whole world differently, more accurately. And he puts down his gun, that instrument of violence and
exclusion so characteristic of the *pusilla anima.*

But what is it that he has seen? We glimpse it in the final snatches
of dialogue. As Bobby Lee, one of the Misfit's associates, comes to take
away her body, he says, "She was a talker, wasn't she?" And the Misfit
responds, "She would have been a good woman if it had been somebody there to shoot her every minute of her life."[87] The killer knows
exactly what had happened in this awful exchange in the shadow of
death; he knows that the grandmother had discovered solidarity and
compassion precisely when the image of Jesus, fired by the ultimacy
of the moment, had worked on her. Then Bobby Lee, exulting still
in the excitement of killing, exclaims, "Some fun!" And the Misfit,
in the grace-filled final line of the story responds: "Shut up, Bobby
Lee. It's no real pleasure in life." Earlier we had seen the unambiguous
choice: either you give away everything and follow Jesus or you get
whatever pleasure you can from stealing and killing. This is presented,
accurately, as an exclusive option, a strict Kierkegaardian either/or. It
is therefore clear at the end of this terrible story that the Misfit has
seen the necessity of following Jesus. In the very act of killing the old
woman, he realized that there is no real pleasure in the outrages of
the *pusilla anima,* no joy in the violence and defensiveness of sin, and
therefore he is opened to grace. Was it perhaps the woman's outreach
in compassion that convinced him of it? Or was it her simple and
desperate evocation of Jesus? Whatever it was, it served to clear his
vision and to prompt him to put down his gun. Ironically, this awful
tale is a comedy, for the two protagonists are, in the end, oriented toward salvation. And each has been for the other the conduit of grace
and *metanoia.*

What I have hinted at in this necessarily cursory reading of
O'Connor's disturbing and wonderful story and what I want to make
explicit now is just how the three aspects of revelation in Jesus are
at play here. Christ is, first, the one who prompts the crisis. In the
presence of Jesus, both the grandmother and the Misfit realize the imbalance of their souls and both are prompted to change. Second, Jesus
functions as the paradigm of the new humanity. The Misfit implies

that the only proper response to Jesus is to abandon oneself completely and *follow* him, that is to say, to do what he did. But what he did is clearly expressed as well: he went into death and brought from it life. The new humanity, which Jesus bears to us, is therefore the life of compassion and active identification with those who are far from God, those who are in death. Finally, and perhaps most elusively, Jesus reveals the God who is really God. The divine power is not a distant indifferent force, but rather the transcendent love that comes, immanently, into the limitations of fear and death, thereby throwing the world of sin off balance. "A Good Man Is Hard to Find" reveals that God is that ungraspable but unavoidable force, that unsettling, unnerving, unpredictable love that can blow like a tornado through the lives of sinful people. O'Connor's God — the God of Jesus Christ — is not the negligible supreme being. He is relentless, all-enveloping, all challenging grace, the power that goes into death and brings out of it life.

Let us now follow these themes of judge, new humanity, and icon of the true God as they play themselves out in the New Testament.

It has certainly become unfashionable to speak of Jesus as judge. He is celebrated as brother, friend, fellow-sufferer, person for others, but judge remains, for many, a problematic image. Does it not call to mind the vivid depictions of the Last Judgment found on the facades of most of the medieval cathedrals, those horrible scenes of sinners being drawn by cackling devils into the terrors of Hell while Christ dispassionately watches from above? Does it not seem irreconcilable with the picture of the gentle and compassionate Jesus?

Though it might cause some cognitive dissonance in the late twentieth-century Christian mind, the idea of Christ the judge remains absolutely central to the witness of the Gospel. Not only are there numerous explicit references to Jesus as righteous judge, but, in a real sense, every word and action of Jesus is a judgment. To say that Christ is the judge of the world is finally to say what we have been arguing throughout this book, namely, that *metanoia* is necessary. Jesus of Nazareth is the coming together of the divine and the human, the concrete display of God's intentions for us human beings and indeed for the world. As such he is the light in comparison to which the shadows of sin and rebellion and disorder deepen.

Both Kierkegaard and Barth contend that we didn't truly know our sin until Christ appeared, since, before Jesus, we had no final and radical criterion by which to judge our inadequacy. And therefore it is in the light of Jesus that we see, really for the first time, how far we are from God, how dramatically we need to change. The very rightness and *ordo* of Christ confounds the disorder in the sinful consciousness, compelling, at worst, violent reaction and, at best, conversion, the taking on of a new mind. In one of his magnificent sermons on Genesis, Origen reminds us that God made the world through the Word and thus that the Word is the criterion of measure for all finite things, the standard of beauty and correctness which they, to varying degrees, imitate. And so, he says, that same Word has come into a now fallen world, clothing itself in flesh and matter, appearing as the divine "judgment," the power that effectively restores the lost balance. The primal Word by which the world was made is also the incarnate Word by which the world is remade.[88]

It is, in this sense, that Jesus Christ is judge. Christ must not be imagined as a divine power arbitrarily passing sentence on a cowering humanity or self-righteously pouncing on a hapless sinner. Rather he should be appreciated as the uncomfortable reminder of just how constraining the *pusilla anima* is. As such, Christ is, precisely as judge, a conduit of grace, a pathway that opens up to salvation. He is the one who, salvifically, "throws everything off."

And we can see this disconcerting quality right from the beginning. In the prologue to his Gospel, John speaks of the Word taking on flesh, pitching his tent among us and *shining a light in the darkness*. This is a poetic evocation of Christ's mission to go to the darkest places of the *pusilla anima* and to illumine them. And it is a foreshadowing of the terrible conflict that Jesus' appearance will engender: light and darkness are mutually exclusive, the one cannot exist in the presence of the other. So there is no room for Christ in the confines of an ego-centered world; so, in the dramatic narrative of John's Gospel, that world must retreat or be transformed in the presence of the judging light.

In his commentary on the Infancy narratives of Luke and Matthew, Raymond Brown reminds us that the Christmas stories are not charming and innocent tales, fables that we can blithely tell our children.[89] There is, in fact, a darkness that broods over both accounts, an anticipation of the spiritual conflict Christ's incarnation precipitates. In Matthew's version, we learn of King Herod's reaction to the arrival of a newborn king of the Jews. "When King Herod heard this he was perturbed and so was the whole of Jerusalem" (Matt. 2:3). The aged and frightened Herod symbolizes the fearful ego that has, for so long, ruled the soul. The people of Jerusalem, who are disturbed with him, stand for all of the energies of the psyche — mind, will, imagination, sensuality — that have grown accustomed to the domineering leadership of the self-elevating ego. When the new king arrives, the old king trembles because he knows that his realm is desperately threatened. The new being which Jesus represents, the coming into union of the divine and the human, is the light that only deepens the darkness of the old mind. What the Herod story anticipates, of course, is the enormous reaction that Jesus will awaken throughout his life and ministry: all those in the grip of the *pusilla anima* will be disturbed by him, "thrown off" balance.

And thus it is interesting to note what Herod does. Furious and deeply shaken by Christ's arrival, he seeks, with shocking violence, to stamp him out and orders the massacre of all the male children in Bethlehem under the age of two. Herod is like a wounded animal, lashing out wildly in order to preserve his life. So the *pusilla anima* will react, sometimes violently, when challenged by the arrival of the judge. It is not accidental, of course, that this account echoes the story of the birth of Moses in Exodus. There the pharaoh represents the self-elevating ego that has effectively enslaved all the powers of the psyche and put them to work for his own purposes, building "fortified cities" in order to secure his position. And Moses, like Christ, symbolizes the coming of the new organizing principle of the psyche, the king who will lead the energies of the soul from slavery to freedom. Foreshadowing Herod, the pharaoh seeks, not to compromise with this threat, but to eliminate it utterly and accordingly orders the slaughter of children. The judge is never a welcome guest in the home of the *pusilla anima.*

We find something similar in Luke's reference to Jesus' rejection from the inn at Bethlehem. The crowded boarding house in the city of David represents, in the interpretations of many spirit masters, the bustling and overcrowded soul, the psyche in which a cacophonous plurality of voices is heard and in which there is no room for the sacred presence. When the criterion of justice in the soul arrives, the unjust soul makes no room for it. If we widen our angle of vision, we see that Herod's Jerusalem and the inhospitable Bethlehem inn are the world in the grip of original sin, the world that has lost sight of holiness and justice and which stands in fear, incapable of saving itself. Interestingly, the judge arrives in this hostile environment and cleverly hides himself in out of the way places — the humble stable in Luke's account, Egypt and Nazareth in Matthew's — biding his time until the moment of confrontation arrives. Like an advance party of an invading force, he quietly ensconces himself behind enemy lines and waits patiently for the battle. The Gospel writers are under absolutely no illusions about the power of sin and the false consciousness: they know its native resistance and they realize the stealthy game that must be played in order successfully to root it out.

And from the beginning of his public ministry Jesus is opposed. It is decidedly not the case that Jesus passes through a blissful "Galilean springtime" of acceptance and success only to be met, at the end of his career, by rejection in Jerusalem. Rather, rejection accompanies him from the outset, hounding and bedeviling him. The judge, from the moment of his appearance on the public scene, draws the rats from their holes.

We see it in the first chapter of Mark, in the account of Jesus' expulsion of the Caparnaum demoniac just after the call of the first disciples (Mark 1:21–28). Christ enters the synagogue at Caparnaum and preaches with great persuasive power, undoubtedly announcing the call to *metanoia* with which he commenced his ministry. A man with an "unclean spirit" begins to shout, disrupting the discourse: "What do you want with us, Jesus of Nazareth? Have you come to destroy us?" Again, we should not be surprised that the clean spirit of the *magna anima* awakens and stirs to protest the unclean spirit of the *pusilla anima*. The shouting of the demon is a sign that the judge is at work.

As we have been hinting, judgment is always for the sake of salvation, since it is a bringing to light of that which has lain destructively in the dark. What Jesus helpfully illumines in the soul of the possessed man is disclosed in the sufferer's anguished question, "What do you want of *us?*" The narrative makes it clear that it is an individual who speaks and yet he refers to himself in the plural. To be in the psychological and spiritual disorder of sin is to have lost the divine center. What characterizes the *pusilla anima* is a tragic splitting and disassociation, an uprooting from the source of life which is God. Unanchored, the sinful ego thrashes about, linking itself now to this value now to that, listening to a myriad of competing voices, allying itself with a succession of gurus, teachers, and guides. The "I" of the properly centered soul (the "I" which is Paul's Christ living in me) becomes a splintered "we." And, as the possessed man well understands, it is indeed this "we" that Jesus has come to destroy, or better, to forge into a new unity around him. With force and angry insistence, Jesus commands the disorder: "Be quiet! Come out of him!" It is intriguing to note that Jesus demands, first, silence. The hurly-burly of the competing inner voices must be stilled if the true center is to be realized. So many of the spirit masters imitate Christ in their insistence on silence as a prerequisite to spiritual development, knowing that only in the calming of the darting "monkey mind" can the deepest "I" emerge.

It is, of course, by the sheer authority of his *magna anima* that Jesus effects the reordering of this man's soul. As the note sounded by the first chair violinist draws the entire orchestra into tune, so the power of Christ's divine center draws the demoniac into centeredness. But it is not surprising that the transition from the small to the large soul is not an easy one: "and the unclean spirit threw the man into convulsions and with a loud cry went out of him." Simply hearing of the Christ child propelled Herod into an animal rage and an orgy of violence; so here the *magna anima* forces a painful, literally convulsing, rearrangement of the psyche. The onlookers realize immediately that something decisively new has happened: "Here is a teaching that is new and with authority behind it: he gives orders even to unclean spirits and they obey him." The Council of Trent taught that we are so mired in the soup of sin, so determined by the power of the *pusilla anima*, that none of our efforts of mind, will, art, or religion could finally deliver us. We are part of a dysfunctional family, and no one tainted by the dysfunction could ever finally free us. And so the power of Jesus is "something new," a *magna anima* that bears a divine authority and comes, so to speak, from another world, from decisively outside of the dysfunction. The judgment of Jesus, the people see, is not like the ineffectual judgments of the rabbis and the Pharisees; no, it is a "teaching" that is from above and hence of healing power.

The medieval rose windows are not only beautiful works of art, but also sublime examples of soul-doctoring, and their transformative power mimics that of Christ in the story just told. Invariably at the center of a rose window is a depiction of Christ (sometimes on the lap of his mother). Around this central point are arranged the numerous "medallions," depictions of prophets, kings, saints, and sages, in striking, almost musical, harmony. When one stands before a great rose window, such as the north window at Notre Dame in Paris, one is hypnotized, transfixed, indeed brought to peace, by this serenity and balance. The window is intended to be a picture of the well-ordered soul, the psyche that has centered itself exclusively on Christ and whose energies and powers have found their harmonious place around that center. Contemplating the icon, the viewer is transformed by its power. The demoniac cured by Jesus is a radically dysfunctional person brought to centeredness around Christ. The medieval work of art is thus a prolongation of the soul-doctoring effected by Jesus.

We find a similar dynamic of judgment in the strange story of the cure of the Gerasene demoniac (Mark 5:1–20). Jesus makes his way into the country of the Gerasenes and is confronted by another man with an unclean spirit, this one living among the tombs. Mark tells us that this unfortunate was chained and fettered, though he often broke these bonds, and that he spent his days howling among the tombs and gashing himself with rocks. Like the Caparnaum demoniac he knows that Jesus represents a threat to his twisted *ordo:* "What do you want with me, Jesus, son of the Most High God? Swear by God that you will not torture me!" When Jesus asks his name, the man replies awfully: "My name is Legion for there are many of us." Now we saw in the previous story the theme of the splintered soul, and that motif is undoubtedly reiterated in this account of "Legion," but there is something else at work here.

One wonders why the man has been chained. Is it for his own protection or is it perhaps because someone wants to keep him there? Is this agonized and self-mutilating man, in a curious sense, serving a purpose? Is he there among the tombs on the outskirts of the town for a reason? Theorists as diverse as René Girard, Carl Jung, and Walter Wink have written persuasively on the theme of scapegoating violence. All three agree that scapegoats perform a decisively important function in the development and maintenance of human societies, effectively channelling away the rivalry, competition, fear, and violence that would, otherwise, tear a community apart.[90] A certain strained peacefulness reigns when warring factions in a society can discharge the tension between them onto a scapegoat — usually a person or group that is already threatening in its otherness. Jung speaks in this context of "shadow projection," the tendency of individuals and collectives to project onto a convenient scapegoat all of those qualities that remain problematic and unintegrated in themselves. This discharges the negativity of the shadow but in a way that is, obviously, nonproductive to the projector and damaging to the scapegoat. Nevertheless, there is a short-term benefit to the process, and this explains the *necessity* of keeping the marginalized scapegoat, so to speak, within view. The one who neutralizes the unbearable tensions of a community is, to some degree, cast out but he is also clung to desperately, since without him the group would revert to self-destructive violence.

Thus we find the psychologically and culturally complex scapegoating of Jews in Christian Europe and of blacks in this country. In each case the hated "other" effectively united the warring factions in the majority culture by providing them with a common enemy, and thus both Jews and blacks were, while ostracized and persecuted, curiously admired, even lionized, by their persecutors. (Think here of the wonderful and horrifying scene in *Schindler's List* where the Nazi camp commandant seeks intimacy with his Jewish housekeeper and then, moments later, savagely beats her.) The hated were, to be sure, on the margins, but they were prevented from wandering too far.

And thus is the Gerasene demoniac — precisely as a scapegoat — chained to keep him close? Can we not imagine the citizens of the town coming out to gawk at the poor soul, much as the children in *To Kill a Mockingbird* watched and taunted Boo Radley, their fearsome, fascinating bogeyman. In the context of this discussion, the tortured man's name takes on new resonance. He calls himself Legion for there are "many" in him. Could the many in question be each of the citizens of the town who have, to one degree or another, projected their shadows onto him? Could his name designate the crowd because it was the crowd, in its collective hatred and violence, who created him? René Girard makes the intriguing suggestion that the demoniac's gashing of himself with stones recalls the original stoning by which he was driven from the town by the mob.[91] It is furthermore interesting that Jesus casts the legion of demons into a herd of pigs, since the pig was, for the Jews, unclean, a sort of scapegoated animal. Finally, we note what is, at first glance, the surprising reaction of the townspeople upon learning of the man's cure. Instead of rejoicing in his good fortune, they are disconcerted and beg Jesus to leave their region. In light of the reading we have been offering, this reaction is entirely understandable, for the last thing the Gerasenes want is the restoration to sanity and sociability of their scapegoat. Without him and his hatred-channelling role, the town might revert to the chaos of factional violence. Begging Jesus to leave the area is an indirect admission on their part that his intervention and presence have thrown off the subtle balance upon which the survival of the town depends.

Once more, the judge is at work. The Gospel writers consistently reveal to us how impatient Jesus is with the demonic whenever he confronts it, whether on the personal or, in this case, on the societal level. The Kingdom of God is opposed to the *pusilla anima* and the proclamation of the Kingdom disrupts and unveils the games, structures, social expressions, and strategies of that little mind. By curing the Gerasene demoniac, Jesus announces his intention to break the pattern of scapegoating and thus to show the people of the village a new way of being in community. Instead of projecting their violence and negativity onto an innocent other, they should turn to the difficult but ultimately soul-enlarging task of self-criticism and *metanoia*. We can hear, in this account, an echo of his admonition: "Remove the plank in your own eye and you can see more clearly the speck in your brother's eye" (Matt. 7:5). Rooted in the *magna anima*, secure in the unconditional love of the divine, one has the requisite courage to face the inner darkness and one is liberated from the hopeless pattern of casting blame and inventing scapegoats. But, once more, it is Jesus the judge who makes this possible, who, through the power of his soul, illumines the dark and unveils the game.

Jesus' judgment of the social manifestation of the *pusilla anima* is also evident in the somewhat comical account of the healing of the blind man at Bethsaida in Mark's Gospel (Mark 8:22–26). The sightless man comes to Jesus seeking a cure and the first thing that Christ does is to lead him out of the village. Then after putting spittle on the man's eyes and imposing hands on him, he asks, "Can you see anything yet?" The man, who was beginning to see, replied, "I can see people; they look like trees to me, but they are walking about." Laying hands on him a second time, Jesus effects a total cure and finally the man sees "plainly and distinctly." Dismissing the man, Jesus says emphatically, "Do not even go into the village."

Now blindness is a rich biblical image for lack of spiritual sight, the inability to see things as they are. When we examined the decrees of the Council of Trent on original sin, we saw that one of the effects of the Fall was a loss of holiness, that is to say, seeing with the eyes of Christ, appreciating the world as a participation in the creative energy of God. All of us sinners, to varying degrees, are blind to this metaphysics of creation and tend to see the world from the standpoint of the self-elevating ego. What this tightly packed Markan narrative discloses is one of the *origins* of this spiritual debility: too much time in the village. It is most significant that the account of the healing is bracketed by two distantiations from the city. Jesus leads him away from the village and then sternly warns him not to return. Is it possible that the soul blindness of this man had been caused by too much time in the city? Had he been immersed too completely in the attitudes, prejudices, conventional viewpoints of the town? Martin Heidegger speaks of the tyranny of *was man sagt*, of "what everybody says," and Carl Jung knows the dangers of surrendering to the collective consciousness, to the mass movements and general attitudes that surround us.

In terms of our study, the village evokes the collective power of the *pusilla anima*, all those ways that we are, unconsciously for the most part, influenced and shaped by the sinfulness of our society. The shared and mutually justified attitudes of hatred, violence, division, and ostracization — all the effluvia of the small mind — are like a blinding sand storm. Again, Trent is useful here: sin is passed on *propagatione et non imitatione*, by propagation and not simply by imitation. The sinful "city" has us; our minds are, willy-nilly, shaped by it, and therefore it is impossible for us to extricate ourselves from it. In the striking symbolism of the Markan story, Jesus the healer and judge has to lead us blind people out of the city and give us sight — and then strictly enjoin us not to return to the blinding ways of the village. We unfortunate village dwellers must, through the power of Christ, put on the mind of Christ. And then we must live in a new town, the community of love and justice which is the church. It is this city of vision that effectively challenges (and judges) the enduring power of the blinding society.

What is so important here is this: the *magna anima* is a holy mind, that is to say, a mind set apart. Anchored in the unconditional love of God, realizing its groundedness in the sacred power, this mind is able to perdure in relative isolation, counterculturally unconcerned by the sinful attitudes that threaten to condition it. At the beginning of the Sermon on the Mount in Matthew, Jesus tells his followers that they shall be "the salt of the earth" (Matt. 5:13). Normally, we construe this saying to mean that Jesus' disciples are to be "down to earth" or "savory," but the image, more straightforwardly interpreted, carries a very different sense. In the ancient world, when a conquering power overran a city and wished completely to negate that city's influence, it would eliminate the people, destroy the place, and then *salt the earth* so that nothing would ever grow there again. Thus when Jesus urges his disciples to be salt for the earth, he is not trading in folksy pleasantries; rather, he is encouraging them to be forces for destruction and elimination. Filled with the power of the *magna anima,* they are to be courageous and independent upsetters of the status quo, troublemakers, naysayers. They are to make sure that, in the fields of the *pusilla anima,* nothing more shall grow. Like Christ himself, they are to be profoundly annoying to a world constructed around sin.

We have seen how Jesus judges the disorder in the individual psyche and in the collective consciousness of the "town." We can also see, throughout the Gospels, how, with a sort of awful power, Jesus judges religion itself, that very institution that, though pledged to the cure of the *pusilla anima,* most effectively fosters it. There are numerous accounts of Jesus' confrontation with religion and its official proponents, the scribes, elders, and Pharisees. For our purposes, we shall concentrate on only one of these stories, Luke's rich and paradigmatic narrative of the woman in the house of Simon the Pharisee.

Luke tells us that Simon had invited Jesus to a meal. It is most important to note that eating etiquette and behavior are of tremendous symbolic importance in the Gospels for they bespeak one's attitude toward the Kingdom of God. Jesus is at table with Simon, presumably in an elegant house and in a relatively formalized setting, and in walks a woman "who had a bad name in town." We can easily imagine the shock and discomfiture that her arrival precipitated, this intrusion of an uninvited and unwanted guest into a proper and carefully planned dinner party. Then the woman intensifies the unease in the room when she stands behind Jesus, weeping onto his feet, drying them with her hair, and then anointing them with oil. Insulted and moved to self-righteous indignation, Simon thinks to himself, "If this man were truly from God he would know what sort of woman this is and how inappropriate is her behavior." There are several aspects to Simon's reaction, each one reflective of a dimension of the religiously toned *pusilla anima*. Simon is, first of all, dismayed at the social upset this woman's appearance has caused. His party was carefully designed to be only for the best, only those who met his probably exacting standards of social and religious behavior. When the woman with a bad reputation crashes his dinner party, she throws into sharp relief the exclusiveness and snobbishness that characterize the host. Her presence sullies the "cleanness" and distinctiveness that mean so much to Simon precisely as a Pharisee. The sinful woman's intrusion into his sanitized world — and Jesus' obvious acceptance of her — dramatically judge the violent exclusiveness of Simon's religiosity.

Secondly, Simon's attitude toward Jesus is revealing. He notices — and undoubtedly rejoices in — Jesus' apparent inability to read the heart of the intruder. Simon had invited this new spiritual phenom to supper in order to size him up, to determine whether he belongs in the inner circle of correct believers, and he is watching this scene unfold with great interest. It is clear that Jesus is not as discriminating as Simon himself, not as insightful in his assessments, not as religiously careful. Once more, ranking, ordering, and excluding are paramount in Simon's mind. But Jesus the judge decisively intervenes at this point: "Simon, I have something to say to you."

He then proposes to the Pharisee the parable of the creditor who forgave two debtors, one who owed him five hundred denarii and the other who owed him only fifty. "Which of them," Jesus asks, "will love him more." And Simon correctly responds, "the one who was pardoned more." Then Jesus turns to the woman who, we recall, is standing behind him, and says, "Simon, you see this woman?" The "topography" here is not incidental. Jesus is between the Pharisee and the woman and thus, when he invites Simon to look at her, he forces him to see her "through" Jesus.[92] Simon has seen her in a conventional way, in the manner dictated by his religious consciousness, and thus he has appreciated her only as an unwelcome troublemaker, a hopeless sinner. Jesus compels him to look again, but this time with new eyes, with, in Origen's sense, the vision of holiness. And what is disclosed from this privileged point of view? "I came into your house," Jesus says, "and you poured no water over my feet, but she has poured out her tears over my feet and wiped them away with her hair. You

gave me no kiss, but she has been covering my feet with ointment."
She is filled with a love for Christ that overflows in acts of self-offering
and service; she breaks open her own heart in gratitude. But Simon
has shown scant hospitality to his guest, offering little if anything of
himself to Christ. The abundance of the woman's love discloses something to Jesus that had obviously been invisible to Simon: she has
been forgiven much. "For this reason I tell you that her sins, her many
sins, must have been forgiven her, or she would not have shown such
great love." It is most important to note that Jesus does not, strictly
speaking, forgive her sins; rather, he notices that she has been forgiven. And the evidence for it is her self-forgetting love.[93] She loves
so passionately and so courageously (risking the disapproval of Simon's
elegant guests) precisely because she has been so graciously and abun-
dantly forgiven. It is decidedly not the case, Jesus implies, that love
precedes divine forgiveness as a sort of prerequisite; on the contrary,
forgiveness precedes love as the condition for its possibility. It is not
the case that one's moral life must be upright in order to win divine
favor; rather the sheer gift of God's favor tends to produce an upright
moral life, a life of love.

How does all of this constitute a judgment on Simon's religiosity?
The Pharisee is so concerned with propriety, cultic purity, moral excellence that *he simply doesn't see* the presence of grace around him.
Among the presuppositions of Simon's religion is the fundamentally
egotistic conviction that divine favor is won through human achievement. It is this illusion of the *pusilla anima* that Jesus punctures. As
long as divine love is appreciated as something that flows from ethical excellence, the sinful ego remains regnant, and the freedom and
sovereignty of God are denied. The ethical component of religion is,
for Simon and likeminded people, a tool by which the unconditioned
ego grasps and manipulates the divine. The Pharisee's blindness to the
implications of the woman's excessive love is tantamount to his blindness to the authentic workings of the God who is really God. Bolstered
by his religion, Simon is still playing the game of Eden.

There is still another demonic component to Simon's religion. Unlike the woman, Simon is not rich in love and therefore he is not
aware of the workings of God's forgiveness in him. In Jesus' language,

he has been forgiven little. Now is this because there is little in him that needs forgiveness? Simon's behavior as described in this brief narrative would suggest not. But it is the Pharisee's religion — his carrying out of the moral law in strict detail — that convinces him of his own self-righteousness and thus renders him indifferent to the divine forgiveness, at least in his case. His own cultic purity brushes forgiveness off the stage and thus produces what we see disclosed in the story: a man weak in love. In the language of this book, Simon's Pharisaical religiosity has blinded him to the need for *metanoia*. He is desperately in the grip of the *pusilla anima,* but the defenses around the little mind are so powerful that the divine grace cannot penetrate in a healing way. What he is tragically unable to see — and this is the heart of the matter — is the joyful and grace-filled process of *metanoia* that unfolds before his very eyes in the gestures of the forgiven woman. It is Jesus the judge who shines light into the darkness of Simon's religion itself, into its exclusiveness, violence, self-righteousness, and egotism.

What emerges from even the most cursory survey of Jesus' judgments is the inevitability of his rejection. From the beginning of his life, Jesus represents a direct threat to the organization of the sinful psyche and to the institutions that flow from that *pusilla anima.* His presence causes shouting, convulsions, resentment, and hatred; his words stir up, disturb, unnerve, and consistently provoke. The *salvator,* the healer, is sometimes like a bitter medicine, a "jagged little pill" whose ultimate effect is beneficent but whose immediate effect is painful, even revolting. And therefore it is no wonder that the body politic — Sanhedrin, Romans, Pharisees, scribes, Zealots — tried to vomit him out. To stay with this vivid analogy, Jesus the judge was the agent whose purpose was to induce vomiting, to prompt the throwing up of the poison.

What, finally, has Jesus the judge revealed? He has demonstrated just how narrow and confining are the ways of the small soul. Like Dante, he has gone deep into the Hell of hatred, exclusiveness, violence, and fear and disclosed the pathetic and weeping Satan that reigns there. He has brought to light the games of Eden still being played, the grasping and hiding that are sadly in our bones. He has shown the dreadful imbalance and lack of holiness that poison our consciousness, and he has consequently channelled the divine anger, shouting at and commanding the demonic powers. By compelling us to see what we have done to ourselves, he stirs the *magna anima*, the almost forgotten treasure in us, and opens the door to *metanoia*.

Chapter Twelve

JESUS THE PARADIGM OF THE NEW HUMANITY

The Sermon on the Mount

If the call is to change of consciousness, there must be something wrong with our minds. It is Jesus the judge who, in myriad ways, signals the presence of the remnants of Eden in our souls, disclosing what is so desperately the matter with us. If the call is to change of consciousness, then there must be, by the same token, something right in our minds, there must be a seed in us of what we might become, a hunger in us that aches for fulfillment, an image of God that must be polished to a shine. It is Jesus the paradigm of the new humanity who brings this seed to growth, who feeds this hunger, who realizes this image. The coming together of divinity and humanity, he both judges and lures, showing both how far we have strayed and how fully we might live. One of the gravest mistakes we can make in any Christology is to imagine Jesus simply as God in the costume or livery of humanity. Jesus is not primarily divine and incidentally human; rather he is, as we will explore in greater detail, fully divine and fully human. And this implies that he reveals precisely what God wants us to be, God's creative intention vis-à-vis humanity and the world.

We don't look through the humanness of Jesus of Nazareth and see nothing but the icon of God; on the contrary, we look at Jesus, God and human, and see the full radiance of who we are destined to be. In a word, Jesus Christ discloses what we have identified as the unstated *telos* of the entire biblical narrative: theonomy. His way of being in the world is not the willful autonomy of Adam and Eve, not the self-deification of the ego, but rather, the living out of the surrender to the

183

divine power which is the root and ground of one's own deepest freedom. Christ lives out of that center, that fountain, that virginal point,
that interior castle which is the very being of God and, in that identification, he shows with blazing clarity just what an authentic human
life looks like. On every page of the Gospels we see this manifestation, this never before glimpsed form of the new humanity. For our
purposes, we shall focus on the strange and thrilling Sermon on the
Mount in Matthew's Gospel, a speech-act in which Jesus displays the
odd coherence, the upside-down *ordo* which "throws off" all that we,
under the influence of Eden, imagined humanity to be.

※|※

In Matthew, Jesus' laying out of the program of the Kingdom of God
takes place on a hill, on an elevation above the flat earth (Matt. 5–7).
The mountain is a standard biblical symbol for the locus of encounter
with the sacred, since it is the place where heaven and earth seem
to meet. I would compare the symbolic locality of the Sermon to the
Lord's mountain in Isaiah, that high place to which all nations shall
stream and from which clarity of vision regarding human relations is
alone possible. Jesus invites his disciples into the rarefied space of an
elevated, transformed consciousness, and it is from that perspective
that he speaks.

The Sermon begins with the eight beatitudes, the richly poetic
spelling out of the form of blessedness (happiness or spiritual good fortune). I interpret Jesus here as indicating the form of the theonomous
soul, what we would be like if the rivalry with God ceased, if grasping and hiding were abandoned. Thus, "how happy are the poor in
spirit; theirs is the kingdom of heaven." The principal move of the
fearful soul is to grasp and hoard. Aware of his own finitude and incompleteness, the sinner spontaneously seeks to fill up the inner abyss
with pleasures, accomplishments, social status, the esteem of others,
sexual conquests. The grasping ego thinks that if it makes of itself
a treasure trove it will forget its incompleteness and loneliness. Of
course we know that this is not the case, precisely because what the
soul longs for is not anything finite but the infinite. What it longs to

do ultimately is to forget itself, its cravings, its needs, and to open itself to the inrushing of the divine power. In Jesus' words, it seeks to
be poor. When the soul turns itself into a vacuum, an empty space,
then the divine wine can flow in and intoxicate. And this state of
affairs *is the Kingdom of God,* the coming together that has appeared
paradigmatically in Jesus and that is now offered as a power to be
shared.

He continues: "Happy are the gentle: they shall have the earth for
their heritage." One of the basic styles of the *pusilla anima* is aggres-
sion. When the ego has made itself the center of its universe, then all
other things and people are potential or actual rivals, and they must
be kept at bay. The chronic attitude of the sinful soul is suspicion
of the other, and this reaches its fullest expression in warfare, cold or
hot, indirect or direct. The *pusilla anima* knows that only the wary and
the violent "inherit the earth." Jesus throws this attitude off balance
by proclaiming that the gentle will be the true rulers of the world. If
the soul is rooted in the sacred reality, this beatitude implies, then it
need not be afraid. Borne up by the power that continually makes the
entire cosmos, it can rest easy, confident that whatever might come,
it is, in the final analysis, safe. And from the base camp of this deep
peace, the *magna anima* can reach out in love to all humanity and all
of nature. In this sense, it is indeed the gentle soul that inherits the
earth, that makes it a friend and not simply a conquered prisoner of
war. From the confines of the fearful *pusilla anima,* the "earth" is coldly
objectified as, at best, a subdued rival, whereas from the open space of
the *magna anima,* the cosmos is a friend and a fellow.

One of the most confusing and ironic of the beatitudes follows:
"Happy are those who mourn: they shall be comforted." Nowhere perhaps do we see more clearly how Jesus confounds the expectations
and assumptions of a sinful world: that which seems most opposed to
happiness (mourning) is in fact essential to it. The universe that we
inhabit is one characterized by conflict: it is simply impossible, in a
net of contingent and mutually dependent realities, for all goods to be
realized at all times for all things. In point of fact, a good for one is
invariably bought at the price of someone or something else's depri-
vation. Thus the cure of cancer through surgery or chemotherapy —

a great good for the patient — is a calamity for the cancer cells, and one person's landing of a coveted job implies, *ipso facto*, that many other people will be disappointed. To live in this world, in short, is to suffer and to mourn. One of the strategies of the *pusilla anima* is a weird sort of denial of this inevitability. Fundamentally afraid, the sinful ego is unable to admit the reality of evil, loss, or tragedy, convinced that such an admission would lead to a breakdown of its fragile inner structure. Accordingly, it creates a fantasy world of unrelieved success and accomplishment, a clean, well-lighted place where no rot creeps in. This is where we can see, not the violent and aggressive face of sin, but rather its benign and cheerful facade. In the film *Ordinary People,* a family tragedy of Sophoclean proportions unfolds behind the screen of affluence and relentless good cheer. One son — a hero of great promise — is killed in a boating accident, and the other son, Conrad, wrestling with dreadful survivor's guilt, attempts suicide and then struggles painfully, always on the brink of collapse, to bring his life back to order. When his parents attend a trendy cocktail party, they are questioned by a concerned neighbor: "How is Conrad?" Reflexively and defensively, they respond "Great! He's doing just great!" To admit the truth that Conrad is not doing at all well, and that in fact his suffering is part of a much greater family calamity, would simply be too much for their fearful egos to bear. They couldn't stand the embarrassment that such an admission would cause. In a word, this family, like many others, is unable to mourn.

Grounded in the still point which is the inner divine, a soul is able to grieve, since it knows that no suffering, however dreadful, can finally destroy it or undermine it. The properly centered psyche can accept the inevitability of pain because it is in possession of a joyfulness deeper than any negativity: "No storm can shake my inmost calm while to that rock I'm clinging...." And therefore, this soul is not apt to deny, repress, or project mourning in a counterproductive way. Rather, it can take suffering in, honestly accept it, turn it over, learn from it. In the well-ordered consciousness there is a certain equanimity with regard to both pleasure and pain, neither one permitted inordinately to dominate. In the face of his sufferings, Job can say, "The Lord has given; the Lord has taken away. Blessed be the name of the Lord" (Job 1:21). He demonstrates thereby that, despite the calamities that beset him, he is rooted in a peaceful place that remains untouched by the shifting fortunes of the world or the passing emotions of the psyche.

Jesus continues to paint his portrait of the *magna anima* with the next beatitude: "Happy those who hunger and thirst for what is right." Righteousness, justice, *ordo* are all deep concerns of the biblical and theological traditions. What we have seen in our discussion of sin is precisely the undoing of the *ordo* that God has established for us, the right relationship that is our joy. To be correctly balanced is to find oneself in the very act of losing oneself to the ever greater reality of the indwelling God. This acrobatic leap of self-forgetfulness is the "justice" of which the Council of Trent speaks, the weird and uncanny balance that is human fulfillment. Jesus is telling us that we are blessed in the measure that we long to be delivered from the pain of sinful imbalance, that we "hunger and thirst" for God's Kingdom. One of the surest tendencies of the *pusilla anima* is, as we saw in the case of Herod, to become complacently and defensively ensconced in the kingdom of egotism, to rest in the ersatz peacefulness of sin. Not to hunger and long for deliverance is to be in what Paul Tillich called the state of "self-complacent finitude," the bland acquiescence to disorder that is the surest block to transformation.[94] One of the clearest signs that the power of grace is at work is the profound dissatisfaction that one begins to feel with the sinful status quo of the psyche. To know that one is a slave and to feel the agony of one's chains is a necessary preparation for Exodus. Therefore Jesus knows that it is a blessing to be continually longing for the perfect balance between creature and Creator, the harmony of God's justice.

The next beatitude, "Happy are the merciful; they shall have mercy shown them," is, in many ways, the fundamental expression of the *magna anima*. Joseph Campbell once commented that all religions and spiritual traditions come together in their insistence upon compassion, fellow feeling. To know that we are one with everyone and everything else in the cosmos is an essential dimension of the transfigured mind. The saved consciousness is one that knows its rootedness in the bearing power of God, that same power that grounds every other expression of finitude in the universe. Hence, the *magna anima* realizes its essential and inescapable connectedness to all things, the fact that its own deepest center coincides with the deepest centers of everything else. We saw this awakening in Thomas Merton's Fourth and Walnut experience, his shattering of the myth of separateness and spiritual superiority. Compassion, the suffering with another, is not therefore simply an ethical commitment; it is a behavioral and attitudinal implication of the deep metaphysical awareness that we are all brothers and sisters in a sense that is infinitely richer than the merely biological.

It is obvious that the *pusilla anima*'s attitude is distinctly unmerciful. When one has made himself the supreme being at the center of the universe, he labors under the illusion that there is no connection between his heart and those of others, and hence he does not "feel with" anyone else. He is, at best, relieved that the suffering of another is not his own and, at worst, delighted that the other's pain will weaken him. When one has locked herself into the fortress of the self-elevating ego, she sees the other, not as second self, but as threat. Discontinuity and defensiveness accordingly become the dominant spiritual motifs. Judgment, distantiation, arrogance, violence, and rivalry — all evident in the aftermath of Adam and Eve's sin — take the place of mercy and poison the moral atmosphere.

It is important to note the logical structure of this beatitude: the one who is merciful will have mercy *shown him*. It seems to be the case, Jesus implies, that acting out of mercy, living in the deep center, effectively awakens an awareness of that center in others. When I touch another in authentic compassion, I break through the veil of illusion produced by the *pusilla anima,* and I force that person to live with me in our shared center. In short, my mercy practically compels the other to show mercy. It is as though my stubborn refusal to live in the world created by sin draws the other, by a sort of magnetic force, out of that world. Compassion is thus the powerful note that stirs a *vibration sympathique* in the surrounding strings and cords of the human family. How happy are we, Jesus says, if we know how to live in that powerfully influential place "outside the village" of the small mind.

"Happy are the pure in heart: they shall see God." In some trans-
lations of this beatitude, purity of heart is rendered as "singleness of
heart." What Jesus praises here is the undoing of the demonic attitude that we analyzed above: how blessed we are if we can anchor
the soul in the reality of God alone and not allow it to be split and
divided in its ultimate loyalty. The single-hearted is the one who, in
Augustine's phrase, loves God first and everything else for the sake of
God. Such a person's "heart" or center is uncomplicated, unsullied,
pure. There is, in her, a simplicity that mimics the ontological simplicity of God: as God gives birth to her in creation, she allows herself
to be born; as God looks at her, she simply looks at God. And this
is why the beatitude implies that the person whose heart is pure will
"see" God. There are in such a soul no distractions, no distortions, no
obstacles; there is only knowing and being known, seeing and being
seen. It is in this context that we can understand the almost universal
description of the saints, despite their differences in personality and
despite the sometimes tumultuous upheaval of their lives, as "simple"
and "serene." The saint is someone whose heart is "clean" and who
hence radiates the simpleness and peacefulness of God even in the
least peaceful of circumstances.

The next beatitude, "Happy are the peacemakers: they shall be
called the children of God," is richly amplified in the course of the
Sermon itself. Once more it spells out an implication of living out
of the divine center, in this case enormous transformative power at
the interpersonal and societal levels. The beatitude places emphasis,
not so much on the peacefulness of the centered person, as on his
peace-*making* quality. The one who has broken through the illusion
of sin is capable of creating an environment conducive to peace, a
place where the compassion and nonviolence of the *magna anima* can
flourish.

The Sermon on the Mount comes to its rhetorical high point with
the radical assertion, "You have heard it said 'an eye for an eye and
a tooth for a tooth' but now I tell you do not take revenge on some-

one who wrongs you. If someone slaps you on the right cheek, turn
and give him the other. And if someone takes you to court for your
shirt, let him have your coat as well. And if one of the occupation
troops presses you into service for a mile, go with him two" (Matt.
5:38–42). Nowhere perhaps do we feel more acutely the sting of Jesus'
judgment than in these words, for they so dramatically contradict the
received wisdom of the *pusilla anima*. The "justice" that the sinful
mind demands — violence for violence, outrage for outrage — is explicitly judged by Jesus since it does not flow from the compassion
place that is the center. Proceeding as it does from the fortress of the
self-elevating ego, this phony justice simply fosters more division and
more hatred, as both the playground bully and the practitioner of su-
perpower *Realpolitik* know. To fight fire with fire simply confirms the
illusion of separation produced by sin. Or, as Gandhi put it, "An eye
for an eye, making the whole world blind."

Is Jesus therefore recommending a turning away from injustice and
violence in an attitude of passive acquiescence? A careful attention to
the language of Christ shows that this is hardly the case. In his remarkable books on the "powers," Walter Wink has demonstrated the
properly provocative quality of Jesus' sayings in the Sermon.[95] It is
certainly clear, he argues, that Christ urges his followers away from
the path of violent resistance to evil, but he by no means advocates
a "flight" from injustice, a cowardly turning away from evil. Such a
course would, like the way of violent resistance, only confirm the aggressive person in his injustice. Passivity in the face of hatred amounts,
once again, to the acceptance of an illusion. Rather, in calling for us to
turn the other cheek and hand over our shirts and go the extra mile,
Jesus is, in fact, advocating a provocative, "in-your-face" challenge
to evil.

Wink reminds us that, in Jesus' time, the left hand, considered unclean, would never be used to gesture in any way in a social context.
Accordingly, if someone were to slap another on the *right* cheek, he
would be striking with the back of his right hand. But such a move
was a sign of contempt, since the back of the hand was used by a
superior to show his dominance over someone of an inferior class
or status, as a husband would hit his wife or a master his slave.

Thus, given the social setting of the Sermon, the opening phrase of Jesus' famous dictum could be translated: "if someone treats you aggressively as an inferior. . . . " And then the recommendation to turn the other cheek takes on great significance. If someone demeans you and violently affirms his superiority, Jesus implies, position yourself in such a way that he cannot continue to do so. When one turns the other cheek, he clearly precludes the possibility of being struck with the back of the hand and thus he announces his refusal to cooperate with the injustice that the aggressor perpetrates. This is not fighting, but it is certainly not fleeing. It is standing confidently and courageously in the face of violence and proclaiming one's refusal to accept it and its presuppositions. The turner of the other cheek tells the aggressor that the world in which one person can dominate another is a false world, and his unexpected gesture helps to lift the veil, to dissipate the shadows. By refusing either to fight or to flee, one becomes, moreover, a most effective mirror held up to the aggressor. By neither justifying the violence nor avoiding it, the follower of Jesus' recommendation compels the violent one to see and feel what he does, to sense painfully the implications of living in the confines of the *pusilla anima*. At the very least, the victim refuses to live in the realm of illusion, and, at best, he helps the victimizer out of his delusion.

Walter Wink offers a particularly illuminating example of the multifaceted power of Jesus' way. The young Bishop Desmond Tutu, long before he emerged as a world figure, was making his way along a narrow wooden sidewalk in South Africa. He came suddenly face to face with a white racist who was proceeding in the opposite direction. "Move off the sidewalk!" the man said, "I don't give way to gorillas." Unfazed, Tutu calmly stepped out of the way, gestured broadly for his tormentor to pass and said, "Ah, yes, but I do."[96] His humorous words, of course, carried a sting and signalled his nonviolent yet courageous refusal to live in the world produced by the fearful ego. His "turning of the other cheek" was hardly passive; it was rather unnerving, unsettling, deeply challenging.

What is wonderful is that we have seen, in our own century, remarkable examples of the power of Jesus' provocative third way.

Gandhi in India, Martin Luther King in the United States, Tutu him-self in South Africa, John Paul II in Poland all practiced a form of Jesus' nonviolent noncooperation with evil. The fact that all four of them prevailed against some of the greatest powers on earth proves that Christ's way is not the program of a dreamy idealist but rather the canny and effective strategy of the *magna anima*.

Jesus sums up his teaching on this score with the still disturbing words: "You have learned how it was said, 'You must love your neigh-bor and hate your enemy.' But I say this to you: love your enemies and pray for those who persecute you." It should be clear that this "love" of one's tormentor has nothing to do with bland sentimentality or passivity. It is instead a "harsh and dreadful" thing, a willingness to stand provocatively in the face of evil in order to transform it. Only the properly centered person, only the one who is rooted in the divine ground, has the capacity to endure the storm of oppo-sition and resistance that will ensue. But more to the point, only that person has the compassion requisite even to make the effort. We remember how immediately after the sin of Eden enemies sud-denly sprang up: nature and human beings, man and woman, human beings and God all became antagonists. Clinging gave rise to fear, and fear gave rise to objectification and distantiation — and all of it proceeded from the illusion of the self-elevating ego. Thus when Jesus pronounces blessed those who love their enemies, that is to say, those who seek to turn enemies into friends, he does so much more than make an idealist ethical recommendation. He declares the fun-damental instinct of Eden illusory and thus hastens the arrival of a new world.

There is no need to dwell at length on the final beatitude — "Happy those who are persecuted in the cause of right: theirs is the kingdom of heaven" — since we have explored it implicitly under the heading of Jesus' judgment. What Jesus states is that those who live in the new *ordo*, who see aright in accord with the *magna anima* will be, not only resented or opposed, but actively persecuted. They will be, like Jesus himself, hunted down and pursued, even to the point of torture, imprisonment, and death. But this very persecution, as we have seen, is a source of joy since it precipitates the breakthrough of the Kingdom. If one is living his life in such a way that he is admired by all and fully at home in the world, he is living, almost certainly, in the realm of illusion. When his lifestyle awakens the resentment and opposition of his neighbors, he is most likely moving toward the divine *ordo*. In Plato's parable of the cave, the hero escapes from his chains and discovers that he and his fellows have been living in a realm of shadows. He climbs up into the bright light of the real world and re-turns to share the liberating good news with his former colleagues. Much to his chagrin and surprise, he is met, not with enthusiastic acceptance, but with derision and finally persecution. Most of us pre-fer the comfort of our illusions to the challenging novelty of the real. Hence the one being lured into Jesus' new Kingdom of freedom must be ready to accept the hatred of those who prefer their chains. W. H. Auden knew that "we'd rather be ruined than changed / We'd rather die in our dread than mount the cross of the moment and let our illusions die."

What we see in the Sermon, in sum, is an opening up of a new spir-itual space. We witness the coming together of divinity and humanity in such a way that the latter is elevated, expanded, and fully real-ized precisely in surrender to the former. What appears is the world in which both the supreme being and the supreme ego — in all of their prickly defensiveness and exclusivity — have been dethroned. What is revealed is the joyful ecstasy that is the true meaning of both divine and human existence.

Many have commented over the centuries on the utopian idealism, the practical impossibility, of the Sermon on the Mount. How could anyone realistically live out its demands and expectations? But these objections come from the perspective of the *pusilla anima*, from that frame of mind that cannot imagine a world other than the blocky antagonistic one produced by sin. To appreciate the power of the Ser-mon, one must undergo *metanoia*, shifting one's consciousness and escaping from the cave of fearful illusion. When one enters into the flow of sheer relationality, when one realizes that real freedom and power come from letting go, then one sees the demands of the Ser-mon, not as demands at all, but as descriptions of a new world, heady wine for new wine skins. The Misfit had it right: either we remain in the violent world of sin (finding pleasure in killing) or we throw away everything and imitate Christ. Having shown us the way, having opened up a new humanity, Jesus compels us to follow him. He has come not for the healthy but for the sick. His judgment is diagnosis; his radiant display of the new mind is the profoundest doctoring of the soul.

Chapter Thirteen

JESUS THE REVEALER OF THE TRUE GOD

Christmas, Chalcedon, and the Cross

How can Jesus be both judge of a fallen humanity and the paradigm of a new humanity? He can play this dual role because, in the deepest sense, he discloses to us the God who is really God. As we have repeatedly emphasized throughout this book, false conceptions of the human and the divine are correlative: the more we misconstrue ourselves, the more we misconstrue the nature of God and vice versa. Jesus can reveal who we most authentically are precisely in the measure that he discloses who God authentically is. In his own person, Jesus breaks the twin idols produced by the *pusilla anima:* the phantoms of a separate ego and a supreme being.

We have argued that the God who unravels sin is the strange and unexpected sacred who can be named only in a bipolar way. The divine that is both immanent and transcendent, both sovereign and humble, both serene and creative is the power that alone can frustrate the sinner's desire either to grasp or to hide. The ego fortress is undone, we concluded, only by the God who is described as Being itself and Love. What I want to make clear now is that this conception of God comes, not from philosophers (though it can be given philosophical expression) and not from mythology (though it is to some degree in continuity with the mythological imagination), but rather from Jesus Christ. It was in relation to him that the first Christians realized the height and depth and breadth of the love of God, the ranginess and surprise of the divine existence. It is not as though Jesus simply gave vivid expression to the Old Testament idea of the sacred; rather he

195

revolutionized that idea, turned it on its head, revealed its inadequacy. And all of this turning around and breaking open occurred in the event that Christians, with a sort of disarming laconicism, refer to as the Incarnation, the enfleshment of God. Let us look at this phenomenon first from a biblical standpoint and then from a doctrinal point of view hoping to see what it is exactly that Christians learned about God from the "coming-together" that occurred in Jesus of Nazareth. In so doing, we perceive how the event of the Incarnation is the richest "salve" for the soul.

We have already seen how the judging power of Jesus is emphasized even in the stories of his birth. Now we want to explore how these accounts, in a richly symbolic way, disclose something of the salvifically bipolar nature of the divine. Let us look first at Luke's detailed and theologically subtle narrative (Luke 2:1–20). "Now at this time Caesar Augustus issued a decree for a census of the whole world to be taken." Luke puts his reader in exalted company and in a cosmic context. We are in the presence of Caesar Augustus, the most powerful man in the world, the one whose armies controlled the Mediterranean basin and whose thoughts and wishes determined the movements of millions. And we hear that this potentate has decreed a census, not of one province or city, but of "the whole world." His reach, his authority seem to know no bounds. In accord with this decree, a newly married couple from a tiny town in a dusty outpost of the mighty empire make their way to the Davidic village of Bethlehem. And there, as the Scriptures had predicted, the Messiah is born.

What does this teach us of God? Even the most powerful person in the world, even the king of kings, even the mighty Roman emperor acts, mysteriously, according to the plan of God. It appeared to be an arbitrary decree, an expression of the sovereign will of the ruler of the world, but in fact it was a chess move in the elaborate game of God. Precisely here, in the preparation for Incarnation, we find most emphatically stated the sovereignty, serenity, and self-sufficiency of the divine. No one or no thing is forcing the hand of the almighty;

on the contrary, even the greatest powers on the earth are operating according to his designs and intentions.

When the divine child is born, an angel appears to shepherds who are keeping night watch in the fields, and the "glory" of the Lord shone around them. As is invariably the case in Scripture, the recipients of this angelic manifestation are "terrified." Angels — those beings who stand close to the face of God, sharing far more intensely than we in the heat and light of the sacred — symbolize the terrible majesty of the divine, its sublimity and awesomeness. Angels are transcendent realities, agents that go beyond the confines of this realm of experience, and, accordingly, they speak of the universal reach of the divine authority. God works not only through the most powerful figures on earth but through the extraterrestrial powers as well. And this sublime authority is even more stunningly revealed: "and suddenly with the angel there was a great throng of the heavenly host, praising God and singing: 'Glory to God in the highest heaven.'" Like the angels in Dante's vision of the heavenly empyrean, these Bethlehem angels cluster together forming an intense circle of light and sound — a living icon of the divine glory. Would it ever have occurred to any of the shepherds to question, control, limit, or manipulate the divine power that was thus disclosed to them? Would any of them have doubted its sovereignty and sublimity? Did they not, in fact, assume attitudes of awed respect and obedience in its presence? ("Let us go to Bethlehem and see this thing that has happened which the Lord has made known to us.") Once more, precisely in and around the event of God's enfleshment, we see overwhelmingly powerful symbolic allusions to the serenity, self-sufficiency, and sovereignty of God.

But, and here is the poetic tension of the account, these clear references to the otherness and strangeness of God are coupled with the most remarkable descriptions of God's intimacy with us. When the humble mother arrives in the city of David, she gives birth to a son and "wraps him in swaddling clothes." The mighty power of God has descended upon the earth — an event that had, in various inchoate ways, been fearfully anticipated for centuries — and it appears as a tiny, helpless infant, powerless, utterly dependent, indeed tied up. The God who works through the cosmic powers and through the greatest of earthly authorities allows himself to be wrapped in the swaddling clothes of our frail humanity. As many commentators have pointed out, the bands wrapped around the infant Christ foreshadow, dreadfully, the burial cloths that will one day encircle his crucified body. At Bethlehem, God enters, by anticipation, into all that frightens and shocks us, all that hems us in. What is clear through this symbol of the Christ child is that the self-sufficiency of the divine by no means excludes the passion of God for the world and its suffering. Being itself creeps into the crevices of the human condition, into its darkest and most terrifying places.

And then he is laid in a manger, the rude place where the animals eat. It was Luther who commented that the humility of God is no more dramatically revealed than in the *Krippe Christi*, the crib of the Christ child. God becomes a little baby, but, more to the point, a baby who offers himself as food for the world. Stooping down from the heights of his self-sufficiency, God deigns to feed the universe with his very self, to be, in the strictest sense, devoured. As becomes blazingly clear especially in the Johannine Gospel, there is nothing harmless about Jesus' offer of himself as bread for the life of the world. In conformity with the realism of the language, he will be consumed, chewed up, swallowed. Once more, the seemingly innocent Infancy narrative foreshadows the dying of Christ on the cross, the moment when he becomes, in the richest sense, nourishment for the world.

And a similar tensiveness is apparent when we turn to one of the best-loved details of the Christmas story found in the Matthean account (Matt. 2:1–12). *Magoi* from the East see the rising of a star, and they know that it announces the birth of a great king. Prompted by this cosmic sign, they set out on a long journey to see the child and pay him homage. The initiative, as always, is the sovereign God's. They had been searching the skies and longing for a portent, but it is only when God is ready to disclose himself that they see. And what they see is, like the angelic vision at Bethlehem, an indication of the all-embracing, cosmic scope of the divine authority, for God uses, not only earthly events and personages, but heavenly displays to reveal his purposes. There is nothing that escapes the press of his power, nothing that cannot be brought under his provident direction. But what do these *magoi* discover after having followed the cosmic sacrament of the self-sufficient God? They find, not a worldly potentate, not the heir to wealth and political power, but a helpless infant in the arms of his humble and somewhat puzzled mother. The God who commands the heavens is a baby too powerless to speak. And then they open their gifts: gold for a king, frankincense for God, and myrrh for the one who will die. The first two offerings witness to the serenity, sovereignty, and self-sufficiency of the power that is disclosed here, and the last speaks of its humility, passion, and creativity. They see in this child, with a sort of inchoate intuition, that the King and God who rules the planets is willing to go into the darkness of godforsakenness out of love. Once more, the story of Incarnation bristles with the language and imagery of bipolar extremism.

And what happens to the reader in the presence of these stories is, once again, metanoetic. The God who is disclosed in the unheard of event of the Incarnation is one who, in the most dramatic sense, cannot be grasped (for he controls the stars, the angels, and the most powerful forces in the world) and cannot be avoided (for he becomes in the humblest way one of us, stooping to the lowest position). The God, whose bipolar tensiveness was hinted at on Sinai and throughout the Old Testament experience, is now revealed as unsurpassably immanent and transcendent, supreme and lowly. And in response, one can do only what the shepherds and the *magoi* do: bow down in surrender to such a power. Curiously, however, the surrender of the shepherds and the kings involves a tensive stance, both above and below the one they worship. In one sense, these adults are superior to the tiny baby (for God has taken the lowest position) and in another sense they are inferior to him (for God is revealed precisely here as sovereign majesty). They tower over him *and* they offer him homage. This strange attitude — neither controlling nor avoiding, neither overwhelming nor ignoring — is the proper stance of the soul vis-à-vis the sacred. The soul had been crippled at Eden; the doctoring begins in earnest at Bethlehem.

※

Most Christians naturally and spontaneously enter into the dynamics of the Christmas stories, but few, I would wager, feel attracted to the stark and conceptual Christological formulations of the Council of Chalcedon. Yet a very similar point is being made in both writings: the God of the Incarnation is too strange for the sinner. Both celebrate the frustrating and illuminating bipolarity of which we have so consistently spoken. Let us turn to an examination of this famous formula of faith in the hopes of uncovering its spiritual and transformative purpose.

Within the confines of this book, we cannot examine in a detailed way the historical setting for the Chalcedonian doctrine. Suffice it to say that it came at the end of a long period of debate and discussion in the early church concerning the nature and salvific significance of Jesus Christ. To simplify somewhat, two camps battled for supremacy over the course of two centuries: one placing greater emphasis on the humanity of the Lord and the other on his divinity. Arius, the fourth-century heresiarch, proposed a sort of compromise according to which Jesus is somewhat divine and somewhat human. Arius's position, to give it its due, had a certain coherency in the context of the ancient world, since it was borrowed from a mythological framework. In the legends of the Greeks, many gods and goddesses "mixed themselves" with humans producing all sorts of divine/human hybrids, quasi- and demigods. Arius proposed to his Hellenistic-Christian world a similar theory of the mingling of nature and supernature.

Of course it was the Council of Nicea that famously refuted Arius's view with the counterclaim that Jesus is *homoousios* with God, "one in being" with the Father, not a demigod but fully divine. In the wake of Nicea, the debate continued to rage, Arians and semi-Arians fighting defenders of *homoousian* orthodoxy, such as Athanasius the bishop of Alexandria. At the center of the controversy was the nagging problem of relating the true and complete divinity of Jesus with his undoubted humanity. How could these two come together without contradiction, compromise, or mutual exclusion? At the Council of Chalcedon in 451, Christian bishops and theologians of both the East and the West met to resolve the difficulty, and their statement of belief has emerged as a sort of classic expression of Christian faith on the question of the ontology of Jesus. It is interesting to note that the Chalcedonian fathers provided, not so much a philosophical *expla-nation* of how the divine and human come together in Christ, as an ecstatic proclamation, born of faith.[97] Standing in the rich tradition stretching back to the Scriptures and the first witnesses to Christ, they gave voice to the fundamental Christian conviction that, in Jesus, di-vinity and humanity coexist in a noncompetitive way and that, as we have often emphasized, the fullness of each is revealed precisely in their coexistence.

The "definition" of Christ offered at Chalcedon can be stated rather briefly:

> One and the same Christ, Son, Lord, Only begotten, made known in two natures which exist without confusion, without change, without division, without separation; the difference of the natures having been in no wise taken away by reason of the union, but rather the properties of each being preserved, and both concurring into one Person and one *hypostasis* — not parted or divided into two persons, but one and the same Son and Only-begotten, the divine Logos, the Lord Jesus Christ.[98]

The first, and in some sense elemental, affirmation of this statement is the oneness of Christ. In Jesus we are dealing, not with two things or two persons, but with one basic reality or power of existence. And it is this unified ground that the Council fathers identify as the divine person of the Logos. In the language of Greek metaphysics, "person" refers to an instantiation of a rational nature, the specification and concrete expression of an abstract form. Thus the "person" of Socrates is a particular focusing of the general species of humanity, the recep-tacle, if you will, into which the form of human being is poured in his case; it is that which makes Socrates this one individual and iden-tifiable human being. The center and source of unity in Jesus is the divine "person" of the Logos, but there is a key difference with re-gard to Christ, for his person bears or instantiates, not one nature, but two — and here we see the real novelty of the Chalcedonian for-mula. No Greek philosopher would speak of a single person bearing multiple natures, though it was a commonplace to hold that a single nature could be instantiated in multiple persons, as Plato, Aristotle, and Socrates are all instances of the one nature of humanity. As is so often the case, Christian dogmatic language twists and breaks the language of philosophy even as it uses it. In Jesus, one person "lights up" two distinct natures, divine and human, allowing both to come to expression in all of their distinctiveness and uniqueness. Accordingly, Jesus is fully human, that is to say, in possession of a human body, mind, will, and passion, as well as subject to all of the characteristic limitations of being a creature. As Karl Rahner points out, despite the union of natures spoken of at Chalcedon, Jesus remains a creature who confronts the divine across an infinite abyss. The ontologically limited and culturally determined humanity of Jesus is not overwhelmed or swallowed by his divinity.

But Jesus is also in possession of a divine nature, that is to say, of all that characterizes and renders distinctive the being of God. In him, the sacred reality that transcends the universe and yet pours itself out in creative love, is alive, operative, personally present. And the onto-logical proximity of the human nature of Jesus does not compromise or overwhelm this divinity. He is not a demigod or a lesser divinity, but rather "fully divine." As the surprising formula states it, the two natures — human and divine — exist in personal union, but without "confusion, change, separation or division."

On the surface of it, what is being proposed here is nonsense. How can two mutually exclusive realities — one finite, the other infi-nite — come together as one? It seems as though this formula violates the most elemental principle of logic, the law of noncontradiction. What is being proposed here, to borrow the language of Hans Urs von Balthasar, is a "theo-logic," a new way of thinking about the real based upon an ecstatic sense of who God truly is. We saw that one of the chief effects of the originating sin is the tendency to objectify the divine. Once we have established our egos as sovereign and cen-tral, God necessarily appears as a supreme being, either threatening or irrelevant. From the standpoint of the self-elevating *pusilla anima*, God is a being with whom we have, at best, an extrinsic relationship; he is "out there" and "over and against us." To be sure, this attitude born of sin affects decisively the way we think theologically: we can-not imagine that God is the immanent/transcendent ground in whom we find our own center. We cannot conceive of the intimacy with the sacred that can be ours. And consequently, we find it terribly difficult to accept the ecstatic metaphysical poetry of Chalcedon, the language of divine/human unity.

But, from the standpoint of *metanoia,* from the perspective of the new mind, we see that God is not a competing supreme being, but the power whose very closeness to us enhances our humanity, whose very proximity makes us most fully ourselves. And we see, at the same time, that God is a reality that can work its way into every corner of creation without ceasing to be itself. In a word the "natures" of God and creation can come together without compromise and contradiction, precisely because God is not a being but the mysterious power of Being itself. The Chalcedonian fathers proclaim, in their sober philosophical language, the undoing of Eden; they see as reality what the sinful mind can appreciate only as illusion or nonsense. And this new vision, these new eyes, *come from Jesus Christ,* from the God/human intimacy that is his very being. In the startling and unique way of being that was Christ's, the first believers glimpsed the theonomy that was offered but lost at Eden, that was held out alluringly throughout the Old Testament, that indirectly animated and gave purpose to all the finest expressions of the religious imagination of humanity.

Let us make this a bit more explicit with regard to the reality of God. We see, in the Chalcedonian formulation, the unheard of closeness of God to the world. What we have termed the creativity, passion, and humility of the sacred are clearly on display in the language of hypostatic union. In Christ we see just how low the divine can stoop — even to the point of "becoming" what is not divine. What is perhaps less obvious is the equal, though implicit, emphasis on the transcendence of God that is contained in Chalcedon. The realm of finitude is characterized by mutual exclusion. One finite thing is defined, appropriately, over and against all those other things that it is not: to be a particular chair is *not* to be any other chair or any other thing. More to the point, one finite reality cannot become another without some radical change taking place: a chair becomes a table or is reduced to ashes only by ceasing to be a chair; a wildebeest "becomes" a leopard only by being devoured. Because of the mutual exclusivity that marks all limited things, relationship between them is always difficult if not dangerous.

But the Council of Chalcedon boldly proclaims that, in Christ, two natures, divine and human, come together in personal unity in such a way that one can speak of God becoming a creature. Yet this becoming in no way compromises the integrity of the natures; nothing is ceded either on the part of God or on the part of the human nature of Jesus. But this entails that *God is not in any sense a worldly nature, decidedly not a finite form.* If God were a thing alongside of others, a supreme being among beings, then the union of God with a creature would be possible only through some radical compromise of either God's or the creature's ontology. As in mythological conceptions, the divine would have to supplant or push out some dimension of the nondivine as it makes its way into the world. But it is just this notion, just this style of thinking, that is consciously rejected at Chalcedon in favor of a properly "theo-logical" solution. The God who can establish the intimacy with the race experienced in Jesus Christ must be, not any sort of being, but a power of existence that, in the most dramatic sense possible, transcends finitude. God must be, not a being, but Being itself. And therefore, like the Infancy narratives, this formula implies the serenity, self-sufficiency, and sovereignty of God just as surely as it implies the tensive qualities of God's humility, creativity, and passion. The bipolarity hinted at on Sinai in the revelation of the burning bush now comes to full expression: the God capable of hypostatic union is very strange indeed, strange enough to save us from our sins.

The God of the Incarnation is thus the power that "throws everything off," that calls into question everything we assumed about the structure of reality. We live, not in a world of division, presided over by the supreme being, but rather in a universe of interrelationship and "charged with the grandeur of God." God can become one of us, and therefore our minds have to change; the Word has been made flesh, and *metanoia* is the only valid response.

What we have uncovered in both the Infancy narratives and the Chalcedonian doctrine is the revelation of God as a tensive play of immanence and transcendence, as Being itself. At the end of part 2 we showed how the Christian tradition sees the connection between this relatively provisional name and the truest or highest name of God as love. Love is that attitude that is both passionate and freeing, both self-sufficient and intimately involved with the other, beyond arbitrariness and manipulation. Like the conviction that God is Being itself, the conviction that God *is* love comes from Jesus Christ, but more specifically, from the climactic and defining event of Christ's life: his death on the cross. It was Martin Kähler who commented that the Gospels are passion narratives with long introductions, hinting thereby that the central preoccupation of the earliest Christian writers was what happened at the end of Christ's life. The drama surrounding his passion, his dying, and his rising was, from the beginning, the focal point of Christian contemplation and the ground for the deepest and most characteristically Christian belief that love is God's truest name. It is upon this breakthrough happening, this scandalous revelation that we will now concentrate.

As we have discussed, Jesus was a problem, an annoyance, a thorn in the flesh. As the living embodiment of God's *ordo*, Jesus shook the disorder of the sinful world. And therefore it is no surprise that this judging quality, from the beginning of his ministry, oriented him to the cross. As many have indicated, one does not have to hold to Jesus' divine omniscience to explain his foreknowledge of his terrible end: any perceptive observer of the religious or political scene could have seen what was in store for him, given his countercultural and disturbing work. Jesus was indeed rejected by everyone — his most intimate followers, his countrymen, people of all political stripes and persuasions, the Roman occupiers — because his light was incompatible with all forms of darkness.[99] In this sense, the cross was nothing but the consequence of his convictions, his cutting words, his divine judgment on sinful humanity.

But the first Christians saw something more in the cross, something awful and strange: it was not simply a human tragedy, but rather the climax of a kind of divine comedy. At the deepest level, the cross was the reason for the Incarnation, the "place" to which God longed to go, the throne that he wished to mount. As Jesus says so often in the Gospels, the passion is the "hour" for which he came, the undoubted climax of his life and ministry, that indispensable element in his work of revelation. And more to the point, this hour is appreciated as something *that God the Father wants.* The cross does not simply happen to Jesus as an unfortunate and tragic accident; rather, it is, in a mysterious way, willed by God precisely as the *telos* or goal of his self-disclosure.[100] As we have argued, Jesus is the judge of a disordered world and the paradigm of the *magna anima,* but his commonest self-designation is, undoubtedly, "the one sent by the Father." Jesus recognizes himself as the obedient servant, the one sent into the world to do the will of the Father, and this will is that he come, finally, to the cross. There is an awful "necessity" concerning the dying of Jesus, almost a predestined certainty, a terrible "must" that comes, not finally from human beings and their sin, but from God the Father and his demand.

And we see this same theme in Paul and the early fathers of the church. If the Gospels are passion narratives with long introductions, the Pauline epistles are abstract kerygmatic proclamations of the passion with practically no introduction. Paul seems almost blithely indifferent to the words and works of Jesus, concentrating almost exclusively on the power flowing from his cross and resurrection: "I preach one thing: Christ and him crucified." If God has spoken in Christ, it is from the cross; if there was a "reason" for his coming, it was the paschal mystery of his dying and rising. Giving voice to a patristic commonplace, Leo the Great says "nec alia fuit Dei Filio causa nacendi quam ut cruci possit affigi." (There was no other reason for the Son of God being born than that he might be fixed to a cross.)[101] In other words, the agency that presided over both the Incarnation and the passion was the same: the divine will. Oddly, almost scandalously, the dying of Jesus is appreciated as something that God the Father desires; it is seen as a sacrifice that is "pleasing" to him. How can we make sense of this?

Jesus was the bearer of the divine presence, the bringer of God's healing and forgiving love. Where and to whom did he carry this power? By his own admission, Jesus went, not to those who are well but to those who are sick. He went especially to those who felt far from God: sinners, the poor, the despised, the outcast, the crippled, the hopeless. Jesus' mission — his deepest sense of self — was to bring the love and mercy of God precisely to the godforsaken. Christ was the Father's outreach in love to those who were alienated, for whatever reason, from the divine mercy. Consequently, he identified himself as the good shepherd, the one who abandons the ninety-nine who are safe to find the one who is lost, and as the woman who sweeps the entire house in order to find the one lost coin. But what is the place that is furthest from God? What is the condition of soul that is most godforsaken? It is the house of death. The fear of dying and the fact of dying are the greatest prompts to sin, for they compel us most powerfully to cling to ourselves. Horrified at the prospect of annihilation, we furiously and relentlessly reinforce the castle keeps of our egos, filling them with food and drink and gold, defending them against all enemies. Under the shadow of death, we cower and brood; in the ice of the fear of death, we stand immobilized and weeping. This dark, cold, and dreadfully defended castle is the terrible place that is furthest from the love of God, and it is to that place, consequently, that the Son of God, in the thoroughness of his *kenosis*, is sent.

What most besets us, what stands most awfully between ourselves and God, what practically compels the curving in on the self that is the essence of sin, is the fear of death. And hence it is into that fear that the Word of God journeys. All of Christ's sallyings forth into sickness, alienation, self-righteousness, and poverty are but preliminaries to the final assault on the stronghold of death itself. It is as though he moves first through the outer defenses, that is, the myriad effects of sin, before coming to the citadel: the origin of all sin which is the terror of dying. And how does he fight? He fights by bringing to these dark corners the light of the divine compassion. He walks calmly into those places that are — so it seems — at the furthest remove from God, and simply brings the divine presence; he approaches those who are — so they think — most alienated from the sacred, and he throws around them the everlasting arms of the divine mercy. In the words of Flannery O'Connor's Misfit, the one caught in the trap of the small soul, he "raises the dead . . . and he shouldn't have done that."

Read "liturgically" the event of the cross begins on Holy Thursday night. Jesus gathers his disciples around him and — reading John and the Synoptics together here — performs two characteristic and symbolic acts. First, he identifies himself with bread shared and with wine poured out as a libation, and, second, he bends low and performs the servile act of washing his friends' feet. In both acts, Jesus signifies the downward trajectory of his mission: he is the one who has been sent from the very heart of God to go to the lowest places (literally, under our feet). His very life is food and drink for others; his very soul is self-emptying service. The Lord and Master — the one who is equal to God — does not deem equality something to be grasped at and becomes instead the slave of all.

The movement downward continues in the garden of Gethsemane. Here the mission of service becomes clearer: he is to take on, to feel from within, the rejection, aloneness, and alienation of the sinner. He begins the process of, in Paul's still shocking language, *becoming sin.* Accordingly, he isolates himself even from his most trusted followers — Peter, James, and John — and in solitude throws himself on the ground. Aloneness is the typical condition of the sinner, the one who has lost the center and hence the sense of connectedness to all things. Like Dante's Satan, the sinner is condemned to a sort of solitary confinement, locked up in the prison of his own fear. And the feeling of being pressed to the earth, weighed down, is also typical of the sinner. We saw in the *Divine Comedy* that the saved and the angels fly, taking themselves, as Chesterton indicated, so lightly, whereas the damned and those on the lower levels of purgatory move, if at all, slowly and painfully. Fear is a sort of weight that keeps one nailed firmly in place, unable to soar. And so Jesus, alone and face down, assumes symbolically the attitude of sin.

And more to the point, as he contemplates what he must endure, he feels the weight of God's demand pressing on him and enters into the psychological state of the sinner. As we saw in our discussion of Eden, the one who has fallen feels the divine demand, not as the expression of his own deepest liberty, but as an outside imposition, the terrible intrusion of a lawgiver and judge. So Jesus, sweating blood in the garden of Gethsemane, feels something of this sinner's anguish. The Father's will is beginning to appear to him as alien, a heteronomous outrage. In submitting to it only after a struggle, the Son shows his awful solidarity with us poor banished children of Eve for whom the acceptance of God's will is almost always painful. In the spiritual and theological literature of the tradition, it has been suggested by some that Jesus in the garden feels the *poena damni* (the suffering of the damned) and the *timor gehennalis* (fear of Hell). Others maintain that, given his intense unity with the Father, it would be inappropriate to speak straightforwardly of such a dramatic experience of separation from God. They prefer to say it is "as though" Christ sensed the suffering and fear of Hell.

With Hans Urs von Balthasar, I would hold that the Gospel writers know nothing of the "as if" quality of Christ's abandonment.[102] What he begins to experience in Gethsemane is the depression and terror that follow from God-abandonment; the Son, out of love, is truly entering into the fear of separation that marks all of us sinners. And we must not interpret away the anxiety of Christ in a monophysite direction, as though Jesus, in his humanity, did not confront the dark abyss of what lay ahead of him, as if he knew perfectly well that all would turn out for the best. The drama and saving significance of Gethsemane are lost if the Son of God did not personally experience the very sadness and terror of the human sinner before the uncertainty of life. We must not look too quickly to the "meaning" of Gethsemane, for its deepest significance is the real confrontation of God with the meaninglessness that bedevils us.

At the climax of the Gethsemane scene, Jesus is confronted by Judas and the mob who have come to arrest him. In the wonderfully ambiguous gesture of the kiss, Judas both reverences Jesus and hands him over to the temple guard. The word *paradidonai* (to hand over, to betray) appears numerous times and in various grammatical forms in the Passion accounts: the temple guards *hand him over* to the Sanhedrin who *hand him over* to Pilate who *hands him over* to be scourged and who finally *hands him over* to be crucified. Throughout the events leading up to his death, Jesus is tossed around like a plaything, becoming increasingly passive and silent, incapable of disposing of himself.[103] Here he once again enters into the spiritual and psychological world of the sinner. Having lost the link to the divine, the sinner is without anchor, "tossed about" from influence to influence, from person to person, never able confidently to take hold of his life. Jesus identifies with this splintered consciousness as he is repeatedly "betrayed." But there is something even stranger and more awful at work here. The ultimate betrayer of Jesus is neither Judas nor the high priest nor the Sanhedrin nor the Romans, but rather the Father. If Jesus is the one sent by the Father to go into the godforsakenness of the sinner, then the Father "rejects" him, turns his back on him, delivers him over to his torturers and murderers. In the terrible language of Scripture, God does not "spare" his only Son but gives him over for our sake. Just as in the Old Testament narratives Yahweh delivered Israel over to its enemies on account of its sins, so the Father delivers over the Son who "becomes" sin. Jesus himself signals the priority of the Father's handing over in his dialogue with Pilate. The Roman governor, in a menacing tone, reminds the helpless criminal that he has the power to release him or crucify him, and Jesus laconically replies that Pilate would have no power over him unless it had been granted "from above." The earthly betrayers are, in the deepest sense, but the agents of the Father's desire that the Son go into godforsakenness. We must not, of course, literalize this symbol in an emotional direction, as if the Father hates the Son, engaging in a sort of divine child abuse. On the contrary, we see in this motif of divine "betrayal" the willingness of God to break his own heart out of love, to enter personally into the experience of being alienated from God.

After the garden, the betrayals, the trials, and the scourging, Jesus is led to crucifixion. It is worth reiterating the frankly horrible quality of this form of execution, for our constant exposure to depictions of the crucifixion have dulled our sensitivity to its terror. For the first several centuries of Christianity, Christ crucified was never represented artistically for the brutal reality of crucifixion was still too fresh and vibrant in people's minds. Nailed through in acutely sensitive areas, the crucified experienced intense pain, but this discomfort was exacerbated, becoming literally excruciating (*ex cruce*, from the cross), when he was compelled to get his breath by rocking his body up and down on the pivots of his pierced wrists and feet. This torture went on and on, sometimes for several days, until the unfortunate crucified one, utterly worn out from the effort, was unable to draw himself up to breathe. Thus crucifixion amounted to a dreadfully painful and agonizingly slow asphyxiation. It is no wonder that the Romans permitted this form of execution only for the worst criminals and never for a citizen of the empire; and it is hardly surprising that the Jews considered someone crucified to be especially accursed of God.

We can sense some of the horror surrounding crucifixion in Paul's famous kenotic hymn in the letter to the Philippians: "It was thus that he humbled himself, accepting death, even death on a cross" (Phil. 2:8). We can almost hear Paul lowering his voice as he evokes the worst imaginable form of death with those final words. It is into this limit case of physical torment that the Son of God goes. One of the dangers of our pious representations of the cross is prettification, putting, as Goethe said ironically, roses around the cross. The spare, understated accounts of Christ's death in the Gospels do not justify such a spiritualizing banalization of the awful event. When we strip away the roses from the cross, we see with much greater clarity the nightmare of physical suffering which the heart of God took on. But what was the purpose of this identification? One of the most powerful occasions of sin is the agony of physical suffering. When we are in physical pain, we have the tendency to turn in on ourselves defensively and fearfully, even to doubt the mercy of a God who could allow such suffering. Moving into our pain so dramatically, the Son of God "divinizes" even this state, showing that it is not a place untouched by the divine presence. Instead of using suffering as an occasion to repudiate God, we can see it as a place of springs, precisely because it is a place into which God himself has gone.

This physical agony of Christ is only an aspect of the whole, but a corner of the icon of the cross. At the darkest heart of the event of the cross is Jesus' feeling of total abandonment by the one whom he called Abba, Father, the one around whose love his life and message revolved. Far surpassing his physical torment was this psychological and spiritual agony of rejection by God, the feeling of being cut off from the one who had been the rock, the sure ground, the source of all. At the limit of his inner torment, Jesus calls out, "God, my God, why have you deserted me?" At that moment, something awful occurred, something the full meaning of which the world will never entirely grasp but on which the salvation of the world depends: God was abandoned by God.[104] In the agonized cry of Christ on the cross, the Son of God — the very Word and heart of God — knows what it is like to feel abandoned by the divine mercy. And thus he "feels" by the deepest sort of identification, the full weight of sin. In Mark's Gospel, this relatively articulate confession of abandonment is followed by an animal groan — the sheer wordless despair of the sinner — and then by death.

What we see on the cross of Christ is therefore the inner tension of the Godhead at its fullest pitch of intensity: the Father has sent the Son out from himself into that state which is most alien to the divine, into hostility to God, into God-abandonment. And the purpose of this awful distantiation is none other than the tracking down of the most recalcitrant sinner. In Christ, the divine power stretches out from its transcendent perch and goes, in the most immanent/intimate sense possible, into those states that seem furthest from the divine love, embracing and surrounding those places and occasions of sin. Into the condition most conducive to sin, into the very rebellion and isolation that is characteristic of the *pusilla anima,* God in Christ has gone. And in this identification he has sanctified what appeared beyond sanctification; he has rendered God-inhabited what appeared godforsaken. In "becoming" sin, Christ has surrounded and hence chained up sin, rendering it powerless. It is only in light of this awful event that Paul can sing his ecstatic hymn: "For I am certain that neither death nor life, neither angels nor principalities, neither height nor depth, nor any other creature can separate us from the love of God that comes in Christ Jesus our Lord" (Rom. 8:38–39). Embracing the utter darkness of physical pain, psychological agony, and even metaphysical despair, the Son of God shows that there is no place, no condition, no state of being that is beyond the outreach of the divine. And therefore, despite the fantasies of Eden, there is no place, in heaven, on earth, or under the earth, to hide from God. In the terrible cross of Jesus, God has conquered sin by throwing his arms around it.

At this point, it would be valuable to say a few words about the much controverted doctrine of satisfaction ascribed usually to St. Anselm, but often presented in a way that betrays the deepest intentions of that great medieval doctor. According to the customary version of the satisfaction theory of the cross, the Son of God's violent death somehow mollifies the infinite anger of God the Father, "satisfying" his just concern for retribution and restoring his offended sense of honor. Jesus takes on himself the terrible punishment that sinners deserved and suffers in their place, allowing God the Father to vent his frustration on him rather than on them. Without descending into all of the complex questions of hermeneutics and theology that surround this theory, I will try to specify how this approach should and should not be understood. It is in the first place essential to notice that, according to the New Testament authors, Jesus becomes on the cross, not a sinner, but *sin*. Accordingly, when God the Father sends forth his wrath on the Son, he is not, in a petulant way, expressing his violent displeasure with a sinner. Rather, he is, in the deepest sense possible, demonstrating his hatred of sin, his profound impatience with the disorder prompted by egotistic rebellion. In the Son's embrace of the cross, God goes into that which is most opposed to God, sinking into the *tohu bohu*, the utter confusion, of the *pusilla anima*. The "hatred" of God is seen in the terrible stretch of the Trinity, in the heartbreak of the Father and the Son. It is as though the cross reveals the full tragedy of sin, because it is in the cross alone that we see the awful lengths to which God had to go to save us. Augustine is able to tell his Christian flock to "love the sinner and hate the sin" precisely because this is what God has done on the cross: in the act of becoming what is other than God, God shows his deepest passion for those who have wandered far away from him. Hence it is decidedly not the case that God the Son has satisfied the anger of God the Father in a primitive and emotional sense, allowing him to "vent" his rage over his infinitely offended honor. On the contrary, in

Christ, God "vents" his anger at sin, revealing with utmost passion his displeasure with our condition, and in that very process he changes sin, dethroning it and relativizing it, turning the desert into a place of springs.

And thus we can understand Anselm's use of the very biblical idea of justice in connection with the cross. As we saw in our discussion of Trent, justice refers to the right relationship, the harmony, between God and human beings which was forfeited through the grasping and hiding of sin. It is into the injustice, the profound imbalance, that God goes in Christ, identifying with it in order to rectify it. In the face of the objection that God could simply have declared sinners just without passing through the drama of the cross, Anselm said that in his justice God cannot call the odd even, pretending that sin does not exist or that its offense is less than terrible.[105] He could not simply pronounce clean the diamond that had fallen into the muck. Instead, he had to go personally to retrieve the diamond and then to clean it off, and this is what happened on the cross. God went to the lowest place, to the very center of the dysfunction, in order personally to reestablish the right rapport between himself and the world. Justice is restored, not through the emotionally satisfying imposition of punishment, but through God's self-emptying uplifting of the fallen sinner, the divine breakthrough into the web of deceit, dysfunction, and anxiety which is the human condition.

In Mark's account of the passion, the Roman centurion, upon witnessing the death of Jesus and the strange happenings surrounding it, cries out, "Truly this man was the Son of God" (Mark 15:39). To that point, Jesus had consistently forbidden anyone to identify him as the Messiah, fearing, the Gospel seems to insinuate, that any such proclamation would be misconstrued in a political or triumphalist direction. It is ironically fitting that the only witness whose voice is not silenced is the one who speaks in the presence of the dead Christ. He can give witness freely precisely because it is in death that Jesus' messianic identity is properly and unambiguously revealed. He is the one who had been sent to do the will of the Father, and that will was that he go to the darkness of godforsakenness out of love. Only in his death, only therefore in the practically infinite tension between the Father's command and the Son's obedience, is the person and mission of Christ visible: he is the justice that throws everything off.

Now none of the above would make any sense were it not for the resurrection of Jesus from the dead. If Jesus had not returned from the realm of abandonment and death, he would be, as Albert Schweizer memorably put it, but one more person ground under by the wheel of history. And if that were true, then everything he announced and embodied would be falsified and the sinful take on the world simply confirmed. If this great servant of God was simply abandoned and forgotten in death, then God is indeed, at best, a distant and arbitrary force, the one to be either mastered or avoided. The fact that, two millennia after the event, we still meditate theologically on the horrible death of a first-century religious reformer is itself an indication that *something else* happened here. The first Christians were formed, galvanized, defined by their conviction that the one whom "they" hung on a tree has not been forgotten but instead raised up by God. They claim, first and foremost, not a beautiful ethic or a reconfiguration of the social/political situation or a new spiritual path, but rather that Jesus of Nazareth, the crucified, is alive through the power of the divine. And because of this, God and humanity have to be radically reconsidered.

It is only in light of this faith in the resurrected Christ that the cross appears, not as a dumb tragedy, but as a revelation of God's heart. To be sure, the resurrection, as numerous commentators have pointed out, is not the resuscitation of a corpse or the appearance of a ghost (nothing as mundane or ordinary as that) but rather the definitive return of Jesus to the Father, the exaltation of the crucified to a mode of existence qualitatively different from earthly existence. It is the breakthrough of the eschaton and hence the manifestation of God's deepest intentions for all of us, indeed for the entire cosmos. Having gone to godforsakenness, the Son returns to the Father's glory, now carrying with him all that he had embraced, gathering up all things, times, and people into the divine life. The hound of heaven went to the bottom of Hell itself and found even those furthest from the divine love and then, in the resurrection, carried them back to God. Hence it is the resurrection of the Son by the Father that fully displays the Trinitarian nature of God. The Father and Son can be separated, almost to the breaking point, the Son going into the outer darkness of what is alien to God, but it is the love between Father and Son — the Spirit — that keeps them from breaking apart. The Spirit is the glue, the link, the tensive love, that presides over the sending and the returning of the Son; it is the love between the Sender and the Sent into which the whole world has been invited. And thus it is in the Spirit that the Father raises the incarnate Son to life. That God *is* love, that is to say, a play of lover, beloved, and shared love is disclosed in the rhythm of the paschal mystery, the *exitus* and *reditus* of the Son of God. Augustine and Aquinas can speak of the Trinity, the dynamic relationships of self-knowledge and self-love in God, because of what has been disclosed in the dying and rising of Christ.

And this in turn tells us something about ourselves. Because we have been embraced and gathered up into God, because there is "room" for us in the divine life, we know that God cannot be a distant supreme being and we cannot be — at the end of the day — rivals of such a power. Rather, we know that we are most ourselves precisely when we find our place within the roominess of the divine existence. The terrible rivalry, the Promethean struggle, the awful illusion that God is a threatening supreme being — all of it is shattered, broken through, by the cross and resurrection of Christ. The *metanoia* of which Jesus so consistently spoke is now possible. And could this be why, upon the death of Jesus, the curtain in the temple, that which blocked universal access to the holy of holies, is torn in two from top to bottom? In the broken heart of God, we now have access to the divine life. Prior to this event, God could be seen only in the dark light of sin, and our only viable options were hiding or grasping. Now, through the graceful self-manifestation of the divine, we can stop our games of self-deification and relax.

Let us look at just one of the mysterious texts describing the resurrected Christ in order to enter more fully into the transforming power of resurrection. The account in Luke 24 of Jesus' post-Easter appearance to the eleven is, like all the resurrection stories strange, multivalent, tensive. It is clear, in the very complexity and uncanniness of the narrative, that something unheard of is being hinted at.

The disciples are gathered in the upper room, the place to which they had retreated in fear after the crucifixion. Despite the locked doors, Jesus stands in their midst. The frightened group, huddled defensively in locked quarters, is a symbolic evocation of all of us locked in the fortress of the *pusilla anima:* terrified, alone, unable to move. The risen Christ, however, breaks through these fortress walls effortlessly because they are, finally, an illusion. He has gone with divine love to the darkest and most frightening place and has returned in the power of the Spirit, and hence there is no more locked fortress, no more upper room, no more sanctuary of sin. He has, as Paul will say to the Ephesians, broken down the walls of hostility that kept God and humanity apart. When he confronts the disciples he says, simply and directly, "Peace be with you." This peace, this *shalom* is the universal well-being that had been longed for throughout the Old Testament, that had indeed been sought ever since Eden. It is the serenity that comes from participating in the very life of God, something that stubbornly eludes us as long as we live in the narrow confines of the *pusilla anima.* In John's account of this scene, Jesus breathes on his friends and they receive the Holy Spirit, that link between the Father and the Son which is now the space in which we all can live. To be within the intimacy of the Father and the Son is what it means to live in Shalom; to live in the ample space of the Spirit is to realize the *magna anima.*

When they encounter him, they think they are seeing a ghost and are, accordingly, terrified. It is worthwhile dwelling on this fear. On the one hand, it is a terror born of the confrontation with the strange and unknown, that which does not fit into customary categories. But on the other hand, it is a fear derived from guilt. In some ways, this account would fit into a classic genre of ghost story: those that emphasize vengeance from beyond, the return from the dead of someone who had been unjustly killed and who angrily seeks retribution. When Jesus came to his moment of trial, when he was attacked by authorities and powers of all stripes, one of his disciples betrayed him, another denied him, and the rest abandoned him, fleeing for their lives. Thus when he returns from the dead and presents himself in the upper room, are they terrified because they think he has come for payback?

The wonderful good news, of course, is that he confronts those who betrayed, denied, and abandoned him, not with violence or even righteous indignation, but with the simple word "peace." To be sure, he shows them his hands and his feet, that is to say, the marks of his death, for he doesn't want them to forget what they did to him. God's own heart appeared in human form, bearing a word of reconciliation and love, displaying for all a new vision of humanity, and the world killed him. "The Lord of life appeared and we put him to death." Christ crucified and risen is indeed, like the earthly Jesus, judge. But, as we saw earlier, Jesus' judgment is never for its own sake, never its own end; rather, it is always a preparation for deeper life and *metanoia*. In him we see our sins, but much more importantly we see the God who has gone into sin itself to rescue us and who therefore comes bearing the peace that surpasses all understanding. We can begin to sense here the source of the ecstatic religious experience of the first believers: we killed God and God still loves us; we performed the most heinous, unthinkable act, and we are still offered peace; we have tried, as thoroughly as possible, to distance ourselves from God, and he returns. Once more, the risen Christ, the new Adam, undoes the damage of Eden and shakes the soul out of its sleep.

What finally breaks open the heart of the sinner is the open heart of God revealed in the crucified and risen Christ. Correlative to the rebellion of Eden is the conviction that God is jealous, distant, and resentful. In relation to this illusory God, the soul becomes sick, warped almost beyond recognition, turned in on itself, frozen in egotism. When Jesus came preaching the Kingdom of God, he attacked this idol and healed the sickness that it prompted. In his presence, people felt the pain of the old self (they were judged) and they glimpsed the possibility of a new being (the *imago* was stirred in them). And when they were near to his heart, they experienced the open and generous heart of God, the divine love that wants nothing more than to lure people into intimacy. They sensed that the spiritual anchors of their lives — the fearful *pusilla anima* and the frightening supreme being — were phantoms, false gods. And when they stood in the presence of the crucified but risen Lord, they knew definitively that the suggestion of the snake of Eden is a lie and that the true God is no competitor but rather mercy within mercy within mercy. Jesus was the Misfit who convinced them, by his very strangeness, that their upright world was in fact upside down.

Face to face with the *icon* of this Jesus, *metanoia* occurred, their sin-sick souls found peace, and they learned once again to see. The whole of Christianity is an attempt to hold up this same icon: the judge of the world, the Son of Man, the Word spoken by a heartbroken God.

Conclusion

TO LIGHT A FIRE ON THE EARTH

We are locked in ice, and we beat our wings in vain; we live in the narrow space of the upper room, and we are armed with rifle and compass. We are tossed on the roiled waves, and the fear of death stalks us every moment. Like the boy in Faulkner's story, we hunt down the divine, and like the grandmother in O'Connor's tale, we spend our lives trying desperately not to be misfits. We are prisoners, and we have lost the key; we are members of the dysfunctional family of sin. The good that we would do we are incapable of doing, and the evil that we would avoid we are incapable of avoiding. We can share the desperation of Paul and say with him and with the entire Christian tradition: "Who will deliver us from this body of death?"

This book is based upon the conviction that there is something profoundly the matter with us, a virus of the soul that will kill us spiritually and that we are incapable of eradicating ourselves. We stand in need of soul-doctoring; we are called to a change of heart. We are blind, and we cannot make ourselves see.

We are all shining like the sun; we are all the children of God. There is in every one of us a mark, a seal, a reminder — an *imago* of the Mercy that continually creates us. Despite our pusillanimity, our smallness of soul, there is, in all of us, a *magna anima* whose power is finally irresistible and whose light is finally unquenchable. Even in our fear, we have the capacity to be grasped by Beauty, to acknowledge our dependency on the Other, to be a sheer transparency to the Love that moves the planets. We might be killers, but we are killer angels.

This book rests upon the conviction that real *metanoia*, the transition from a mind of fear to a mind of trust, is possible. Due to the playful, strange, unpredictable, and relentless love of God, the *imago* in us can be polished and the great soul can emerge.

Who will finally deliver us from the body of death? Paul's answer is as provocative as his question: "Thanks be to God through Jesus Christ our Lord!" The *imago* emerges, not through our efforts of mind, will, or imagination, not through the rearrangement of social and political institutions, not through the declarations of churches, but through the incongruous jest of the Incarnation. God and the world, the infinite and the finite, heaven and earth, fulfillment and hope — those contraries that no thinking person ever imagined capable of union — come together. And in this wild juxtaposition, in this cosmic misfit, this enfleshment of the heart of God, the soul is doctored.

This book shares with the whole Christian tradition the conviction that it is in Jesus Christ that we have found the healer, the bearer of the *salus*, the doctor of the spirit, the salve for the blind eyes of the soul.

And the power of Christ is everywhere. It is in cathedrals and epic poems, in rose windows and the lives of saints. It is in tragic/comic stories, in birdsong and medieval towns. It is in autobiographies, treatises of aesthetics, existential laments; it is in the feeling of absolute dependency and in the shock of nonbeing. It is in sermons, images, stained glass, gargoyles, and domes; it is in songs and conciliar statements. It is in the still surprising pages of the Bible. It is in the pronouncements of popes and the soul-hunger of the poorest of the poor.

This book is animated throughout by the conviction that these sources of Christ's healing and transforming power must be tapped and their energy unleashed. For too long, the new being has been locked away in libraries, archives, and shuttered churches. What would happen if we had the courage and the intelligence to hold up these icons of faith? What if we dared to be who Christ wants us to be: salt for the earth and light for the world? Something tells me we would foster *metanoia*; we would facilitate the emergence of the *magna anima*; we would light a fire on the earth.

Finis Operis

NOTES

1. See, for example, "Sermon 22" in *The Classics of Western Spirituality: Meister Eckhart: The Essential Sermons, Commentaries, Treatises and Defense*, ed. Bernard McGinn (New York: Paulist Press, 1981), 193.

2. All citations from the *Divine Comedy* are taken from: Dante Alighieri, *The Divine Comedy*, vol. 1, trans. Mark Musa (New York: Penguin Books, 1984).

3. Ibid., 67.

4. Ibid.

5. Ibid., 68.

6. Ibid., 69.

7. Ibid., 90.

8. Ibid., 381.

9. Ibid.

10. Ibid.

11. Ibid.

12. Pierre Teilhard de Chardin, *The Divine Milieu* (New York: Harper and Row, 1968), 49–50.

13. Thomas Aquinas, *Summa theologiae*, Ia, q. 2, art. 3.

14. Teilhard de Chardin, *The Divine Milieu*, 74.

15. The Council of Trent, *Decree on Original Sin*, DS 788.

16. Jeffrey Schwartz, *Brain Lock* (New York: Harper Collins, 1996), 70–78.

17. Michael Shaara, *The Killer Angels* (New York: Ballantine Books, 1974).

18. Thomas Merton, *The Seven Storey Mountain* (New York: Harcourt Brace Jovanovich, 1948).

19. Ibid., 83.

20. Ibid., 6.

21. Ibid., 11.

22. Ibid., 41.

23. Ibid.

24. Ibid., 122.

25. Ibid., 178.

26. Ibid., 179.

27. Ibid., 193.

28. Thomas Merton, *Conjectures of a Guilty Bystander* (New York: Image Books, 1965), 156.

29. Ibid., 157.

30. Ibid.

31. Ibid., 158.

32. Hans Urs von Balthasar, *The Glory of the Lord* (San Francisco: Ignatius Press, 1982).

33. Hans Urs von Balthasar, *Theo-Drama: Theological Dramatic Theory* (San Francisco: Ignatius Press, 1990).

34. Ibid., 24.

35. Ibid., 21.

36. Ibid., 25.

37. Ibid. 32.

38. Rainer Maria Rilke, *Letters to a Young Poet,* trans. Stephen Mitchell (Boston: Shambhala, 1993).

39. James Joyce, *Ulysses* (New York: Vintage, 1990), 783.

40. *Theo-Drama,* 211.

41. Friedrich Schleiermacher, *On Religion: Speeches to Its Cultured Despisers,* in *Friedrich Schleiermacher: Pioneer of Modern Theology,* ed. Keith Clements (Minneapolis: Fortress Press, 1991), 82.

42. Ibid., 83.

43. Ibid., 84.

44. Ibid., 85.

45. Ibid.

46. Friedrich Schleiermacher, *Glaubenslehre,* in *Friedrich Schleiermacher: Pioneer of Modern Theology,* 99.

47. Ibid.

48. Paul Tillich, *Systematic Theology* (Chicago: University of Chicago Press, 1967), 1:191.

49. Ibid., 163.

50. *The Catechism of the Catholic Church,* paragraph 28.

51. Joseph Ratzinger, *Introduction to Christianity* (San Francisco: Ignatius Press, 1990), 69.

52. William Faulkner, *Go Down, Moses* (New York: Modern Library, 1995), 185.

53. Ibid., 187.

54. Ibid., 195.

55. Ibid.

56. Ibid., 197.

57. Ibid.

58. Ibid., 200.

59. See Robert Barron, *Thomas Aquinas: Spiritual Master* (New York: Crossroad, 1996), 135–36.

60. Paul Tillich, *Dogmatik: Marburger Vorlesung von 1925* (Düsseldorf: Patmos Verlag, 1986), 41ff.

61. Thomas Aquinas, *De Potentia,* q. 5, art. 1.

62. Karl Rahner, *The Foundations of Christian Faith* (New York: Crossroad, 1984), 76–77.

63. *De Potentia,* q. 3, art. 3.

64. John Henry Newman, *The Grammar of Assent* (Notre Dame, Ind.: University of Notre Dame Press, 1979), 99.

65. *Dogmatik,* 148.

66. St. Anselm of Canterbury, *Proslogion,* in *St. Anselm: Basic Writings* (La Salle, Ill.: Open Court, 1974), 7.

67. Robert Sokolowski, *The God of Faith and Reason* (Notre Dame, Ind.: University of Notre Dame Press, 1982), 8.

68. *De Potentia,* q. 1, art. 6.

69. *Summa theologiae,* q. 9, art. 1.

70. *Systematic Theology,* 3:245.

71. *Summa theologiae,* q. 25, art. 3.

72. Richard Rohr, from a conference delivered at Mundelein Seminary, March 1997.

73. Robert Bolt, *A Man for All Seasons* (New York: Vintage Books, 1960), 6.

74. Thomas Merton, *Thoughts in Solitude* (New York: Farrar, Straus and Giroux, 1983), 83.

75. St. Bonaventure, *Itinerarium Mentis in Deum,* in *Bonaventure,* The Classics of Western Spirituality (New York: Paulist Press, 1978), 102.

76. G. K. Chesterton, *The Everlasting Man,* in G. K. Chesterton, *Collected Works* (San Francisco: Ignatius Press, 1986), 2:359–60.

77. St. Augustine, _De trinitate,_ trans. Edmund Hill, O.P. (New York: New City Press, 1991), 272.

78. St. Thomas Aquinas, _Summa contra gentiles,_ Book 4: _Salvation_ (Notre Dame, Ind.: University of Notre Dame Press, 1975), 79–90.

79. Mihaly Csikszentmihalyi, _Flow_ (New York: Harper Collins, 1990).

80. Flannery O'Connor, "A Good Man Is Hard to Find," in Flannery O'Connor, _The Complete Stories_ (New York: Farrar, Straus and Giroux, 1974), 117–33.

81. Ibid., 118.

82. Ibid., 122.

83. Ibid., 127.

84. Ibid., 131.

85. Ibid., 132.

86. Ibid.

87. Ibid., 133.

88. Origen of Alexandria, _Homilies on Genesis and Exodus_ (Washington: Catholic University of America Press, 1982), 47–71.

89. Raymond E. Brown, _The Birth of the Messiah_ (Garden City, N.Y.: Image Books, 1977), esp. 48ff. and 249ff.

90. See Walter Wink, _Unmasking the Powers_ (Philadelphia: Fortress Press, 1986), 43–50.

91. René Girard, "Generative Violence and the Extinction of Social Order," _Salmagundi_ (Spring–Summer 1984): 210.

92. This idea was drawn from a conference given by John Shea at the Center for Development in Ministry, Summer 1994.

93. See Paul Tillich, _The New Being_ (New York: Scribner's, 1955), 4–14.

94. Robert Barron, _A Study of the De potentia of Thomas Aquinas in Light of the Dogmatik of Paul Tillich_ (San Francisco: Edwin Mellen Press, 1993), 47–50.

95. Walter Wink, _Engaging the Powers_ (Philadelphia: Fortress Press, 1992), 175–84.

96. Ibid., 191.

97. Aloys Grillmeier, _Christ in Christian Tradition,_ vol. 1: _From the Apostolic Age to Chalcedon (451)_ (Atlanta: John Knox Press, 1975), 545.

98. Heinrich Denzinger, _Enchiridion Symbolorum Definitionum et Declarationum de Rebus Fidei et Morum_ (Freiburg im Breisgau: Herder, 1957), no. 148.

99. Hans Küng, _On Being a Christian_ (Garden City, N.Y.: Image Books, 1984), 177–210.

100. Hans Urs von Balthasar, _Mysterium Paschale_ (Edinburgh: T. & T. Clark, 1990), 12–20.

101. Ibid., 21.

102. Ibid., 104–5.

103. Ibid., 107–12.

104. G. K. Chesterton, _The Everlasting Man,_ 344.

105. St. Anselm of Canterbury, _Cur Deus Homo?_ in _St. Anselm: Basic Writings,_ 203ff.

INDEX

ALSO BY

ROBERT BARRON

THOMAS AQUINAS
Spiritual Master

"Spirituality with spine.... Barron's solid and accessible study
is itself a fine example of what he admires in his master."
– Michael Downey, *America*

"A valuable and successful attempt to represent Aquinas
in a refreshing and original manner as one of
the Christian tradition's great spiritual masters."
– *Theological Studies*

Winner of the Catholic Book Award for Spirituality

0-8245-2507-8; $14.95

Please support your local bookstore, or call 1-800-395-0690.
For a free catalog, please write us at
THE CROSSROAD PUBLISHING COMPANY
370 LEXINGTON AVENUE, NEW YORK, NY 10017

We hope you enjoyed And Now I See.... *Thank you for reading it.*

crossroad